SUPPLY CHAIN RISK MANAGEMENT

Agile Strategies for Stakeholders

SUPPLY CHAIN RISK MANAGEMENT

Agile Strategies for Stakeholders

Ayse Kucuk Yilmaz
Eskisehir Technical University, Turkey

Marc Helmold
IU International University of Applied Sciences, Berlin, Germany

Tracy Dathe
Macromedia University of Applied Sciences, Berlin, Germany

World Scientific

NEW JERSEY • LONDON • SINGAPORE • BEIJING • SHANGHAI • HONG KONG • TAIPEI • CHENNAI • TOKYO

Published by

World Scientific Publishing Europe Ltd.
57 Shelton Street, Covent Garden, London WC2H 9HE
Head office: 5 Toh Tuck Link, Singapore 596224
USA office: 27 Warren Street, Suite 401-402, Hackensack, NJ 07601

Library of Congress Cataloging-in-Publication Data
Names: Küçük Yilmaz, Ayşe author | Helmold, Marc author | Dathe, Tracy author
Title: Supply chain risk management : agile strategies for stakeholders /
Ayse Kucuk Yilmaz, Eskisehir Technical University, Turkey,
Marc Helmold, IU International University of Applied Sciences, Berlin, Germany,
Tracy Dathe, Macromedia University of Applied Sciences, Berlin, Germany.
Description: New Jersey : World Scientific, [2026] | Includes bibliographical references and index.
Identifiers: LCCN 2026006451 | ISBN 9781800619197 hardcover |
ISBN 9781800619203 ebook | ISBN 9781800619210 ebook other
Subjects: LCSH: Supply chain management | Risk management
Classification: LCC HD38.6 .K83 2026
LC record available at https://lccn.loc.gov/2026006451

British Library Cataloguing-in-Publication Data
A catalogue record for this book is available from the British Library.

For any available supplementary material, please visit
https://www.worldscientific.com/worldscibooks/10.1142/Q0564#t=suppl

Desk Editors: Murali Appadurai/Pui Yee Lum

Typeset by Stallion Press
Email: enquiries@stallionpress.com

Preface

In our book, the concept of corporate sustainability is discussed together with the risk paradigm because sustainability requires the management of multidimensional and different risks. The strategic, economic, environmental, and operational dimensions of sustainability and the effects of the risks within the scope of these dimensions on each other and interactively on the business are discussed. Thus, decision-makers are trying to gain maneuverability with a holistic risk management perspective. Enterprise risk management (ERM) has the core goal of adding value to the business. In this respect, risks associated with value potential should be viewed as opportunities.

Acceleration of digitalization and artificial intelligence development is transforming industries in many ways, such as in human resources, management systems and functions, production tools, and managerial approaches. Given the high momentum of change, it has become difficult to make long-term predictions. Industries and organizations in related sectors face unprecedented levels of complexity and multiple, varied risks that require technological literacy. It is within the definition of doing business to predict and identify all risks faced by today's industry and business environment holistically and systematically, as well as to manage their effects with an optimal managerial strategy. This book presents the concept of ERM with its conceptual and philosophical emphasis on sustainability and supply chain risks.

Understanding the conceptual basics and their relationship with sustainability is an important need for implementing risk management within infrastructure. For this reason, in our book, sustainability and ERM are discussed together, and the reasonable assurance provided by ERM regarding sustainability risk is discussed with its conceptual and theoretical foundations. ERM is a managerial approach that should be understood in terms of its unique terminology and processes. Importantly, although the general algorithm remains the same, the processes need to be shaped specifically for each institution. To fully and accurately understand ERM in these aspects, the conceptual process and the tools, techniques, and models used in various stages of the process are presented together.

Various ERM frameworks that organizations can adopt to systematically manage risks are also presented in detail, and alternative guidelines and related approaches for institutions are introduced. Humans are a source of risk and, at the same time, the risk managers. For this, we have included risk models based on ergonomic and human factors in our book. These models clarify the need to consider human capabilities and limitations in risk management and risk analysis. Culture is one of the key issues in management and strategy. It is particularly important to understand its scope, as culture plays a decisive role in the establishment and execution of risk management as intended.

If risk management can be applied throughout the organization, it can create a risk culture, thereby increasing corporate performance and building capacity. In these aspects, we examine organizational culture and performance management in separate sections. Non-technical skills such as collaboration, communication, leadership, decision-making, teamwork, and situational awareness, which we call NOTECS, are needed to achieve supply chain risk management (SCRM). Developing the capacity for these skills is presented with the details of the skills.

A risk management-based approach has become a necessity to manage digitalized global supply chains. Next-generation resources will affect all elements of the supply chain, from warehousing to transportation, and will differentiate risks. For this reason, a comprehensive SCRM framework and process are discussed in detail, and a new risk taxonomy developed through discussions of sustainable energy sources is presented. As digital technologies continue to transform industries, this transformation will have implications for SCRM under scrutiny. This chapter discusses how these technologies can both introduce new risks and offer innovative solutions to manage them.

Finally, emerging trends in SCRM are discussed, and projections for the future are also included in our book. Assessments and predictions regarding sectoral risks related to the supply chain and industries are presented in our book. With all these aspects, this book is designed as a comprehensive and strategic guide for leaders, professionals, decision-makers, academics, and researchers, as well as anyone who wants to understand and manage with greater awareness the life chain, which is based on SCRM.

SCRM constitutes a new maturity level of the supply chain. Optimal application is directly related to understanding all aspects of its managerial, organizational, and behavioral components. Supply chain is the basis of life and industries, while its risk management serves as a framework for all of them. We present the fundamentals of management and strategy in industries, which contribute to the maturity levels of leaders in managing their supply chain risks in an optimal manner: lean management and maximizing opportunities while minimizing the impact of threats on business and its processes.

About the Authors

Prof. Dr. Ayse Kucuk Yilmaz is a full-time professor in the Faculty of Aeronautics and Astronautics at Eskisehir Technical University, Turkey. She has over 25 years of experience as an academician, researcher, and administrator, including six years as an international airport business manager and eight years in various managerial roles. She has published over 30 books, more than 70 peer-reviewed journal articles, and over 50 conference papers. She also leads Erasmus+ EU projects. Her fields of expertise include management and strategy: enterprise risk management, risk analysis, leadership, lean management, airport management, supply chain risk management, decision-making, multi-criteria decision-making, digital transformation, and digital technologies.

Prof. Dr. Marc Helmold (M.B.A.) is a full-time professor at IU Internationale Hochschule in Berlin. He teaches bachelor's, master's, and M.B.A. courses in business management, operations management, lean management, quality management, and Leadership. He has served in several executive leadership positions at original equipment manufacturers (OEMs) in the automotive, railway, and aviation industries. In addition to his professorial role at IU Internationale Hochschule in Berlin, which he has held since 2016, he conducts lean, quality, and leadership workshops in his own consultancy.

Prof. Dr. Tracy Dathe is a full-time business management professor at Macromedia University, Berlin, Germany. She has a rich background in finance, previously holding the position of chief financial officer (CFO) for a multinational medium-sized automotive supplier. In this capacity, she oversaw commercial management across various legal entities in Germany, China, France, Italy, Sweden, the Czech Republic, Turkey, and the US.

Contents

List of Figures

Chapter 1

DNA of Industries: Supply Chain and Enterprise Risk Management

Industries and all life can **continue with the supply chain** ONLY and ONLY.

—M. Efe Yilmaz, Ayse's son

1.1 Driver of Business

Everything is the beginning of supply: a starting point, a key point, and a vital point. Therefore, we positioned and assigned a value to supply chain risk management (SCRM), as "supply chain" is the DNA of all industries and businesses. The supply chain has many and diverse risks which should be managed to achieve goals. At this point, risk management plays a vital role in the strategic and optimal management of this. In this respect, SCRM is an essential and fundamental element of industry and business management and organizational behavior.

When the supply chain is integrated with risk management, it can provide reasonable assurance that an uninterrupted chain would be created and maintained in accordance with the conditions of the day. Regardless of your industry, whether you are a manufacturing or service business, if you can manage the risks of your supply chain, you can get closer to achieving your business goals.

Enterprise risk management (ERM) is designed to create added value and foster resilience and agility while remaining competitive within its industry. Supply is fundamental to everything. In other words, everything starts and continues via supply. For this reason, the supply can be considered the DNA of industries and businesses.

1.2 Introduction to Supply Chain with Enterprise Risk Management

ERM drives an organization to engage in continuous, multifaceted brainstorming, keeping it aware of its environment and itself. In addition, with ERM, organizations aim to increase their resilience against all potential possibilities and enhance their capacity for readiness by developing different risk scenarios.

ERM is a vital and ongoing event or practice; it is a main part of management systems that has the potential to influence every element of the organization, including its culture, in every way. With its interactive approach, ranging from individual to company and vice versa, in the form of both induction and deduction, and with its philosophy and set of values, i.e. its paradigm, it influences and shapes the organizational structure.

The need to adapt to today's business environment has meant that the institution-wide application of risk management, supported by a contingency approach, is no longer an option. Adapting to changing external conditions requires rapid adjustments to internal conditions based on the situational approach. As a result, the internal and external environments of organizations are constantly evolving, transforming, and changing. This situation increases and diversifies risks. This has made it almost imperative to consider the impact of risks on each other in a holistic sense and to be flexible. Therefore, business managers should see the whole picture and make decisions by analyzing each element with risk management and systematic analysis, adapting to changing conditions in a short timeframe.

Supply chain and corporate sustainability also strongly underline that "it is not only possible to be self-sufficient". Both internal and external conditions need to be considered to ensure that the functions and activities related to the supply chain can continue effectively without interruptions. Therefore, stakeholders need each other. Other people and organizations, which we can call external and internal factors, are risks. Some of these risks exist as threats, and some as opportunities. Managing threats at a controllable level and with the least loss, while at the same time seizing opportunities, is the main goal for both individuals and businesses because this reflects the main rule of sustainability. Because resources are limited, obtaining the right resource and using the obtained resource represent two separate strategic issues. But both are within the scope of risk management because strategic development and decision-making involve making choices. Choice, on the other hand, means choosing an opportunity: giving up other opportunities while selecting only one. Risk management is the direct management of decision-making and selection processes.

1.3 The Supply Chain as DNA for Industries

In this book, we define the supply chain as the DNA of industries, that is, a structure that enables industries and organizations within its scope to fulfill their survival functions and carries the strategic codes necessary for them to grow, become profitable, increase their performance, develop their capacity, and achieve their goals. DNA, which ensures the maintenance of life in organisms, also controls the continuity of metabolic events that occur in the cell. In other words, the supply chain is to industries and companies what DNA is to living things.

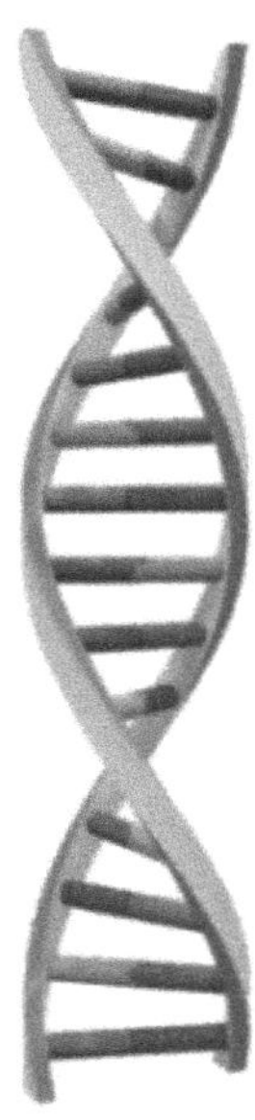

Here, when we define DNA as the supply chain, we are underlining both the vital position and decisive role of the supply chain for industries by making an analogy from a management perspective. In this concept, we can assume that supply chain (SC) as DNA is the basic building block that shows the systematic functioning of industries together with the organizations within the scope of their processes, connections, and interactions among production resources with the processes.

In terms of management and strategy, in a situation where DNA plays a supply chain role, industries, sectors affiliated with those industries, organizations and companies affiliated with sectors, and departments within organizations or companies all function as divisions or units that are part of a larger system. There is a strong interrelation here. The optimal operation of the system and its subsystems depends on being efficient and effective, achieving a balance, and working in harmony with each unit. Just as DNA determines the health and functioning of an organism, the supply chain determines the success of an organization and, therefore, of industries. It ensures that products, services, and information flow at the right time, in the right place, and in the right way. A disruption or deterioration in this flow negatively affects the whole process. The most recent COVID-19 crisis we experienced was the moment when we saw a clear picture of this. In the business environment shaped by artificial intelligence, digitalization, and technology acceleration, there are changes to this building block and critical shifts in the resources that feed it. Companies that cannot manage the risks of this transformation are struggling with crises—and that's exactly what our book is about. Because, in our opinion, risk management is also the genetics of the supply chain. As is known, the genetic code of an organism is the key that determines all of its characteristics, including its biological characteristics and durability. SCRM also identifies the continuous strengths and weaknesses of the supply chain, along with its sources, and offers managerial strategies for maintaining strengths and eliminating weaknesses. There is a risk-based decision-making process integrated with risk management within the supply chain.

Decision-making involves making choices among alternatives which have the potential to contribute to problem-solving. Decision-making is also influenced by the factors that determine how the supply chain works, where weak points are found, and what potential risks it may face. At this point, risk management plays a critical role in protecting the genetics of the supply chain, improving the process and restructuring when necessary, and identifying and seizing on opportunities. In a sense, this is an analysis of the benefits, opportunities, costs, and threats of a potential event as part of the "BOCR" logic; it is an analysis of all aspects of the event that is the source of risk, such as 360-degree scanning, and determining whether the benefits or costs are high, that is, whether it is a risk worth taking. This is possible because risk management can optimize the direction of configuration, improvement, and resource allocation.

Risks are identified, evaluated, and transformed into decisions in the context of corporate strategies. These decisions involve multi-criteria decision-making, and it is especially important that the alternatives are thoroughly evaluated. Without a good identification of the alternatives, the best one in terms of strategy and objectives cannot be selected among the alternatives.

Technological developments, including digitalization and artificial intelligence, have the potential to make changes, similar to mutations, in the genetics of the supply chain. The risk management-based approach also identifies the sources that could affect the essence and components of this system and provides reasonable assurance of identifying the strategies for handling them. From a management point of view, this means the achievement of an uninterrupted and effective procurement process. It covers the entire process from supply sourcing to supply delivery.

Genetic deterioration is one of the most important problems of today. It is possible to protect the genetics of DNA chains, that is, to protect the genetics of the supply chains without preventing them from developing in a way that adapts to the day, with a risk-management approach. The genetics of the supply chain encompasses all the components of the process and its stakeholders, including suppliers, supply chains, customers, logistics companies, information flow, storage, and security. Proper functioning of DNA means that risks are effectively managed. In other words, it aims to prevent any genetic mutation (deterioration, disruption, delay, or quality decrease) in the genes of the chain (supplier relations, production processes, storage methods, transportation strategies, etc.). The risks that will cause this need to be managed. Extreme conditions such as COVID-19, which could create potential events that mutate DNA, resource dependency, and limited resource access cause businesses to enter a crisis. Technological developments and competitors, accompanied by digitalization and artificial intelligence, provide the ability to manage change and market risk necessary for business management. In addition, managing the risk of gaps in the human–machine interface is vital to prevent crises. The human factor, which cannot keep up with technology or has a problem in technological literacy, is a potential source of risk as a primary threat. As can be seen, the risks and effects of each element in management systems are different. The recent Intel crisis is one of the most concrete examples of this (see Özüağ, 2024).

In the ever-changing environment, business is transforming under the effects of digitalization and artificial intelligence; risk management, on the other hand, is a management system that provides reasonable assurance that this genetic structure both develops and remains intact. Just like an organizational defense system that tries to prevent harmful mutations, risk management diagnoses events (sources of risks, which include both threats and opportunities) that have the potential to affect a process and its components at all stages of the supply chain. This identification can be proactive and/or reactive or both.

In this context, managing the genetics of the supply chain is not only to maintain its current functionality but also to increase resilience against future threats, develop capacity, bridge the gap between the human factor and other components of the process, ensure flexibility, and minimize the harmful effects of risks associated with the biggest opportunities.

1.4 Basics of Enterprise Risk Management and Decision-Making

Supply chains are basic (fundamental) to sustaining industries. Today, crises arise from the inability to supply and manage the risks associated with supply sources.

Advanced technological developments are changing the environment for calculating the probability, predictability, and evolution of risks and their consequences. Technology and digitalization are influencing the types of risks, their potential for emergence, the predictability of their evolution and transformation, and the assessment of the severity of their impact. The time to make predictions and calculate probabilities is shorter than it was in yesterday's industrial environment. At the same time, it is more difficult to make this calculation than under yesterday's conditions. The industrial and business environment is moving away from predictability. Therefore, more agile and resilient SCRM must be the primary system for all industries and businesses. Because the existence of industries cannot be sustained without supply, scarce resources, risks to resource availability, and the transformation of new generation resources are changing the direction of investment, supply conditions, and the supply process.

The combination of technological advancements, environmental concerns, and increasingly digitalized supply chains requires a systematic, holistic, and well-designed approach to risk management. This book focuses on ERM in supply chains, serving as a guide to the future with strategic insights and designed to provide innovative processes and practices based on ergonomics.

Basically, *ERM* emphasizes how organizations create tangible value through a risk-management-based approach and associate strategies with decision-making processes.

Decision-making processes are part of our daily lives. Decision-making is essentially the process of considering all possible options to achieve an optimal solution to the problem(s) or event(s) that are the sources of risk, choosing the best one among those that can be considered, and implementing that choice using appropriate resources in a timely and appropriate manner, while monitoring, controlling, and evaluating the results. Completing this process as quickly, accurately, and with the best use of resources possible is a prerequisite for successful decision-making. We know that sometimes decisions have to be made quickly. Any time spent waiting for a decision is time lost. The speed at which risky events or problems requiring decisions occur and the range of their potential impact can also vary. From this point of view, the difficulty and criticality of each decision are constantly changing.

Due to the multitude and variety of variables, managing and making decisions in the multidisciplinary and multicultural dynamic environments of industries and their sectors is risky. Decision-making is not merely about making a choice; it is about identifying alternatives, balancing available information and scenarios—including forecasts and alternatives—with a visionary perspective and integration. As industry and business conditions are dynamic and changing, objectives and sub-objectives related to these objectives may need to be redefined as new information is received and scenarios are developed. This means that a company's risk management processes and levels are constantly evolving.

"Multidisciplinary" refers to collaborating and integrating different fields and disciplines within industries. This involves bringing together experts from different fields, such as engineering, physics, computer science, and management, to collaborate, influence, and support each other in developing and improving technology, operations, safety, and management in an industry, e.g. aviation.

The ERM process provides a common language throughout the organization. The process, which is applied throughout the life cycle of enterprises, should be designed to be flexible and institution-specific enough to be developed and implemented with the same effectiveness in different conditions. ERM ensures that all potential risks that support or threaten the corporate performance of organizations are identified together with their sources, and the best management options are selected for these risks. It improves readiness against corporate risks, both proactively and reactively. Thus, the frequency of encountering shock situations that will create a crisis can be reduced. Shocks or crises are stopping points and interruption points for organizations whose durations are not known exactly. The breaking points of the supply chain are interruptions or stoppages. ERM provides reasonable assurance that these downtimes are minimized. In addition, since the ERM system works with scenarios, it also increases resilience to critical, unexpected, or sudden events and the crisis period experienced during and after such events. In unavoidable crises, it is effective in shortening recovery time and reducing the amount of loss and damage.

Building on this framework, we present the outlines of a step-by-step ERM process, providing a practical guide to implementing risk management initiatives. We also detail and further discuss various ERM frameworks and guidelines, providing readers with a toolkit for tailoring risk management to their specific organizational needs.

The decision-making process regarding models, tools, and techniques to be used in risk management is another important process, as these choices ensure that risks are correctly identified, assessed, and managed. Using the wrong model, tool, or technique may lead to inadequate handling of risks and increased potential losses. Therefore, the selection of the right tools and techniques directly affects the success of the risk management process. In addition, risk management tools and techniques require significant resources. In terms of the correct use of resources, the issue of which tools, models, and techniques to choose represents a risky decision-making issue. Here, we share the details for the optimization of these choices.

We focus on transforming organizational culture by exploring how multidisciplinary and multicultural perspectives shape risk management practices. We seek to analyze and examine the relationship between business performance and risk management, emphasizing the strategic importance of aligning risk management with business objectives.

As risk management emphasizes, the structures of organizations are not only affected by their activities, products, and functions. Culture, as one of the shapers, directly or indirectly affects all elements of the organization. This cultural influence is also a shaping factor for business behavior, teamwork, feedback aspects (up, down, or both up and down), reporting styles, communication channels, and the chain-of-command structure. The most appropriate structure is selected to support the achievement of organizational goals, the use of resources and capacity, and performance management. At this point, another important determinant involves the establishment of risk management and the design of a structure suitable for obtaining the expected benefits from it. The design, implementation, and continuous implementation of ERM, as an "essential part" of the company, requires the use of a significant number of resources. With the necessary infrastructure in place, the risk management process can be implemented. At this point, a good analysis of the company itself is one of the determinants. With techniques such as SWOT analysis, the company has the chance to identify its own strengths, resilience, and weaknesses, which could create fragility. This will be an important input for managing organizational risks.

Analysis and assessment of risks include both the qualification and then quantification efforts of risks and are aimed at facilitating their management. In this context, risk quantification includes the determination of the probability of occurrence of risks and the severity of their effects on the achievement of the objectives, ranking risks according to their priorities, selecting critical risks from the listed ones, and developing separate models for those selected risks. After these studies, the modeling studies carried out separately are integrated in order to obtain a holistic picture and establish the corporate value connection, and the quantification studies are completed (Yilmaz, 2017).

1.5 Organizational Behavior: Human Factor and Risk Management

The human factor is one of the most difficult risks to manage due to the dual role of humans (both as a source of risk and as a manager of risk) in ERM, as well as their variability and controllability. In addition, people are different from each other. This makes them an inimitable capability, i.e. a source of opportunity. But the same "uniqueness" also affects people's potential for optimal manageability through generalization. Especially in industries operating in a global environment and their sectoral organizations, diversity risk management is also included in the scope of risk management due to cultural differences and multicultural environments. Organizational behavior is one of the major topics or issues for any industry because culture, attitudes, and norms also have an impact on people's work behavior. Training and upskilling can help individuals and managers keep up with the pace of the day, but behavioral change and personality are another matter. For these reasons, organizational culture, performance management, and non-technical skills are among the topics covered in our book. For example, one of the training exercises given to pilots is cabin welding training. This training emphasizes the importance of teamwork, lean hierarchies, and collaboration. Although all of the pilots nod their heads in agreement with this cooperative and simple environment while in class, they may not be willing to apply what they know when they start flying—ego speaking: "there's only One Captain here!" In fact, this is also true for some managers. Let's consider what could be the proportion of people today who really "want" to "share" their leadership. For these reasons, ergonomics or human factors, which are important links in the chain, are a topic of study under SCRM.

Organizational structures, communication channels within those structures, and the health of communication, i.e. whether people listen to each other or not, affect the risk culture. And we know that people often only seem to listen to each other. Communication is effective in decision-making as a source of risk for all industries.

Understanding that technical skills alone are not adequate for effective risk management, we emphasize here the role of non-technical skills—such as collaboration, communication, leadership, decision-making, teamwork, and situational awareness—in managing risk.

The supply chain is the DNA of industries and their sectors. It is a fact that supply chains are not mutating but transforming. The evolution and digitalization of people, business environments, and resources also require the adaptation of supply chains in a flexible, agile, and maneuverable way. At this point, supply chains need to be reshaped as components of SCRM. Designing the framework of the supply chain specific to businesses, keeping the process dynamic and integrating it into all managerial approaches and practices, is vital for managing risks on an enterprise scale and therefore ensuring an uninterrupted, efficient, and durable supply chain process. While designing the framework, the wishes, needs, and objectives of the enterprises are taken into consideration. Each business is unique because its human resources are different. In other words, each business needs to design its own risk management framework. This is a multi-stage and risky process.

New-generation energy sources are an important force that directs investments. The direction of investors determines the areas of business development. In this respect, investment risks have a feature that needs to be examined and affect all of us directly or indirectly. In this regard, a comprehensive risk analysis of next-generation "green" energy resources, such as using sustainable aviation fuel, is a critical issue for industries and economies.

Supply chains impacted by digitalization and artificial intelligence affect the achievements of business strategies and, therefore, industries. It is important to consider all aspects of digitalization and artificial intelligence, which are central to today's conditions, to develop and increase the level of awareness about them.

Because technological developments also differentiate risks and affect their management, without faster, more agile, and more flexible systems, crises and the destruction they will cause will increase. If SCRM is implemented effectively and thoroughly, the duration of relevant crises and the damage caused by them will decrease. Because crisis management is a subset of risk management, the latter also analyzes each risk event or risk source in terms of the crises it will create.

Risk management, with all these economic, behavioral, managerial, and strategic aspects, is in the DNA of business life and our lives. The more aware we are, the more effectively we can minimize threats, see opportunities better, and seize the opportunities. This is a good, complex journey.

Case studies and/or best practices are considered to illustrate key concepts and provide practical examples of risk management in action. It is my hope that this work will serve as a valuable resource for professionals, academics, and students alike, offering both theoretical insights and practical guidance for navigating the complex world of ERM and sustainable supply chain practices.

Professionals and students in both management and strategy may benefit from this book, which contributes to the literature that focuses on the supply chain through ERM in industries. This is based on the premise that SCRM is a complementary concept and that sustainable, non-technical, skills-based approaches bring out the decisive role of decision-makers as risk leaders in industries.

In industries, operations and activities are carried out primarily by teams. In this team-based work environment, it is important that teams are formed correctly and that team members have the right skills and knowledge in order to accomplish their tasks in the most effective manner possible. Non-technical skills, besides technical capabilities of human factors, are vital in all industries.

Organizational culture is determinative of human behavior. The ability to do business in a multicultural environment is also a requirement for both managers and employees. In a highly digitalized environment, risk leaders in the aviation industry need to adapt to it. As globalization increases and technology advances, it may not be possible for a single leader to reach everyone in the right way at the right time, so distributed leadership is considered as a new management strategy. Resource management is the most important risk management area in all industries. Lean management is an increasingly valuable approach in aviation, as business is conducted with scarce resources worldwide, and those resources are diminishing. Since aviation is a high-cost, high-risk industry, it is especially important for its leaders to develop and implement strategies that focus on risk management and lean management practices. The goal of leaders is to ensure that all business activities are conducted in the most sustainable, safe, economical, and optimal manner by effectively managing risks.

"Risk management is everyone's job!" and also, everyone is a risk manager! This is because the whole organization has responsibility for implementing SCRM throughout its lifecycle. In this view, the source of power is shared responsibility for risk management throughout the organization.

Risk management is effectively implemented in an environment where everyone is a risk manager as part of the corporate culture of shared risk management. When leaders and employees take ownership of risk management, then this holistic system can provide "reasonable" assurance that safety objectives will be achieved (see Fig. 1.1).

Fig. 1.1. The power of shared risk management.

Source: Authors, made with Napkin, June 16, 2025, https://app.napkin.ai/page/CgoiCHByb2Qtb25lEiwKBFBhZ2UaJGUxZDY2ZWZlLTFmYWUtNGYzOC05MmRhLTU0ZGI3N2JhMjIzNw.

Risk management is a vital need for sustainability and corporate performance in the business world. By following the basic principles and process steps of ERM, businesses can identify and assess various risks. In this process, different tools and techniques are used to identify and assess risks, guided by ERM frameworks and guidelines. Risk models based on ergonomic and human factors are developed in accordance with the multidisciplinary and multicultural nature of the organizational culture. Corporate performance and risk management are supported by non-technical skills such as collaboration, communication, leadership, and decision-making, as well as teamwork and situational awareness. SCRM focuses on analyzing next-generation risks, such as green energy sources, and includes the use of digital technologies. Finally, new trends in SCRM and insights into industry risks provide a critical roadmap for a sustainable future in business.

We are aware and awake that high-tech developments are changing the environment for calculating probability, predictability, risk evolution, and their consequences.

Artificial intelligence and digitalization influence the sorts of hazards, their likelihood of emergence, the predictability of their evolution, and their metamorphosis as the severity of their consequences evolves. The time required to generate forecasts and calculate probabilities is shorter than in yesterday's industrial environment. At the same time, the computation is more complicated than it was yesterday. The industrial and business environments are becoming increasingly unpredictable. As a result, a more agile and flexible SCRM system should be the principal system for all industries and businesses. Industries rely on finite resources, accessibility hazards, and new-generation resources to sustain their existence. These factors influence investment decisions, supply conditions, and processes.

Our new "*RAgiLean*" SRCM approach may serve as a helpful guide for managers and professionals as well as researchers of enterprise management and strategy. It focuses on the successful integration of risk management into business functions and systems, with approaches emphasizing industry operational, managerial, and functional issues of supply chain. Companies are starting to focus on ERM, as well as a value-based approach. Constantly emerging techniques are facilitating this task, which is of primordial importance for companies to remain resilient and competitive; however, managing human factors and ergonomic-based risks remains a challenge. Industries and related corporates try to sustain a hypercompetitive environment by applying digital technologies to achieve effective operations and efficient performance. Furthermore, the elegant handling of multiculturalism-based risks is a key priority for the global industry. For this reason, decision-makers and managers must consider managing risks raised from ergonomics.

Finally, the aim of the *RAgiLean SCRM framework* is to provide contemporary guidance to leader managers and decision-makers across all industries, enabling them to perceive, analyze, and manage risk in a multi-dimensional way, and to manage the supply chain as a resilient and agile, lean-based strategy. In addition, in order to support the educational background of managers, RAgiLean SCRM supports managers with master's and doctoral degrees in fields such as management, economics, logistics, and engineering by raising their awareness of current and fundamental issues and developing their skills. It also shows them the areas where they can add value to industries by inspiring them to create value through their creativity in managing their risks.

References

Özüağ, E. (2024). Intel's biggest crisis: Troubled processors and strong competitors. https://www.youtube.com/watch?v=t3l-Lq1Y1IY.

Yilmaz, K. (2017). *Enterprise Risk Management in International Business: Strategy and Organizational Culture Oriented Paradigm*, Literaturk Academia, Konya, Turkey.

Chapter 2

Supply Chain Risk Environment: Evolution toward "RAgiLean" ERM Framework

2.1 Supply Chain Risk Environment and Capacity Building

All social and economic conditions in the world, including climate and resources, are constantly and irregularly changing in way and direction. These complex conditions increase uncertainties, making it difficult to predict and analyze them, as well as to manage the behavior of human resources. It is necessary to develop and implement strategies to manage the risks of this situation and its processes with effective leadership. For this reason, the clearer and simpler all managerial and organizational functions and processes are, the more effectively they can be directed to create value.

Enterprise risk management (ERM) is becoming increasingly strategic, with risk practitioners emphasizing that strategic initiatives critical to growth—acquisitions, for example—present both opportunities and risks. In this context, the holistic risk management approach emphasizes not only protection from negatives but also evaluating the risk capacity of the organization and pursuing growth opportunities with confidence. Experience in the banking and airline sectors shows that being prepared for unexpected disruptions yields tangible benefits in terms of market share gains and economic empowerment. Prepared companies are able to not only weather crises but also turn them into a competitive advantage. Therefore, this progressive approach takes risk management out of a defensive approach and transforms it into a strategic tool; it allows companies to turn potential vulnerabilities into opportunities for growth and leadership (Nystedt *et al.*, 2024).

Risk is the probability of something happening that will impact the objectives. In this respect, risk and risk management are perceptual concepts, especially in terms of awareness and interpretation. Perception management is decisive in the business world and markets because it affects and directs perspectives, evaluations, and decision-making processes. Since it recognizes the impact of the human factor on management and decision-making, as well as the risks in operational processes, organizational structure, and behavior issues, they are within the scope of corporate risk management, and a risk culture has been included in the risk management process as an infrastructure element.

Supply chain risk management (SCRM) is a network system that mediates between suppliers and customers and manages and establishes the organization. It is essential to manage the flow of information and materials among stakeholders cooperating within the scope of procurement, without interruption and in a cost-effective manner. Effective SCRM will also ensure customer satisfaction, and this will contribute to the development and continuity of stakeholder relations and levels of cooperation (Helmold *et al.*, 2021).

In the traditional sense of risk management, risk is considered an adverse event that needs to be eliminated or, if it cannot be eliminated, reduced or mitigated. Strategies to manage this negativity focus on eliminating risk (and, if possible, the sources of risk), removing risk, and/or mitigating or reducing its effects. However, we know that events have a two-sided potential. This refers to the capacity of two-sided potential events to generate both positive and negative outcomes. Furthermore, eliminating risks and risk sources is not logical and is often impossible. An ERM approach is needed as a new approach that focuses on the effects of risks and the opportunities presented by them to effectively utilize limited resources.

Capacity management is the elimination of disruptions and delays in the supply chain and/or the reduction of both the frequency (of occurrence) and the duration of interruptions and delays; it refers to improving results in terms of robust and smooth transportation, storage, transfer, and delivery of products from the first receipt to the final customer, while optimizing resource use and achieving simplicity. As a result, customer trust, strong stakeholder relations, and the opportunity to approach and/or achieve corporate sustainability goals are captured.

The approach is characterized by several commitments, including the annual review of the corporate plan, integration of risk management into both strategic and operational planning, and systematic monitoring of organizational arrangements. Independent reviews through internal and external audits are regarded as an essential component of accountability and assurance. Responsibility for risk ownership is devolved appropriately, with structured training and ongoing support to ensure competence. Importantly, the framework highlights the need for all colleagues to understand both the organizational approach to risk management and the roles of individuals within it, reinforcing a culture of shared responsibility (Audit Scotland, 2024).

2.2 Supply Chain Network Design: Global Market and Chains

The social, environmental, and economic conditions surrounding the business world, including climate and resources, are constantly changing in an irregular, volatile style and direction. These complex conditions increase uncertainty, making it difficult to predict and analyze and, at the same time, to manage human resources behavior. Developing and implementing strategies to effectively manage this situation and the risks associated with the processes involved require effective leadership. Therefore, the more streamlined, agile, and resilient the supply chain is, with all its managerial and organizational functions and processes integrated with risk management, the greater its potential to achieve supply chain objectives and the more reasonable assurance it provides in this regard.

We know that corporate DNA contains organizational behavior instructions, which are related to the development and functioning of the organization. Supply chains are a company's DNA and determine the basic structure of industries, their mode of operation, and therefore their existence and development. A complete and accurate understanding of the supply chain is essential to understanding its power to influence the business world and its potential spheres of influence. The supply chain should be considered a multi-component, interactively interacting network. This is a network designed for the fast, robust delivery of products and services, as well as their raw materials, from manufacturers to the final consumers. To achieve this goal, it uses and benefits from many organizations, people, technologies, and resources, including information. While doing all this, it directs industries as a leader. ERM plays a vital and deterministic role in tailoring supply chains as a "RAgiLean" approach, suitable for the volatile, uncertain, complex, and ambiguous (VUCA) situations of the business world.

Supply chain network design is of vital importance in today's global environment due to the increasing frequency of disruptions such as natural disasters, labor issues, and geopolitical conflicts. Traditional supply chain designs developed under stable conditions are no longer effective in today's volatile environment. Companies must prioritize network design to remain competitive and agile. This enables rapid adjustments in production and distribution in response to demand fluctuations. Regularly reassessing critical decisions, such as supply strategies and facility locations, is crucial for maintaining an adaptable supply chain capable of succeeding in an uncertain environment (GAINSystems LLC, 2025).

2.3 Corporate Capacity Building for Supply Chain via Enterprise Risk Management

The rapid acceleration of change and technological transformation makes it difficult to make predictions and projections in business life, as it makes the environment ambiguous and increases complexity. It has become almost impossible to achieve corporate agility, resilience, and sustainability goals by attempting to manage them alone. For this reason, the development of leadership capacity is a priority in the agendas of business management and strategy. Competition is always one of the agenda items for businesses. When the aforementioned environmental effects and the technology-intensified processes and activities of the enterprise are considered, the vital need for agile and lean leaders who can make strategic decisions becomes clear.

Globalization and digital transformation, as well as the increasing prevalence of green and lean management practices, have made it necessary for all businesses—even those in supply chains across all industries—to implement more systematic, holistic, and transparent stakeholder relations risk management in a comprehensive manner. Because the supply chain is one of the most important sources of risk in terms of stakeholder relations today. Stakeholder relations remain at the top of the agenda of today's leaders.

In today's world, where digital technologies are accelerating and complicating the business environment, organizations must first master their supply chain systems, assessing their strengths, weaknesses, opportunities, and threats, to mitigate supply chain management (SCM) and the possibility of interruptions or disruptions in the supply chain process. It is very difficult for organizations with deficiencies in self-definition to identify supply chain risks completely and accurately, to analyze those risks objectively, and to decide on the best management option. From this point of view, we present the "**RAgiLean**" SCRM framework, an evolutionary paradigm shift in the supply chain and represents a framework that integrates agile and lean management principles to design and operate a more resilient, flexible, improvable, and efficient risk management system (see Fig. 2.1).

The main capabilities of an enterprise depend on its ability to develop its capacity to meet the needs and evolve its supply chain from traditional to digital and virtual design, maximizing its advantage in a market where competitive balances are constantly changing and effectively managing associated virtual and digital dimensions with new supply chain risks,

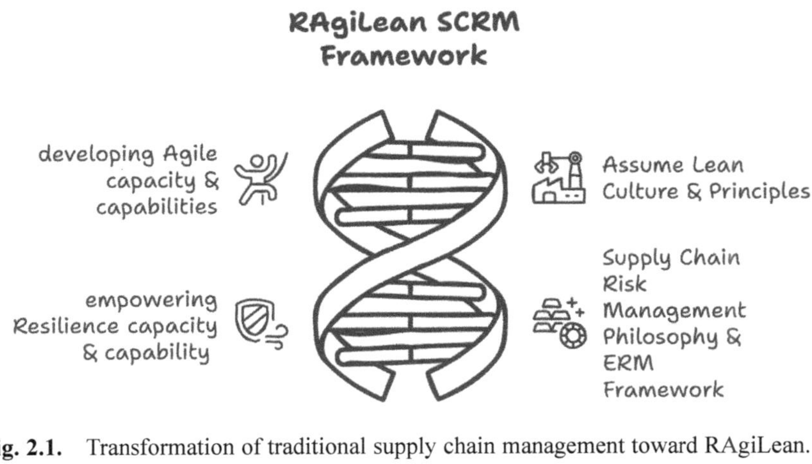

Fig. 2.1. Transformation of traditional supply chain management toward RAgiLean.

Source: Napkin AI used only for visualization; original design by the authors. https://app.napkin.ai/page/CgoiCHByb2Qtb25lEiwKBFBhZ2UaJGMwM2MxYzhhLTFmYzMtNDU0Yi04NGExLTkxZmEyODI5ODQxMQ.

threats, and opportunities (developed from Ambe, 2010). SCM is the centralized management of the flow of goods and services into and out of a company, including all processes related to the conversion of raw materials and components into final products. With SCM, companies can reduce excess costs and deliver products to consumers more quickly and efficiently. Good SCM can help prevent costly product recalls, lawsuits, and bad publicity. The five most critical stages of SCM are planning, procurement, production, distribution, and returns. The supply chain risk manager is responsible for controlling and reducing costs and preventing supply shortages (Fernando, 2024).

Access to resources is becoming more difficult, and production costs are rising, forcing businesses to look for ways to reduce and simplify costs. In fact, lean management is already a savings philosophy that needs to be implemented. However, businesses cannot reach this philosophical awareness without decreasing resources or increasing the costs and difficulties of accessing them. From this point of view, it is more clearly seen that lean, agile, digital, and resilient businesses need the same lean, agile, digital, and resilient leaders. However, the supply chain is not a suitable choice for unconscious cost-cutting. On the contrary, businesses today must invest more in sustainable supply chains, technology, capacity building, digital infrastructure, logistics, and inventory management to achieve their goals. At this point, it is important to define the sustainable supply chain well.

Resilient SCM encompasses the management of material and information flows, as well as cooperation among companies along the supply chain, while considering goals across all three dimensions of sustainable development, i.e. economic, environmental and social, and stakeholder requirements. On the other hand, for sustainable supply chains, environmental and social criteria need to be fulfilled by supply chain members to remain within the supply chain, while it is expected that competitiveness would be maintained through meeting customer needs and related economic criteria (Seuring *et al.*, 2008).

2.4 Building Capacity Strategies and Corporate Resilience

Organizations will need to develop their own capacity strategies based on their specific circumstances and risk exposure. Just as risk management must be integrated with existing processes, organizational capacity for practicing integrated risk management should be built upon what already exists. Assessing and building on existing capacity helps tailor the approach to deal with the organization's specific needs. To build the necessary capacity, organizations may want to determine what already exists, identify where changes, enhancements, or improvements are required, and make the required changes. To build sustainable capacity for integrated risk management within an organization, consideration may be given to two key areas: human resources, and tools and processes (Treasury Board of Canada Secretariat, 2001).

Resilience can be defined as the ability of a person, system, or organization to recover readily when subject to deformation, force, or change. In terms of the supply chain, it can be defined as an ability to adapt readily to change and disruption, as well as manage supply chain risk effectively (River Logic, 2021). In today's global economy, characterized by countries with complex, diverse, and interconnected regional development dynamics, environmental variability with high fragility in certain areas, and differing quality and quantity of raw material and natural resource providers, the ability of organizations to effectively manage risks in their supply chains has become decisive for achieving resilience and agility.

The analysis of supply chain risks within SCRM also provides organizations with the framework they need to tailor the definition and key objectives of SCRM, including the various categories of risks that may affect supply chain operations and the various strategies available to mitigate them. It will be an important convenience for organizations and companies to develop and establish their own SCRM systems to examine the profound impact of global events on supply chain vulnerabilities and basic best practices for risk assessment and mitigation, as well as to use their resources to develop a framework from scratch, i.e. to avoid waste. Importantly, analyzing case studies and best practices for successful SCRM implementations across various sectors plays a role in the SCRM process as an important preparatory stage for a multifaceted understanding of the complex relationship between SCRM and supply chain resilience.

Organizations operating in a digital transformation environment must fully understand the transformative role of technology in developing SCRM capabilities and recognize the need to manage risk by combining reactive and proactive approaches for corporate resilience and agility (Zhang and Wang, 2025). The traditional risk management paradigm of "identify, analyze (evaluate/assess), manage/handle, monitor, and report" is no longer sufficient to address contemporary risks, considering that many current risks are "unknown unknowns". The concept of resilience, which is multifaceted and interdisciplinary in nature, originating from psychology and ecology, is increasingly being adopted in the field of SCM. The phrase "the ability of the supply chain to recover from disruption and return to its desired or original state" is often used to describe supply chain resilience. The presence of supply chain resilience means that the damage caused by systemic risks can be reduced and the system can be recovered as quickly as possible. Its beneficial function in risk management has led to its widespread recognition as a solution for supply chain risk prevention and management in the modern era. Furthermore, it offers new research ideas for dealing with the unpredictability of unpredictable hazards. Therefore, it is imperative to prioritize resilience and agility to effectively prevent and control risks within the industry and supply chains.

2.5 Change of Colors in Economic Geographies: White Collar–Blue Collar

In developed countries such as the US, the geography of manufacturing has changed as the manufacturing economy has been replaced by the service economy. Due to increased global competition and the shift of production to low-cost countries, the US economy has moved away from manufacturing and toward the service sector. This transformation has led to the country losing its role as a world production center but becoming a leader in service exports (Micro-Macro, 2025). The primary factors considered within the scope of production economics include labor costs, logistics, economies of scale, incentives, flexible arrangements, and regional stability, variability, and demand.

Labor costs and skilled labor-oriented progress are important factors in determining which economies countries or companies will prioritize (i.e. whether they will be service-based or production-based). However, this transformation should be considered and interpreted as part of a multidimensional structural change.

Economic changes, geographical distribution, and density of the workforce make it necessary for supply chains to change in accordance with these shifts. Depending on the production density, i.e. blue-collar and white-collar density, supply chains are restructured considering all areas, including locations, processes, and technologies used in processes, in a way that is static or dynamic (Fig. 2.2).

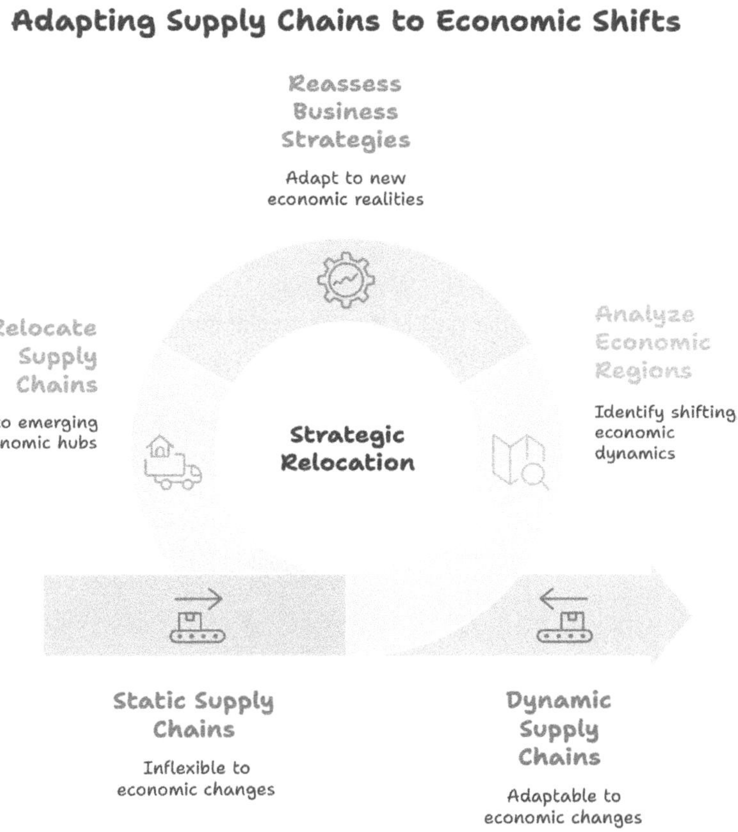

Fig. 2.2. Adapting supply chains to economic shift.

Source: Napkin AI used only for visualization; original design by the authors.

🧑💼 *Change of Colors of Economic Geographies: Change of White Collar – Blue Collar Geography*

The change or reshaping of the geographies of these manufacturing and/or production and service economies has transformed the structure of supply chains into a complex, interconnected network involving many stakeholders in different geographical locations.

The shift in production from the US and Europe has had not only economic but also social, environmental, and geographic consequences. With this change, supply chains are also affected, as the advantages and disadvantages of countries shift. For example, the rise of the service economy has reduced some negative effects in developed countries while also creating new opportunities and advantages. Cities, which were previously production centers, have evolved from blue-collar (worker)-oriented structures to service and technology centers and have become white-collar business areas. Developed countries shifted from low-value-added production to high-value-added sectors such as design, brand management, finance, software, university cities, and R&D. This meant more economic returns with less environmental burden. This has increased environmental pollution and the know-how dependence of other countries on these countries. However, China—a global hub for the production economy—has established integrated supply chains by prioritizing the synergy between production and service sectors, representing a significant portion of global manufacturing volume. Now that China is moving beyond low-cost manufacturing, it has stepped up its initiatives to become a global leader in sectors such as robotics, artificial intelligence (AI), chip manufacturing, e-commerce, digital finance, electric vehicles, and biotechnology.

Meanwhile, since developed countries are also concentrating on service economies, other countries are able to develop their production economies, that is, to significantly strengthen their role in the Eastern global production chain. However, to achieve this, they need to make infrastructure investments, including logistics, and establish agreements to attract investments, provide tax incentives to investors, develop strategies for viable policies, ensure political stability, and develop their capacity to train an educated workforce. It is important for them to switch to medium and high technology, strengthen industrial zones, and encourage increased domestic production. To accomplish all this, it is imperative that they are included in global supply chains. Companies must be able to access markets through international agreements (such as customs unions, free trade agreements, and digital trade agreements) to meet this requirement. This is important in terms of developing logistics infrastructure and a reliable supplier image to access these markets while striving to differentiate themselves through quality, on-time delivery, and green production with strong risk management. Therefore, organizations must manage the risks associated with their global supply chains at the corporate level, in an agile and resilient manner, in accordance with the characteristics of the economies in which they operate.

The economic preferences of developed countries have caused the geographies of manufacturing and service economies to change or be reshaped. These economic geography reconfigurations have transformed the structure of supply chains into a complex, interconnected, and multi-dimensional supply chain network involving many stakeholders across different geographical locations.

In this complex and geographically diverse environment, the supply chain has evolved into an intricate web of interconnected and interactive networks involving a multitude of stakeholders across various geographic locations. This complex network relies on global networks of increasingly diverse suppliers, manufacturers, distributors, and logistics professionals to deliver goods and services to end consumers. While the nature of this interconnectedness fosters efficiency and global reach, it also reveals a multitude of potential areas of pitfalls, opportunities, and threats arising from a mix of vulnerabilities, resilience, agility, and weakness. As the characteristics of economies increase with globalization, the complex interactions in these supply chains create more and more events that are sources of potential risks (opportunities/threats). At this point, it is clear that SCM has been replaced by SCRM.

Supply chains are global, interconnected, and inherently complex to comprehend. The structure and functioning of an organization's supply chain—from internal operations to material sourcing across multiple tiers—are critical to the organization's overall exposure to risk and resilience. It is vital to understand that effective management of supply chain risks requires a deep commitment and sustained effort. While this is not an easy process, the financial implications of an adverse event can be significant, including the loss of potential opportunities and the undermining of long-term stability. Supply chains are the backbone of any organization's ecosystem, providing the foundation for day-to-day operations and facilitating long-term innovation (Solvsten *et al.*, 2025).

Organizational resilience is no longer simply a part of risk management; it has become a top priority in boardroom conversations. In the contemporary business environment, organizations require proactive risk management strategies to ensure operational efficiency and compliance. It is vital that they proactively anticipate, mitigate, and manage potential disruptions, which are only set to increase (Solvsten *et al.*, 2025). SCRM emphasizes a comprehensive, strategic, and updated management system for the supply chain, shaped by experience and adapted to current conditions. Here, with SCRM, we express a framework and philosophy (a way of thinking and understanding) that will guide managers in decision-making moments. This is because the risks and sources of risks (events) that have the potential to affect businesses are no longer just "internal financial and labor-related concerns"; they consist of multi-layered, interconnected, and rapidly changing systemic events.

A smarter, more proactive approach to managing supply chain risks is needed because in today's volatile environment, the ability to quickly adapt and respond to risks within this complex supply chain network has become one of the most important factors in determining long-term success. In recent years, we have directly observed the repercussions of global events on our business. The following factors are causing disruption in the global business environment (Solvsten *et al.*, 2025):

(a) the pandemic caused by the virus known as SARS-CoV-2 (COVID-19);
(b) a growing shortage of workers in the global workforce;
(c) rising inflation rates;
(d) geopolitical instability in various regions of the world;
(e) wars and conflicts in different parts of the world;
(f) the increasingly visible impact of climate change on supply chains;
(g) cybercrime.

When we consider the increasing complexity of interconnected risks, it becomes clear that these challenges are not easy to overcome.

In the current business environment, enterprises of all sizes are confronted with a range of challenges related to geopolitical tensions, inflation, cybersecurity threats, raw material shortages, regulatory changes, digital transformation, and data availability. These factors have the potential to impact operations, revenue streams, and long-term viability. The global supply chain continues to demonstrate signs of uncertainty and complexity, highlighting the need for flexible and adaptable risk management strategies. As insurance markets become more competitive and unpredictable factors become more challenging to anticipate, conventional risk management techniques are facing significant challenges (WTW *et al.*, 2025). At the same time, geographical conditions (such as resources, access to resources, wars in neighboring regions, political stability in neighboring regions, and political cooperation) may also give rise to risks that have the potential to affect the functioning of supply chains. In this respect, it is not enough simply to identify the risks faced by businesses from a supply chain and holistic perspective. With SCRM, modeling the integrated effects of potential risks and developing scenarios by considering their interactions among themselves increases/strengthens the maneuverability of businesses to become more agile and resilient.

SCRM involves the management of risks throughout the process of delivering products from producers to end customers, ensuring that products meet the requirements of end users in a safe, sound, timely, and secure manner. In the software industry, the delivery of products does not necessitate physical access for the execution of attacks on the supply chain. But the software supply chain is more vulnerable to attacks than in other industries, and the consequences of successful infiltration can disseminate rapidly (Ahn *et al.*, 2025). SCRM can be defined as the process of identifying and resolving potential vulnerabilities within a company's supply chain. The objective is to mitigate the adverse effects of these risks on a company's operations, reputation, and financial performance (McGrath and Jonker, 2023).

2.6 Risk Interconnectivity

Interconnectivity between risks is a critical issue in SCM because supply chains often involve multiple, interconnected risks arising from supply-side, demand-side, or unexpected background uncertainties (Mukherjee and Padhi, 2022). The fact that the risks are interconnected indicates the existence of interaction risks. Risks can trigger one another, thereby increasing or decreasing the severity of their effects (low probability). The interaction of risks constituted the main component that could not be considered and therefore managed before corporate risk management. ERM is also an important managerial system that can develop strategies for integrated impact and impact severity by considering the interactions of risks, analyzing, and prioritizing them.

The fact that risks affect each other is not a new concept; however, over the past 20 years, the interdependence of risks has increased as the physical and digital worlds have become more connected. However, many organizations have not developed a process to systematically assess the links between risks. Leading institutions now use a "risk network" approach instead of a "risk profile", prioritizing risks not only based on a matrix of probability and impact but also on their interconnectedness (KPMG, 2019).

In today's fast-paced, globalized economy, businesses must prioritize seamless communication and coordination among all supply chain elements to remain competitive. The use of digital technologies offers real-time visibility and improved efficiency, making supply chains more resilient and successful. The interconnectedness of risks plays a central role in SCRM. In a modern, globalized economy, the importance of seamless integration and cooperation between SCM and logistics has increased and reached a decisive position (Rahman and Faizanuddin, 2025).

Global supply chains are becoming increasingly fragile due to a combination of geopolitical instability, environmental challenges, and economic volatility; these multifaceted crises (or "polycrises") are fueling each other and creating spillover effects. According to a Maersk survey, 80% of shippers see geopolitical tensions as the most dominant risk, while studies from the University of Cambridge show that crises are interconnected and mutually reinforcing. Global service reliability in maritime shipping has fallen to 50–55% by 2024, with capacity constraints and rerouting driving vessel demand three times faster than cargo volume and resulting in fluctuations in freight rates. Resilience in this environment requires improving service reliability through hub-and-spoke network models and adaptive planning, proactively managing demand and risks with AI and predictive analytics, supporting port and terminal operations with robust infrastructure and workforces, and enabling shippers to respond quickly to disruptions with data-driven visibility, third-party risk management, and alternative transportation solutions. The interconnected nature of risks in supply chains makes it essential to make global transportation and supply chains more resilient to future crises through collaboration, data integration, and adaptive strategies (UNCTAD, 2024).

Interconnected risks are defined as an 'interconnected risk structure in which the actions taken to solve one risk affect other dependent risks.' This has the potential to significantly increase the total intensity of catastrophic events. The total intensity of catastrophic events caused by interconnected components affecting supply chains far exceeds that caused by significant natural disasters, such as the 2011 Tsunami in Japan or Hurricane Katrina in the US (2005), Mukherjee and Padhi, 2022.

Risks can be linked in different ways: causal or consequential relationships, based on common causes, or positive/negative correlations. In a positive correlation, risks increase or decrease together; in a negative correlation, an increase in one risk leads to a decrease in the other. The strength of these connections can also vary; strong correlation increases the likelihood that when one risk occurs, the other risk will also be triggered. In addition, the risk velocity dimension of risks is also important. This concept refers to how long it takes for a risk to take its full effect on an organization. Assessing risk velocity helps organizations determine their level of preparedness for high-velocity risk events (KPMG, 2019).

Within a supply chain, every component—be it a supplier, manufacturer, logistics provider, or retailer—is dependent on the smooth functioning of the others. Through a well-established connection, "information flows freely, allowing businesses to react quickly to changes in demand, disruptions, or operational inefficiencies" (Rahman and Faizanuddin, 2025).

These interconnected risks arise from the complexity of supply chain components and can pose significant challenges for the firm. Case examples are presented here, explaining the effects of interconnected risks; the following concrete examples will be useful for a full and accurate understanding of the subject (Mukherjee and Padhi, 2022):

Volvo: The link between dollar value and car sales has led to a loss of revenue, which affects raw material sourcing decisions.

Ericsson: The disruption in chip supply caused a loss of $400 million.

Toyota: Part of the product recall crisis has been attributed to supply chain complexity caused by the interconnectedness of supply components.

Chevron: The production halt due to hurricanes and the increase in oil prices caused the company to lose $400 million.

Cisco Systems: Its outsourcing strategy significantly increased supply chain complexity and the interconnectedness of risks, leading to a 300% increase in inventories and a $2.25 billion loss when the market crashed.

Emerging and interconnected risks are increasingly shaping strategic decisions and long-term resilience within supply chains. Organizations must understand and manage these risks; unrecognized suppliers, overlooking links between risks, or misidentifying emerging risks can lead to vulnerabilities within the supply chain. Regulators no longer just want to see the risk list; they expect businesses to explain how risks are assessed, so it is critical that risks are analyzed with a time perspective and their interconnectedness. While WTW research enables the redetermination of priorities by revealing hidden risk dependencies, properly managed emerging and interconnected risks not only provide resilience to crises but also increase the capacity to seize strategic opportunities within the supply chain (WTW, 2025).

The food, agribusiness, and beverage (FAB) business sector faces interconnected and complex risks, such as economic fluctuations, geopolitical tensions, climate crises, and increased regulations; these risks can quickly create a domino effect in the supply chain and increase costs and operational risks. With global food demand growing by 35–56% by 2050, driven by changing consumer preferences and sustainability pressures, the industry's operational and strategic decisions need to be increasingly precise. While technologies such as digital transformation and AI offer opportunities in the supply chain, cyber threats and digital disruptions increase risks. Therefore, FAB businesses must adopt an innovative and holistic approach in both risk capital and human capital, accurately identify interconnected risks in the supply chain, proactively reassess operations and strategies, and seize strategic opportunities while increasing resilience (AON, 2024).

Interconnected risks affect the raw material procurement decisions of companies in various ways. "Focusing on the strength of this interconnectedness—tightly and (or) loosely connected—between sources of risk can help develop supply plans that are critical to supply chain risks". In addition, the optimal supply choice for a risk-averse manufacturer also depends on the degree of interdependence of risks, as demonstrated by the following examples (Mukherjee and Padhi, 2022):

Supply and background risks: When input price risk and background risk become "tightly" linked, the risk-averse producer may prefer to buy fewer inputs.

Demand and other risks: When product price risk becomes "tightly" linked to input price or background risk, the producer may prefer to buy more inputs. Developing strategies for risks using risk linkages is also within the scope of resilient, lean, and agile SCRM.

Digital technologies such as AI, the Internet of Things (IoT), and blockchain are rapidly strengthening the interaction of risks and their interconnectedness. This is actually one of the main challenges of risk management in today's conditions. By creating a network where physical objects are digitally connected, IoT "increases agility, visibility, tracking—in a sense, simplicity—and information sharing". For example, IoT sensors can monitor the condition of products during transit (such as temperature and humidity), allowing logistics managers to make proactive decisions to ensure product safety and reduce waste. AI plays a crucial role in supply chain optimization by automating processes such as demand forecasting, inventory management, and supplier selection. Furthermore, with AI tools, companies can anticipate and respond to risks such as supplier shortages, natural disasters, or geopolitical issues, ensuring business continuity and resilience. Blockchain technology, on the other hand, could revolutionize connectivity by providing a transparent, tamper-proof record of transactions and movements. This enables secure information sharing throughout the supply chain, reducing the risk of fraud and enhancing traceability (Rahman and Faizanuddin, 2025).

In the context of the supply chain, risk interaction and interconnectivity mean that a risk arising at any point in the supply chain network's administrative functions or operational processes can directly or indirectly affect all other components of the supply chain. Just as the links in the chain are interconnected, an impact occurring in one will also impact the other links. This also applies to risk management outcomes. The strategy implemented for one risk or risk group will act as a potential source of impact on other risks. For example, a problem with raw materials supply can lead to both production delays and increased costs.

Multiple and comprehensive risks exist in the supply chain. SCRM takes this into account. This is why risk categories are developed during the risk identification phase. It is noted that supply chain risks can interact with multiple risks simultaneously. This makes the risk management process and its implementation more complex and challenging. One of the main reasons why not every company successfully implements ERM is that they fail to recognize risk interactions and, even if they do, they lack the competencies to manage them. Digital transformation supports risk identification and agile responses, but companies must master digital systems. Risk interactions are inherent in the supply chain. The increasing variety and number of risks, coupled with the increasing complexity of interactions and interconnectivity, further interconnect systems. Therefore, it is necessary to be able to see and manage both the parts and the whole, and the integrated impact of each on the system, from a holistic perspective. To manage this situation, companies must ensure a transparent flow of information and collaboration among all supply chain stakeholders through a proactive and holistic corporate-wide risk management approach.

2.7 Risk Culture to Corporate Risk Resilience

An organization's culture reflects its core values, behaviors, and decisions. Management decisions are, in turn, a function of the available information, judgment, capabilities, and experience. An entity's culture influences how the organization applies its ERM framework, how it identifies risk, what types of risk it accepts, and how it manages risk (COSO, 2017). An entity with a risk-aware culture stresses the importance of managing risk and encourages transparent and timely flow of information. It does this without assigning blame but with an attitude of understanding, accountability, and continual improvement.

An effective risk management culture is founded on the interaction between people, systems, processes, and the wider environment in which they operate. The framework emphasizes that sustainable risk management requires embedding these elements across the organization rather than treating them in isolation (Audit Scotland, 2024).

Organizational culture essentially defines how employees create, share, and use information. It also determines what information is important and why it is so; it also establishes the context of social interaction and shapes how organizational knowledge is produced. In addition, the culture of "adhocracy" is characterized by a creative work environment and a spirit of risk-taking, and these characteristics help the creation of knowledge within the organization. On the other hand, the culture of hierarchy is defined as the opposite of "adhocracy", and it is emphasized that it has less presence in creative businesses (Aichouche *et al.*, 2022). Risk culture emphasizes that risk management is everyone's responsibility. In addition, the commitment of senior management is the basis and essential to the implementation success of risk management.

Creating positive risk management behaviors and culture helps because it sets an appropriate "tone from the top" and enables an organization to clearly describe the positive attitudes and behaviors it expects to see in risk management. Behaviors and culture are more important than processes. That's not to say that processes and systems and controls are unimportant—far from it. But experience tells us that we cannot foster a risk-aware culture by putting the primary emphasis on the process side.

Leaders need to lead—by example, not by exhortation—encouraging the right approach to risk, percolating deeply into the organization (hard-wired with the right skills and processes) (Risk Culture Lab, 2025).

As emphasized in COSO's guidance, effective ERM depends on establishing a strong risk culture throughout the organization. This risk culture is shaped by leadership style, accountability structures, communication, and incentives that encourage proactive risk awareness and management. Gaps in risk ownership must be addressed to ensure accountability, and executives and boards must play a key role in strengthening discipline and oversight to address significant gaps in risk management capabilities. At higher levels of maturity, organizations foster a culture of continuous improvement, innovation, and collaboration, where best practices are shared and quality is integrated into processes (Protiviti, 2019).

Supply chain resilience requires a culture based on risk awareness in order to build strong defenses against uncertainties and respond quickly in times of crisis. Risk management is inherently probability-based; therefore, companies should not ignore low-probability but high-impact risks and should invest in mitigating these risks using an insurance approach. For example, a pharmaceutical company could lose up to 25% of its earnings before interest, taxes, depreciation, and amortization from a supply shock that disrupts operations for one month. Therefore, scenario development, probability assessment, and incorporating risk costs into business decisions are critical. Leaders must clearly define their risk tolerance and establish a common understanding across the organization regarding which risks should be mitigated and which should be accepted. It is also important to foster an open culture where employees feel comfortable sharing bad news or risk signals and where there is a high sense of ownership. This enables both management and employees to take responsibility and develop rapid solutions when risks arise. This approach requires concrete plans, clear responsibilities and timelines for priority risks, and regular reviews of all risks. The COVID-19 experience has shown that focusing solely on efficiency is not enough; in the face of the unpredictability of global shocks, companies investing in resilience and continuity today will be better prepared for inevitable crises in the future (Alicke *et al.*, 2020).

A strong risk culture contributes to the long-term sustainability of organizations by ensuring that risks are identified, assessed, and managed effectively. When establishing an ERM framework, developing risk awareness, understanding, and a culture among stakeholders is critical. While risk awareness is generally strong among boards of directors and senior executives in the public sector, the operational level tends to focus on specific issues such as health, security, or data privacy. A strong risk culture contributes to the long-term sustainability of organizations through the effective identification, assessment, and management of risks. Key elements of a risk culture include senior management's stance, governance, the integration of risks into decision-making processes, awareness and competency development, and the value added by risk management in daily operations. However, even with strong risk awareness, internalizing this awareness and institutionalizing appropriate risk behaviors within organizations remains challenging, and risk management is often limited to specific areas. Furthermore, decision-makers may encounter cognitive biases such as recency bias, anchoring bias, uncertainty avoidance, and status quo ante. To ensure the sustainability of ERM implementation, institutions conduct practices such as face-to-face training, e-learning modules, communication activities, awareness days, expert talks, online newsletters, and small-group training. The maturity of the risk culture is measured through anonymous surveys, focus group meetings, stakeholder interviews, and independent consultant evaluations. A strong risk culture enables more effective risk management, cross-functional collaboration, strengthened strategic decision-making processes, and the sustainable achievement of organizational goals (KPMG, 2019).

2.8 Supply Chain Risk Management Concept: Opportunities and Challenges

ERM is not a static exercise but a continuous journey to improve an organization's ability to anticipate and manage its risks. ERM is used not only to control risks but also to create value. The benefits of institutions, especially with the updated approach in guidelines such as today's COSO, are as follows (KPMG, 2019):

- **Reduction of blind spots:** By assessing interconnectivity, risk clusters that can have knock-on effects can be recognized earlier.
- **Stronger decision-making:** Integrating risk-based analysis into strategy increases the reliability and speed of decisions.

- **Organization-wide awareness:** Risk culture is developing with the spread of risk awareness not only in senior management but also at operational levels.
- **Efficiency and resource optimization:** Identifying common controls and risk mitigation strategies ensures more efficient use of resources allocated to risk management.
- **Strategic alignment:** Linking ERM outputs with performance management contributes to organizations achieving strategic goals in a more sustainable way.

2.8.1 *SCRM Opportunities and Benefits*

The opportunities with benefits of SCRM include greater resilience through preparedness for disruptions, continuity of operations, and sustained competitiveness. It enables cost reduction by optimizing inventory and logistics, ensures compliance with quality and regulatory standards to avoid penalties and protect its reputation, and helps maintain brand image by proactively addressing risks. Furthermore, by supporting corporate social responsibility and advancing ESG goals, SCRM contributes to sustainable practices and minimizes environmental impact across the supply chain (McGrath and Jonker, 2023):

(a) **Resilience:** The greatest benefit of SCRM is that it increases resilience. By identifying potential risks in advance and creating contingency plans, companies can quickly react to unexpected events, ensure operational continuity, meet customer demands, and maintain competitive advantages.
(b) **Cost reduction:** Effective SCR enables reducing costs by identifying areas of waste and inefficiency. For example, optimizing inventory levels reduces holding costs and the risk of out-of-stocks, while improving logistics processes reduces shipping costs and shortens delivery times.
(c) **Reputation and quality:** Making sure suppliers meet quality and regulatory standards protects a company from expensive recalls and legal penalties. This not only secures the company's reputation but also ensures that quality products and services are provided to retailers and customers.

2.8.2 *Challenges*

Digital transformation and data availability are now top priorities for businesses, and digital tools are becoming central to future supply chain strategies. It is vital that suppliers and customers continue to cooperate in order to maintain resilience. While many companies are still seeking significant change, a gradual strategy adjustment is typically favored over a complete overhaul (WTW *et al.*, 2025).

The primary challenges within supply chains include complexity and a lack of visibility, inadequate risk assessment frameworks, organizational resistance, supplier non-compliance, environmental and regulatory changes, and cybersecurity threats. Real-time data sharing and transparency should be ensured through ERP and other integrated digital platforms to increase visibility. Organizations should not overlook critical threats by developing flexible risk assessment frameworks that incorporate qualitative and quantitative metrics. Risk awareness training, leadership ownership, and cross-functional cooperation should be encouraged to overcome internal resistance and low participation. Clear SLAs should be established, regular audits should be conducted, and performance monitoring technologies should be used to prevent supplier non-compliance and performance issues. Environmental and regulatory changes should be closely monitored and integrated into risk assessment processes. Finally, strong measures should be taken against cybersecurity threats, regular audits should be conducted, and regular training should be provided to employees to reduce risks associated with human error (Ivalua, 2025).

Implementing SCRM can be challenging for companies due to several factors. Modern global supply chains are deeply complex, making it difficult to track details closely at every step from start to finish. Furthermore, if a company does not have access to reliable data on its suppliers, it will not be able to fully and accurately assess risks. Some suppliers may be reluctant to provide data due to privacy concerns or a fear of losing a competitive advantage. And even if they provide enough data to identify risks, they may be unwilling to adopt new practices or alter existing ones. It also comes with costs: new technologies, training, and hands-on monitoring require financial investment that can sometimes prove too much for smaller businesses to accommodate. The more stakeholders involved, the larger the budget required to maintain due diligence across them all (McGrath and Jonker, 2023).

2.9 Capacity Building for Supply Chain Risk Management via Digital Transformations

2.9.1 *Technology Impact on Risks*

Technology is described as a critical enabler of ERM. Enterprise-wide systems and digital tools allow organizations to consolidate risk information, automate controls, and improve real-time monitoring. For example, chief information officers (CIOs) play a key role in aligning IT operations with risk governance, ensuring gaps and overlaps in IT risk ownership are eliminated. The guide also explains how risk management evolves with technology: from discrete and periodic activities to continuous, enterprise-wide monitoring supported by automation, dashboards, and workflow integration. Advanced analytics, integrated measurement methodologies, and digital platforms strengthen risk-adjusted performance management, improve reporting, and embed risk management into day-to-day operations (Protiviti, 2006).

Thanks to technological advancements and transformation, capacity building in the supply chain has been achieved. High technology and AI offer fast, accurate, effective, and powerful ways to analyze supply chains, thereby improving their performance, visibility, and transparency, enabling timely follow-up and analysis of customer demands and requests. Therefore, a high-performance, cost-effective, and accountable SCM system will be established and operated.

Digital technologies (such as robots and automation, IoT, blockchain, AI, advanced analytics, and 3D printing) can play an important role in providing businesses with a strategic competitive advantage by making supply chains more efficient, transparent, and customer-centric. However, each of these technologies must be implemented with careful planning, effective and correct use—that is, mastery of the technology—and strong security risk mitigation. In the technology–human interface, the gap should be as small as possible, and a level of cooperation and harmonious work should be created. Gaps in this interface, called gap, are a source of potential risk (meaning threats).

Technology is a key enabler for building a connected and integrated ERM framework. ERM processes can be enhanced, for example, with more timely and accurate reporting of information from operations and improved consistency of risk management practices, among others.

In other words, technology allows organizations to deploy "sensors" within operational processes and functions, perform analysis on collected data and information, and improve the timeliness of risk escalation and management. Technology can also enable organizations to prepare and report risks in an interactive dashboard format. Risks are updated almost real-time and supported by data and indicators monitored on an ongoing basis (KPMG, 2019, p. 15).

Some technology tools are available to assist in the facilitation or identification phase. Additionally, software is available to assist an organization with the entire ERM process. Gartner Inc. recently reviewed ERM software vendors based on two aspects: completeness of their vision and their ability to execute. Some organizations choose to either develop their own ERM processes tailored to their needs or hire consultants to help with the process. Technology products not only help with the process but also assist with data gathering, modeling, or reporting. One risk software tool, for example, helps with capital optimization and data management. Other technology products are designed to help with issues such as time-series modeling, correlations, and other advanced modeling techniques. Finally, certain industries have software tailored to companies in that industry, such as the online maturity model available for insurance companies (IMA, 2007).

Before investing in a technology solution, organizations should conduct a risk analysis of it because technology may not always produce accurate information, even when it is not malicious. This reveals that the use of AI under human leadership and control/supervision is still necessary. In this respect, the fact that the system is in its most critical position is comforting and important as an indication that we humans are still needed. Organizations need to firmly establish the basic structures of the ERM (risk governance model, documentation of processes, regular risk reporting, communication with stakeholders, and awareness). When choosing a technology, off-the-shelf systems may provide the advantage of fast installation but may be limited in terms of flexibility; custom-developed solutions, on the other hand, do not require a license fee, fully adapt to the institution's workflow, and can be customized. In successful applications, technology does not dictate processes; on the contrary, it adapts to ERM processes. The proposed approach for government agencies is to include technology integration in the ERM roadmap but to advance it in a gradual and deliberate manner (KPMG, 2019, p. 17).

While robots and automation speed up order processing by increasing warehouse efficiency, the IoT improves safety and delivery accuracy by tracking the location and status of products in real time. Blockchain technology builds trust by providing transparency and traceability; AI, on the other hand, improves inventory and demand management while optimizing decision-making processes. 3D printing offers local and flexible production, reducing delivery time and costs and giving a strategic advantage to supply chains (Stackpole, 2020).

Leading AI companies, including Google, Amazon, Cohere, and Mistral, are prioritizing resolving accuracy issues in chatbots by implementing technical updates, enhancing data quality, and introducing verification systems. Despite their efforts, they have not completely eradicated the problem of "hallucinations", or erroneous responses, in AI systems, caused by probabilistic word sequence prediction. Experts explain that these inaccuracies result from the process of selecting the most likely word during text generation, often leading to contextually irrelevant or incorrect information. These issues represent a significant challenge, not only hindering the further utilization of AI in sectors such as healthcare and law—which demand precision—but also underscoring the ongoing struggle to perfect the accuracy of chatbots (Forbes Turkey, 2025).

2.10 Industry Example: Medical Supply Chain and Managing Cybersecurity Risks

The healthcare industry is highly susceptible to cyberattacks, which often target internet-connected medical devices, outdated technologies, cloud applications, third-party services, and the broad supplier networks within healthcare facilities. These vulnerabilities can be exploited in many ways, including servicing supplier assets, weak manufacturer security designs, network installations, borrowed or leased devices, default manufacturer passwords, and supplier applications integrated into health systems. Because the consequences of such risks are severe—ranging from financial losses to the irreparable loss of life—the healthcare industry requires **proactive risk management strategies**. Effective supply chain cybersecurity risk management not only protects patient information and sensitive data from internal and external threats but also strengthens preparedness, business continuity planning, and countermeasures for the

Fig. 2.3. Medical supply chain risk management.

Source: Napkin AI used only for visualization; original design by the authors. https://app.napkin.ai/page/CgoiCHByb2Qtb25lEiwKBFBhZ2UaJGFkNDQwYWE3LTY2NzMtNDM5MC04NzA2LThmNTIyNTQ2NTMwZg.

entire sector (Health Sector Coordinating Council Cybersecurity Working Group, 2023).

Managing supply chain cybersecurity risks in the healthcare industry requires a proactive approach to protect patient information and sensitive data from malicious actors. This is not only operational but also a regulatory requirement under the Health Insurance Portability and Accountability Act (HIPAA). Cybersecurity has gone beyond information technology and has become a common responsibility of all healthcare sector stakeholders. In the US, the U.S. Food and Drug Administration (FDA), the U.S. Department of Health and Human Services (HHS), and the U.S. HHS Centers for Medicare & Medicaid Services (CMS) are increasing cybersecurity requirements for healthcare organizations and suppliers (see Fig. 2.3). In this context, the FDA has published new guidelines, HHS and CMS have made various recommendations, and the HHS Health Sector Cybersecurity Coordination Center (HC3) was established in November 2018. In addition, the National Institute of Standards and Technology (NIST) updated the Cybersecurity Framework (CSF) 1.1 in April 2018 to add the "Supply Chain Risk Management" category, aiming to reduce risk through buyer-supplier relationships and encourage suppliers who offer stronger security solutions (Please see the original report by the Health Sector Coordinating Council Cybersecurity Working Group, 2023).

References

Ahn, J. K., Cho, K., Seo, K., Kim, H.-J., and Kim, S. (2025). Comprehensive analysis and recommendation of supply chain risk management framework for the military domain. *IEEE Access*, 13, 96813–96833. https://doi.org/10.1109/ACCESS.2025.3573515.

Aichouche, R., Chergui, K., Brika, S., Mezher, M., Musa, A., and Laamari, A. (2022, May). Exploring the relationship between organizational culture types and knowledge management processes: A meta-analytic path analysis. *Frontiers in Psychology*, 1313, 856234. https://doi.org.10.3389/fpsyg.2022.856234.

Alicke, K., Barriball, E., Lund, S., and Swan, D. (2020, May). Operations practice, is your supply chain risk blind—or risk resilient? McKinsey & Company. https://www.mckinsey.com/~/media/McKinsey/Business%20Functions/Operations/Our%20Insights/Is%20your%20supply%20chain%20risk%20blind%20or%20risk%20resilient/Is-your-supply-chain-risk-blind-or-risk-resilient.pdf.

Ambe, I. M. (2010). Agile supply chain: Strategy for competitive advantage. *Journal of Global Strategic Management*, 4(1), 5–17.

AON. (2024, July 01). Connected perspectives: Better decisions on interconnected risks for FAB organizations. AON: aon.com. https://www.aon.com/en/insights/articles/connected-perspectives-better-decisions-on-interconnected-risks-for-fab-organizations.

Audit Scotland. (2024). Risk management framework 2024–2026. Audit Scotland. https://audit.scot/uploads/docs/um/risk_management_framework_24-26.pdf.

Committee of Sponsoring Organizations of the Treadway Commission (COSO). (2017). Enterprise risk management: Integrating with strategy and performance. Committee of Sponsoring Organizations of the Treadway Commission. https://www.coso.org/Documents/2017-COSO-ERM-Integrating-with-Strategy-and-Performance-Executive-Summary.pdf; https://www.coso.org/_files/ugd/3059fc_61ea5985b03c4293960642fdce408eaa.pdf; https://www.coso.org/guidance-erm.

Fernando, J. (2024). Supply chain management (SCM): How it works & why it's important. Investopedia. https://www.investopedia.com/terms/s/scm.asp.

Forbes Turkey. (2025, July 23). hallucination" in artificial intelligence: Accurate knowledge generation is still unsolved. Forbes Turkey. https://www.forbes.com.tr/makale/yapay-zekada-halusinasyon-sorunu-dogru-bilgi-uretimi-hala-cozulemedi.

GAINSystems, LLC. (2025, July 30). Supply chain risk intelligence: Practical steps to build resilient operations. GAINSystems.com. https://gainsystems.com/blog/supply-chain-risk-intelligence-practical-steps-to-build-resilient-operations/?gad_source=1&gad_campaignid=22716848818&gbraid=0AAA

AAo32s4iKUHhfp2lCe5ttbBPIDK_N8&gclid=Cj0KCQjwhafEBhCcARIsAEGZEKIBv6Ubk9ENcsneDMuIsrjahrrlVZ-nwUvddfnSULCpszGFBIrkFjkaAkfEEALw_wcB.

Ghadge, A., Dani, S., and Kalawsky, R. (2012, November 2). Supply chain risk management: Present and future scope. *The International Journal of Logistics Management*, 23(3), 313–339. https://doi.org/10.1108/09574091211289200.

Health Sector Coordinating Council Cybersecurity Working Group. (2023, October). Health industry cybersecurity—supply chain risk management guide v2.0. Health Sector Coordinating Council: healthsectorcouncil.org. https://healthsectorcouncil.org/wp-content/uploads/2023/10/HIC-SCRiM_2023-2.pdf.

Institute of Management Accountants (IMA). (2007). Enterprise risk management: Tools and techniques for effective implementation. IMA. https://www.imanet.org/-/media/66fbef31c9f1416b9f57b49798c23ed5&ved=2ahUKEwjt0Zf34MaPAxW_BdsEHYqLCYY4ChAWegQIJxAB&usg=AOvVaw2pb4M0rQ_k1hfV409rj6bg; https://eu.imanet.org/research-publications/statem; https://eu.imanet.org/research-publications/statements-on-management-accounting/enterprise-risk-management-tools-and-techniques-for-effective-implementation?_gl=1*7wmcfd*_gcl_au*MTkzNjI1Mjg2Mi4xNzU3.

Ivalua. (2025, February 25). Supply chain risk management strategies & solutions. https://www.ivalua.com/blog/supply-chain-risk-management/. Accessed September 08, 2025.

KPMG. (2019). Enhanced risk management the journey to ERM 2.0, a guide for the public sector in Singapore. KPMG Services Pte. Ltd, Singapore. https://assets.kpmg.com/content/dam/kpmg/sg/pdf/2019/08/the-journey-to-erm-2.pdf.

McGrath, A. and Jonker, A. (2023, December 2). What is supply chain risk management (SCRM)? IBM. https://www.ibm.com/think/topics/supply-chain-risk-management.

Micro-Macro. (2025, April 14). Mikro-Makro. https://mikro-makro.net/abd-dunya-uretim-merkezi-olma-konumunu-nasil-kaybetti; https://mikro-makro.net/abd-dunya-uretim-merkezi-olma-konumunu-nasil-kaybetti.

Mukherjee, S. and Padhi, S. (2022). Sourcing decision under interconnected risks: An application of mean–variance preferences approach. *Annals of Operations Research*, 313, 1243–1268. https://doi.org/10.1007/s10479-021-04485-3.

Nystedt, J., Wegman, C., and Glodde, M. (2024, May 14). Agile risk management: Preparing for success beyond adversity. Association for Financial Professionals. https://www.financialprofessionals.org/training-resources/resources/articles/Details/agile-risk-management-preparing-for-success-beyond-adversity.

Protiviti. (2006). Guide to enterprise risk management- frequently asked questions. Ucop.edu. https://www.ucop.edu/enterprise-risk-and-resilience/_files/erm_panelrpt.pdf. Retrieved September 08, 2025.

Rahman, F. A. and Faizanuddin, M. (2025). Interconnected supply chain management and logistics: Key to driving business success. *Management* (Montevideo), 3(142). https://doi.org/10.62486/agma2025142.

Risk Culture Lab. (2025, September 08). Management risk in government. Risk Culture Lab & Linkedin. https://www.linkedin.com/posts/risk-culture-lab_management-of-risk-in-government-activity-7367634147093282816-JLB2?utm_source=social_share_send&utm_medium=member_desktop_web&rcm=ACoAAAL8TtwBe_AqaXiG-RnNVSGAETh8qasg8UY. Accessed September 03, 2025.

River Logic. (2021). Supply chain resilience 9 things to consider and how to be successful. http://www.riverlogic.com/. Retrieved at September 27, 2021.

Seuring, S., Sarkis, J., Müller, M., and Rao, P. (2008). Sustainability and supply chain management—An introduction to the special issue. *Journal of Cleaner Production*, 16(15), 1545–1551. https://doi.org/10.1016/j.jclepro.2008.02.002; https://www.sciencedirect.com/science/article/pii/S0959652608000334.

Solvsten, S., McNulty, D., and Milne, A. E. (2025, May 14). Global Supply Chain Risk Report: Navigating Supply Chain Risks and Insurability. University of Southern Denmark Research Portal SDU. 61 p. https://portal.findresearcher.sdu.dk/en/publications/global-supply-chain-risk-report-navigating-supply-chain-risks-and.

Stackpole, B. (2020, February 14). 5 supply chain technologies that deliver competitive advantage. MIT Sloan School of Management. https://mitsloan.mit.edu/ideas-made-to-matter/5-supply-chain-technologies-deliver-competitive-advantage.

Treasury Board of Canada Secretariat. (2001). Integrated risk management Framework. Government of Canada Publications Treasury Board of Canada Secretariat Cat. No. BT22-78/2001. https://www.canada.ca/en/treasury-board-secretariat/corporate/risk-management/guide-integrated-risk-management.html; https://publications.gc.ca/collections/collection_2019/sct-tbs/BT22-78-2001-eng.pdf.

United Nations Conference on Trade and Development (UNCTAD). (2024). Enhancing supply chain resilience amid rising global risks. Erişim adresi. United Nations Conference on Trade and Development (UNCTAD). https://unctad.org/news/enhancing-supply-chain-resilience-amid-rising-global-risks.

WTW. (2025, September 10). Emerging and interconnected risks. WTW. https://www.wtwco.com/en-ca/insights/campaigns/emerging-and-interconnected-risks.

WTW, Wegbrans, H., Delchar, S., Grimwade, M., and Sølvsten, S. (2025). Supply chain disruptions are no longer rare — they're the new normal 2025 WTW Global Supply Chain Risk Survey. Global Supply Chain Risk Report 2025. https://www.wtwco.com/en-gb/insights/2025/05/wtw-global-supply-chain-risk-report-2025.

Zhang, Z. and Wang, X. (2025). Evolutionary game analysis of coal industry chain supply chain risk prevention and control from the perspective of resilience. *Sustainable Futures,* 9, 100678. https://doi.org/10.1016/j.sftr.2025.100678.

Chapter 3

Stakeholder Engagement and Supply Chain Fragility: Enhancing Corporate Performance Through Collaborative Networks

3.1 Stakeholder Engagement as Part of SCRM Framework

The phenomenon of globalization has been demonstrated to result in the establishment of comparable regions across the globe. The increased interconnectedness of the global economy, facilitated by globalization processes, has the potential to extend the reach of products and services to a wider demographic. The advent of online ordering has facilitated the global distribution of products, now procured by companies and individuals worldwide. This suggests that preferences are subject to mutual influence. For commercial entities, the primary objective is market expansion, with the aim of enhancing their social and economic profitability. Following the growth of the market, it is imperative that the supply chain be capable of expanding and managing accordingly. Consequently, the contemporary paradigm of supply chain management has evolved to encompass the notion of supply chain risk management (SCRM). It is imperative for organizations to develop a robust risk management strategy within their supply chains to ensure their continued viability.

The concept of "stakeholder engagement" in the context of the supply chain refers to a company's proactive, ongoing, and mutually beneficial communication, collaboration, and relationship management with all stakeholders involved in or affected by the supply chain.

Stakeholder engagement is a key aspect of business operations, and effective risk management is essential to ensure the smooth functioning of the supply chain. Stakeholder risk management involves the proactive management of risks related to relationships with all parties that directly or indirectly impact the supply chain. These parties include suppliers, logistics providers, customers, employees, local communities, and regulatory authorities. It is crucial for companies to have well-defined risk strategies and objectives in place to ensure the safety and success of their operations. Engagement is considered a form of risk management because establishing and maintaining the same level of trust with all stakeholders simultaneously, being transparent with them, and receiving the same level of transparency from them, sharing information, and regularly communicating effectively are risky processes. Finding the right balance is essential for achieving company objectives. A risk management-based approach also helps to establish balance in the supply chain stakeholder engagement process (see Fig. 3.1).

Companies interact with a wide range of stakeholders. Each stakeholder has specific expectations from the other. Some expectations encompass issues shared by other stakeholders. All stakeholders expect transparency and information sharing from the company, but primarily, they want to trust the company. This aspect of trust may concern financial investments, activities related to environmental sustainability, employee health and safety, or human rights. From an environmental business perspective, stakeholders pressure the company to ensure that the type of energy used in supply chain operations and logistics activities is environmentally friendly and to reduce consumption of scarce resources. In recent years, green and lean management approaches have also focused on savings and the environment. The selection of the least environmentally harmful energy type (sustainable and/or green, hydro, electric, etc.) can lead to expectations of reducing and/or mitigating negative environmental impacts and outcomes, such as a low carbon footprint, low emissions, and effective waste management. Stakeholders also expect to see concrete evidence and/or a demonstration of commitment on all these issues. Local communities also have expectations of companies, requesting that they operate in areas where suppliers are present, protect the

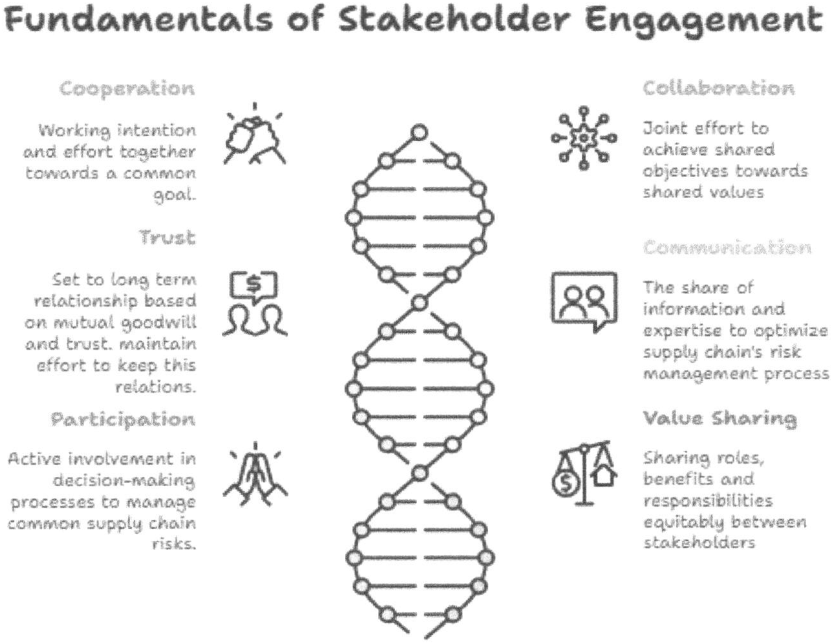

Fig. 3.1. Stakeholder engagement as part of supply chain risk management.

Source: The original design is by the authors; Napkin AI was used for visualization purposes only. https://app.napkin.ai/page/CgoiCHByb2Qtb25lEiwKBFBhZ2UaJDYwYTU0NGMxLTE5MDYtNDljYy1iNDM4LTc2MjVjODIxY2JhNw.

environment, contribute to economic development, increase employment opportunities, and minimize potential negative environmental impacts.

The ability to manage the risks of their supply chains is one of the most prominent corporate performance indicators for companies seeking to continue their existence in the global and digital transformation environment. In this environment, companies must manage not only their own performance but also that of their supply chains. Supply chains are complex, multifaceted systems involving a vast network of customers and suppliers and must therefore be treated as such (Ross, 2008). The supply chain is a stakeholder engagement process where each stakeholder fulfills their role and responsibilities optimally within defined parameters. This includes suppliers of raw materials, spare parts, services and maintenance, resources (such as electricity, water, fuel, internet, and software), semi-finished products, manufacturers, logistics companies, and retailers.

Achieving goals requires a commitment to protecting and maintaining harmony, cooperation, and coordination among stakeholders.

Globalization has played a significant role in facilitating the acquisition of resources by companies, enabling them to streamline their production processes and enhance their operational efficiencies. Furthermore, the companies were operating directly with their clients, thereby circumventing the need for intermediaries. Therefore, they are able to manage the chain with a reduced number of partners, both in terms of location and geography and stakeholder networks, including supply companies. This risk management approach was one of the most effective strategies, considering the conditions of that day, because managing supply chains was much easier since the risks associated with supply were less, both quantitatively and qualitatively. Today's global markets have seen increased risks due to the diversification and expansion of product complexity, spare parts and services, international business operations with large supply networks, and the use of external resources in supply chains. The transformation of complex supply networks has resulted in an increased and shifted risk profile. The increasing variety of products and services, the proliferation of e-commerce, outsourcing, and globalization are just some of the factors contributing to the complexity of the business world. These factors have resulted in an increased distribution of risk throughout supply networks (Harland *et al.*, 2003).

Uncertainty in supply and demand, increased globalization, shorter product and technology life cycles, and complex international supply chain relationships are some of the factors contributing to the dynamism and complexity of the supply chain ecosystem. Companies are facing increased risks due to these factors, including increased interaction among production, distribution, and logistics partners, interaction of components within the entire supply chain system, and technological transformation (Diabat *et al.*, 2012). The increasing dynamics within the ecosystem and the increasing complexity of those interactions further increase the vulnerability of supply chains. It is imperative to recognize that these dynamics also encompass sources of risk, thereby ensuring uninterrupted and targeted operations for supply chains necessitate the implementation of risk management strategies. Identifying risks within such a complex, digitally intensive, and AI-influenced ecosystem is a challenging endeavor. Consequently, the focus on risk management is more accurately and meaningfully addressed than the attempt to eliminate risks.

Stakeholder engagement, cooperation, and collaboration are critical components of successful risk management implementation, and it is essential that each stakeholder fully comprehends these concepts.

Cooperation, the term "cooperation" is used to express a situation in which stakeholders or stakeholder groups in a supply chain work in coordination by sharing a common goal in line with their strategies. Each stakeholder supply chain company in the supply chain network carries out its company-related activities and operations, roles and responsibilities, and enterprise risk management (ERM) across its organization. However, they also serve the common goal of the entire stakeholder network. For instance, effective risk management by a company can also yield indirect benefits for its suppliers. For instance, effective management of risk by a catering supplier for an airline can positively impact customer satisfaction with the airline's catering services. Once again, the more effectively the ground handling company manages its own risks, the greater its contribution to customer satisfaction with the on-time performance of the airline. Each individual is responsible for their own tasks, and there may be limited interaction or information sharing among those responsibilities. The fact that different departments within the same company carry out their own activities and that each department actually serves to achieve the company's goals is an example to understand the concept of cooperation. The marketing, sales, and logistics departments of an e-commerce company are working to meet the year-end sales target. Marketing is responsible for the company's advertising campaigns, while the sales team focuses on customer relationships, and logistics manages the shipping of products. Each individual operates according to their own strategy, yet all contribute to the same objective: increased sales. Cooperation also includes a "working style" of "side by side, not together" and a "focus" on the individual task outputs of the company.

The concept of cooperation encompasses a specific approach to work management, namely a "side-by-side, not together" methodology, emphasizing individual task-oriented outputs within the organizational framework.

Collaboration is a process in which individuals or groups work together in an integrated manner to achieve a common goal. This involves the constant sharing of information, ideas, and responsibility. It also encompasses solving a common problem through the systematic and coordinated efforts of stakeholders. For example, stakeholders can collaborate to develop strategies addressing the risks posed by new-generation sustainable fuels to supply chains. This principle applies to all systems and their subsystems: while each subsystem pursues its own objectives, it also contributes to the overarching goals of the main system through collaborative efforts.

We consider stakeholder engagement as a concept that encompasses cooperation and collaboration, as well as one that includes establishing trust among stakeholders, ensuring transparency among stakeholders, and managing long-term relationships based on trust with the goal of creating shared value together. In this respect, stakeholder relationship risk management, focusing on engagement, collaboration, and cooperation, has become a component of SCRM.

The concept of cooperation is closely aligned with the operational principles of both the company and individual departments. The emphasis is on a collaborative approach, whereby each party contributes their respective share toward a shared goal. Collaboration can be defined as the process of working as a unified team to solve or create a problem or project together. In the context of SCRM, where a greater degree of complexity or creativity is required, it is in the company's best interest to assume responsibility and collaborate closely with all departments. It is recommended that stakeholders collaborate to generate synergy and identify shared solutions to supply chain challenges. Collaborative efforts can facilitate the transformation of differences into opportunities. In response to the prevailing circumstances, the airline industry has established cooperative networks that are designated as "alliances" (see Fig. 3.2).

Airline alliances, particularly, can be regarded as a leading example of supply chain engagement. It is possible to provide examples from several areas, including the utilization of joint sources, standardization and integration, risk management and flexibility, and demand forecasting. Airline alliances (e.g. Star Alliance, SkyTeam, and Oneworld) illustrate this by utilizing or sharing services among their member airlines, such as airport maintenance services, aircraft maintenance, representation, and reception services, ground handling, catering services, and spare parts procurement. This engagement also offers significant opportunities for resource optimization, quality improvement, and cost reduction through cost-savings-focused lean supply chain management. In other words, rather than a single airline, alliance members develop joint supply chain strategies. It is proposed that members of the alliance can achieve faster and more efficient process management by establishing common

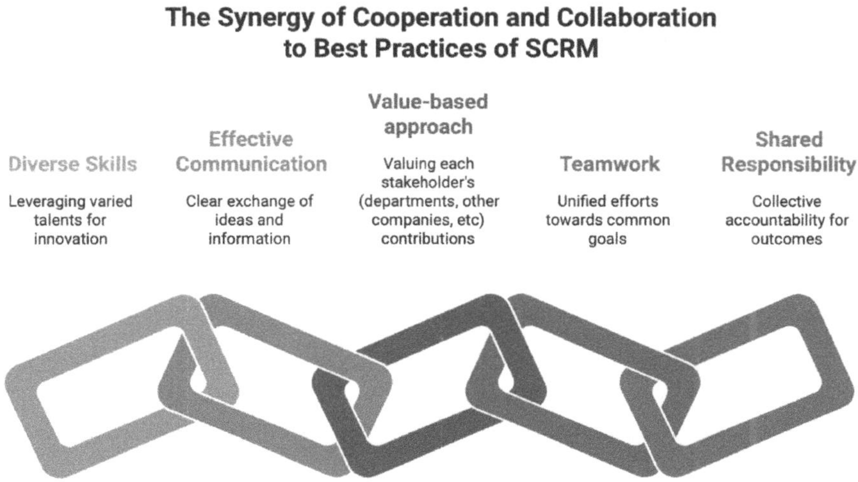

Fig. 3.2. The synergy of cooperation and collaboration in line with best practices of SCRM.

Source: The original design is by the authors; Napkin AI was used for visualization purposes only. https://app.napkin.ai/page/CgoiCHByb2Qtb25lEiwKBFBhZ2UaJDY5ZGZkODgyLTYxYmEtNDU0MC1iZGRhLTMwNzA3NGU5MTNhYg.

reservation systems, baggage management, and MRO maintenance procedures in their operations.

The capacity for transparent and coordinated operation among all supply chain stakeholders is thus established, and this represents a key advantage of the system. Furthermore, suppliers may also choose to specialize by providing similar services to a wider range of customers. In the event of a disruption, they can now apply the same standard to multiple airlines. This finding suggests that supplier specialization enhances supplier capacity, thereby reducing interruptions and disruptions in the supply chain. In the event of a risk materializing within the supply chain of an airline, the members of the alliance can offer support and share resources with the airline in question, with a view of either preventing interruptions or minimizing disruptions. This engagement fosters a reciprocal relationship of trust among relevant stakeholders.

Furthermore, members of the alliance provide mutual assistance in circumstances where spare parts or maintenance are required. This enables the establishment of a resilient and agile supply chain, with the potential to effectively manage supply chain risks. Moreover, the establishment of strategic alliances has been demonstrated to facilitate the optimization of demand forecasting and capacity management. The conception of destinations and routes with greater accuracy is indeed a possibility. Consequently, companies are presented with the opportunity to integrate their supply chains across both the goods/service flow and the demand and service flow areas.

3.1.1 *Industry example: Star Alliance*

The Star Alliance serves as a remarkable illustration of cooperation and collaboration, signifying deeper interaction among its members.

In the context of cooperative endeavors, where independent entities collaborate by sharing resources and synchronizing their operations to accomplish collective objectives, the Star Alliance was founded in 1997 with the overarching goals of "global reach, worldwide recognition, and seamless service". The 25 airlines that are members of the alliance maintain their own independent identities and have created a vast network serving more than 1,160 airports in 192 countries, with 17,837 flights per day. This extensive network facilitates access beyond the capacity of individual airlines to achieve independently, thereby serving as a pivotal indicator of collaboration.

With regard to collaboration, Star Alliance refers to more profound interaction in which partners work together to solve problems or create new value, sharing knowledge and expertise. Star Alliance's commitment to the principle of "hassle-free service" is demonstrated in the text. This commitment is evident in the collaborative efforts of members to address issues such as connecting mileage programs, shared lounge access, and the integration of ticketing systems. These collaborative endeavors offer a unique value proposition that individual airlines would be unable to provide independently, thereby facilitating a unified and seamless travel experience for customers. This represents more than mere coordination; it is a genuine collaboration. In conclusion, the Star Alliance offers a dynamic model in which members collaborate to achieve common goals while developing integrated solutions to create unparalleled value for customers (Turkish Airlines, 2025) (see Fig. 3.3).

The establishment of partnerships and collaborative efforts, such as strategic alliances, is one of the corporate strategies to overcome challenges associated with supply chains. According to predictions by airline

Fig. 3.3. Cooperation and collaboration: Star Alliance.

Source: The original design is by the authors; Napkin AI was used for visualization purposes only. https://app.napkin.ai/page/CgoiCHByb2Qtb25lEiwKBFBhZ2UaJDE2MDAyYjAzLTViMTYtNDFhNC04M2FlLTJhN2JlMWI4Y2M4MQ.

executives, issues within the supply chain of aircraft and parts are likely to persist for a period of no less than two years. IAG CEO Luis Gallego has emphasized that the company's growth plans have been hindered by the aforementioned issues, stating, "There is a requirement for aircraft and engines, and an ambition to expand; however, this cannot be achieved at the current time in the manner that is desired". Air India CEO Campbell Wilson has highlighted the inadequate delivery speed and noted that the supply of seats is causing a significant bottleneck. Güliz Öztürk, the CEO of Pegasus, asserts that even delays of a few weeks can engender significant issues, particularly during periods of peak demand. She highlights the uncertainty surrounding the delivery schedule as the most critical challenge (Harper, 2024).

The primary function (or aim) of the supply system is to ensure the uninterrupted provision of essential services and/or ongoing production. A problem with supply chain stakeholders can cause disruption to the chain or a deterioration in quality. Imagine if the airline catering supplier were unable to deliver the food to the plane in a timely manner or if the food quality was deemed unsatisfactory. It is important to note that this will have a significant impact on the airline's reputation and the perception of service quality. This, in turn, creates a number of potential risks in many areas. Risks may include decreased demand, reputational damage, and diminished investor interest.

3.2 Supply Chain Fragility and Global Impacts on Industries

Fragility is associated with the possibility of disruption or damage to the supply chain. Fragility can be defined as the occurrence of risk within a supply chain, leading to its disruption when that risk materializes. For instance, the most undesirable events for a supply chain are those that result in disruption or interruption. ERM is implemented in the supply chain to address these concerns. Supply chain fragility can be managed across industries, as SCRM is the only management system that can provide reasonable assurance. It is evident that effective management of fragility necessitates the enhancement of a company's supply chain resilience. The achievement of this objective varies depending on the industry, and the process becomes more complex in some cases. Indeed, managing fragility in the supply chain is a complex and challenging process. Industries are characterized by their unique risks, which are driven by factors such as high security, safety and quality standards, global networks, and the products and services they produce.

Risk management is key to ensuring that fundamental strategies are in place to manage this vulnerability. The selection and implementation of the most appropriate strategy is determined by a company's characteristics, risk tolerance, and available resources, as well as the strategies it can overcome. When selecting a strategy, it is important to consider key factors such as supplier diversity, stakeholder interactions and relationships within the supply chain, digital technologies, risk management tools, and the company's flexibility and capacity. Supply chain vulnerability is intrinsic to the chain itself and cannot be entirely eliminated. However, effective risk management strategies, along with the appropriate technology and approach tailored to the company, can ensure the successful navigation of these challenges. As it is impossible to eliminate all risks completely and as risk management cannot provide absolute assurance, residual risks will always remain. However, effective management of vulnerability risk can enhance operational performance and ensure that the company or industry maintains specific quality standards.

Supply chain vulnerability refers to the degree to which a network deteriorates when it encounters unexpected obstacles, such as a sudden weather event, a geopolitical shift, or a local factory closure. It's about fundamental disruptions rather than just minor delays. Due to the systemic nature of modern supply networks, these vulnerabilities are not individual weak links but rather a situation where a disruption spreads throughout the system. Trends such as globalization, lean manufacturing, and single-source procurement have further exacerbated supply chain vulnerability. This makes it imperative for companies to shift from passive crisis management to proactive risk management. Vulnerability can manifest in these key components of a supply chain (Sustainability Directory, 2024):

Sourcing: Dependence on single suppliers or geographically concentrated resources.

Manufacturing: Overreliance on "just-in-time" inventory systems.

Logistics: Disruptions in shipping routes, port congestion, or storage capacity limitations.

Distribution: "Last-mile" delivery issues or errors in demand forecasting.

Fragile supply chains are susceptible to loss of value when confronted with uncertainty and disruptions, whereas antifragile supply chains have the capacity to benefit from them. Many companies are still using traditional, precision-based planning methods, leaving their supply chains in a fragile state. This results in a reactive management style, which is often counterproductive and can negatively impact profits. While certain companies endeavor to establish a robust supply chain, these chains frequently prove incapable of withstanding minor disruptions and are frequently unable to cope with major uncertainties. In order to build a truly resilient structure, supply chain planning leaders must understand the effects of uncertainty and use methods such as probabilistic planning, trial and error, and stress testing. In order for a supply chain to transition from fragility to antifragility, it is imperative that the appropriate balance be achieved between precision and probability in planning, emphasizing resource performance. A holistic, company-wide, and stakeholder-based system is vital in risk management and should be implemented to strengthen supply chains by supporting readiness (Payne, 2025).

While the enhancement of supply chains was a primary factor in moderating inflation in 2023, this trajectory shifted in 2024 as geopolitical tensions and logistical disruptions reintroduced volatility into global markets. This projection is underpinned by the expectation that supply chains will become more vulnerable due to fragmentation within the global economy and the prevalence of disruptions. A salient indicator of this phenomenon is the observation that central banks are now subjecting supply chain operations to heightened scrutiny when evaluating inflation risks. Moreover, events such as the Baltimore Bridge collapse illustrate that logistics flexibility has become even more important than diversifying supply sources. Geopolitical events, such as the Red Sea crisis, are creating a new operational norm, with shipping costs being reflected in prices more rapidly, while the frequency of disruptions due to labor strikes, cyberattacks, and climate change is also increasing. Finally, geopolitical risks, including the future of the US–Mexico–Canada Agreement (USMCA), have the potential to engender uncertainty, particularly for companies pursuing the "near-shoring" trend. The aforementioned factors led to a significant increase in the fragility and complexity of supply chains throughout 2024 (KPMG, 2024).

Managing fragility, planning for resilience, and strategically using the time dimension ensure that the supply chain survives unexpected shocks. Supply chains are complex systems focused on efficiency and are therefore resistant to anticipated risks and vulnerable to unexpected shocks (robust yet fragile). Although the Just-in-Time model provides efficiency, crises can stop the chain if enough resilience is not added. Resilience is at the heart of business continuity, and unlike disaster recovery, it refers to the company's capacity to continue delivering products and services no matter what crisis it experiences. Three key approaches to resilience in the supply chain stand out (BCarm, 2025):

(a) **Outage tolerance:** A maximum tolerable downtime (MTPD) should be determined; flexibility should be provided through buffer stocks, additional facilities, and alternative suppliers.
(b) **Prepare for everything:** The cause of the crisis is irrelevant; the important thing is to maintain the flow of products/services. Disruptions are minimized by prioritizing risks.

(c) **Time management:** Supply chain and delivery processes should be mapped in the time dimension; disruptions and priorities should be identified, and creative, low-cost solutions should be developed.

According to recent statistics, 80% of clinical trials in the life sciences sector are unable to be completed on schedule due to supply chain issues. This is due to raw material shortages, logistical problems, and delivery delays. Pharmaceutical startups struggle more, as they lack infrastructure, supplier networks, and funds to withstand market fluctuations. They often depend on a single supplier or factory. Supply chain issues can lead to data breaches and counterfeit materials. Delays can cause lost sales and increased costs. Temperature-sensitive products can become unusable due to a single error. These risks can be exacerbated by the political climate; tariffs; environmental, social, and governance (ESG) pressures; and cross-border regulations. Financial protection against unexpected events is essential. Life sciences companies can adopt proactive strategies to mitigate these risks, such as strategically storing inventory in multiple locations and diversifying supplier networks. It is also critical to establish a robust risk management framework and develop contingency plans. Technology can strengthen supply chains: artificial intelligence (AI) and machine learning (ML) can improve demand forecasting, blockchain technology can increase the traceability and transparency of products, IoT sensors can track critical parameters, and serialization can prevent counterfeiting. Lastly, risk transfer solutions such as insurance can provide financial protection (Gallagher, 2025).

Supply chain fragility is a significant issue that arises from unexpected events such as natural disasters, geopolitical tensions, and pandemics. To address this challenge, businesses are rethinking their supply chain operations to build resilience. Risk management strategies to mitigate this fragility to improve vulnerability include (GEP, 2025):

- **Nearshoring and nearstoring:** Bringing production and inventory closer to end markets, reducing lead times, and minimizing disruptions. This approach can also provide long-term cost advantages.
- **Diversifying supplier base:** Establishing secondary suppliers in different regions to spread risk. This allows for redirecting production volumes elsewhere if one supplier is affected.
- **Leveraging technology:** Utilizing technologies such as ML to enhance visibility, supply planning, and compliance. ML can classify suppliers

and risks, as well as improve forecasting accuracy by incorporating various data such as weather and macroeconomic changes.
- **Real-time visibility:** Embracing technology that provides real-time visibility, connecting all stakeholders throughout the supply chain. This is critical for accurate forecasting, inventory optimization, and risk mitigation.
- **Convergent goals:** Recognizing that efficiency, resilience, and sustainability are not conflicting goals. Bundling these goals reduces costs associated with inventory losses and provides environmental benefits.

Risk management becomes important with solutions that are proactive, support prediction, include early warning systems, allow uninterrupted and good communication, provide real-time monitoring and prediction-proof visibility, and also identify potential weaknesses. Ultimately, adopting such solutions helps companies transition from reactive crisis management to proactive risk mitigation. Acute climate events such as Winter Storm Uri pose a major risk to supply chains. This 2021 storm hit the petrochemical industry in Texas, presenting a significant case study due to the resulting severe shortages of key components, including resins, and highlighting the fragility of modern supply chains. This severely impacted medical device manufacturing, highlighting the following systemic challenges (EXIGER, 2025):

- geographically concentrated facilities in a single region,
- companies' inability to see beyond their primary suppliers,
- providing reactive responses in times of crises.

3.3 Stakeholder Risk Management as Part of SCRM

The management of risk by stakeholders is based on a thorough analysis of the stakeholders themselves, their respective roles, and the impact they have on the objectives of the supply chain. This analysis encompasses the impact areas, durations, and severity of the stakeholders' actions, and the development of risk management strategies is informed by the findings of this analysis. It is acknowledged that the composition of stakeholders and the supply ecosystem within which they operate are subject to variation. Consequently, stakeholders and risks are not considered to be fixed entities.

The characteristics of these phenomena and their effect on the supply system are subject to change. Therefore, the necessity for continuous monitoring, communication, and reporting is fundamental, with subsequent updates employing an engagement approach. In the context of SCRM, the process encompasses stakeholder risk analysis and the formulation of risk management strategies for stakeholder-related risks. These are then followed by resource allocation and the implementation of risk management strategies. However, in order to gain a more comprehensive understanding of stakeholder risk and its scope and to observe the management process in depth, it is advantageous to establish a detailed framework. Each company can modify this framework based on its own supply chain stakeholders, decreasing or increasing the number of stages accordingly. It is vital to recognize that SCRM employs a comprehensive approach, addressing all potential risks within a corporate entity. Stakeholder risks, both internal and external, are included within the corporate risk map. Stakeholder risks have the potential to impact supply chains in a number of ways, both strategically and operationally. The following section outlines the key framework of the stakeholder risk management process, with the objective of serving as a guide for company decision-makers. The stakeholder risk management framework has been developed in accordance with a four-step methodology (see Fig. 3.4).

Management of risk by stakeholders depends on thorough analysis of stakeholders, their respective roles, and their impact on the supply chain. This analysis covers stakeholders' actions and their impact, duration, and severity, and it informs the development of a risk management strategy. As stakeholders and the supply ecosystem are subject to changes, stakeholders and risks are not fixed. Consequently, continuous monitoring, communication, and reporting using an engagement approach are fundamental.

In the context of SCRM, stakeholder risk analysis and risk management strategies for stakeholder-related risks are integral to the process, followed by resource allocation and implementation.

A detailed framework can be advantageous for a comprehensive understanding of stakeholder risk and its scope and for observing management processes in depth. Each company can modify this framework based on its own supply chain stakeholders, increasing or decreasing the number of stages accordingly.

SCRM employs a comprehensive approach addressing all potential risks within a corporate entity, including stakeholder risks, both internal

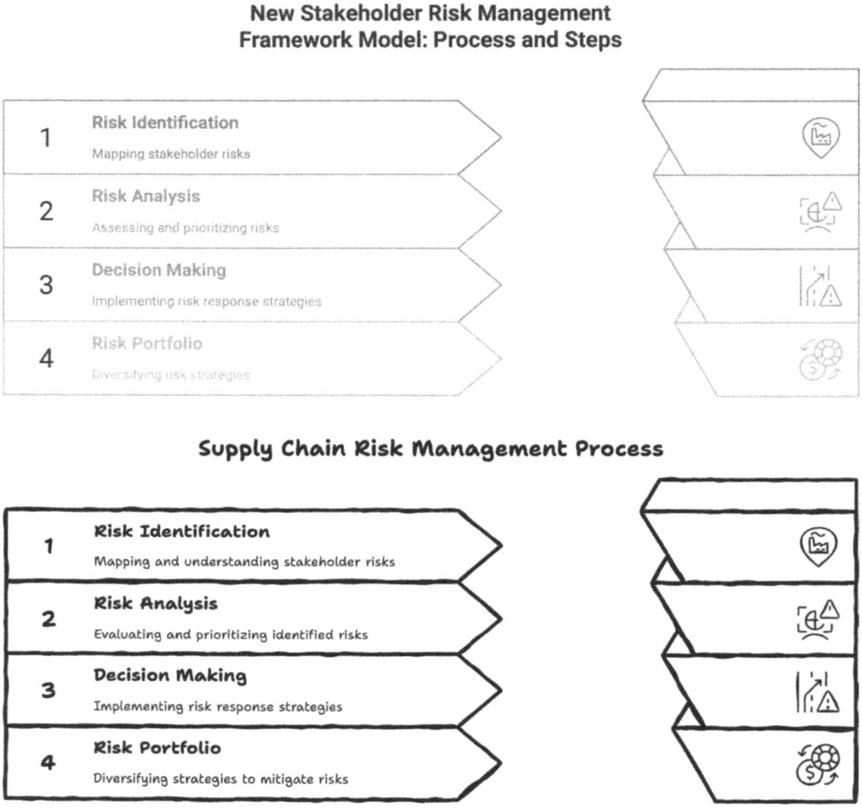

Fig. 3.4. Model of supply chain framework and process.

Source: The original design is by the authors; Napkin AI was used for visualization purposes only.

and external, within the corporate risk map. These can impact supply chain operations and strategies.

This section outlines the key framework of the stakeholder risk management process, serving as a guide for company decision-makers.

Step 1. Risk Identification: Examining the stakeholder ecosystem and developing a stakeholder risk map

In this step, which includes the process of diagnosing and identifying potential risks arising from stakeholders, stakeholder risks are also defined within the scope of institution-wide risk identification studies. The goal of this step is to clarify the situation regarding the potential risks and to reveal exactly what those risks are and where they originate. Detections can be made using many different digital tools and methods. In addition, attempts are made to predict risk scenarios and risks that may be encountered. While doing this, the interaction of the risks we have highlighted in the previous sections must also be taken into account. Risks can create new risks through their interactions. The risk assessment phase involves:

(a) Identification and definition of events related to all stakeholders in the supply chain ecosystem as a source of risk.
(b) Deciding which category external stakeholder risks will be included within the scope of SCRM (strategic risk category, financial risk category, operational risk category, or environmental risk category). According to the organization's risk management model, stakeholder-related risks have the most significant impact on the operational or strategic category. Subgroups of stakeholder risks can also be included in different risk categories. The analysis involves identifying stakeholders with strategic impact and high operational effectiveness, followed by the systematic determination of their categories.

Identifying and managing stakeholders in a supply chain ecosystem is a critical step in SCRM. This process begins by identifying both internal and external stakeholders, direct and indirect, and those in the immediate and distant vicinity of the business. In this step, all stakeholders in the supply chain ecosystem must first be identified and then listed. At this first stage, the list does not need to be in a specific order. It is only necessary to ensure that all stakeholders in the entire supply chain are included in the list, as these stakeholders have the potential to influence the company's supply chain goals in the long term or short term, today or in the future, with high or mild severity. These stakeholders can be suppliers or customers in the supply chain, as well as authorities, social media platforms, environmentalists, tourism professionals, etc., who indirectly affect the chain in managerial or operational areas. As is known, the near and far environment of the business is managed by developing different strategies. It is also possible to categorize it as the near and far environment of the business or as internal and external stakeholders, respectively. We can think of the immediate environment as the business environment. Remote environments also refer to those known as "general" or "macro".

Within the scope of the macro environment, it includes elements such as the legal and regulatory environment, economic environment, social and cultural environment, technological environment, political and international environment, and demographic environment, while the immediate environment includes customers, suppliers, competitors, and financial institutions, which are analyzed in the context of the supply chain. The most optimal categorization can be chosen in terms of risk management strategy. There is no one correct categorization, and it is not necessary to have one. In addition, stakeholders are changing day by day. Their number may change; new stakeholders may emerge, and existing stakeholders may disappear.

While conducting a risk analysis of the company's far and near environment, the company either benefits from its own expertise or works with a consultancy company to have the risk analysis done. They can also work jointly with stakeholders to conduct this analysis. Undoubtedly, all three analysis methods are powerful for preparing the company's risk profile and/or risk map. Each method has its own strengths and weaknesses, or, in other words, threats and opportunities. Outsourcing or collaborating with stakeholders to prepare a risk profile and create a risk map means that those outside the company are also aware of the risk profile. This reminds us once again of the element of trust within the stakeholder engagement concept.

There are many different risks in supply chains arising from the ecosystem, that is, the environment, and the risks have a constantly changing structure. Even if the name remains the same, there are many risks whose content changes partially or completely. The momentum of this change is high in the digital transformation and artificial intelligence (AI) landscape. After the risks are identified in the first step of the process within the SCRM framework, they are grouped under categories. The classification of risks is done at this stage. For example, it should be decided under which category the external stakeholder risks will be evaluated among the risks identified according to the company's own SCRM model. In the basic risk management frameworks, which should be shaped according to the size, goals, and needs of the companies, the impact areas of risks arising from stakeholders should also be evaluated because every risk has a cost. It may also have the potential to influence strategy. Risk can also impact operational processes. Therefore, the effects of the risk should be analyzed by considering the impact areas. A risk can have an impact in more than one area. After these effects are analyzed and calculated, stakeholder risk can be included under the category with the most impact. This shows us that each risk will be multifaceted. The effects of a risk manifest themselves in many areas. When risks coexist, interconnected risks have the potential to affect many different areas, that is, they have the potential to impact multiple domains. This feature of risks is one of the signs that risk detection and analysis are obscured. Detecting risk involves identifying it and identifying its sources . A mistake made at this stage can create a chain effect, as there will be incomplete or incorrect input for analysis. In risk management, it is important to proceed quickly but in a controlled manner at all stages of the process.

In the categorization of multifaceted risks, each company can act according to its own strategy. Assigning stakeholders' risks to the category of the area that is affected the most or whose consequences are felt the most is the most preferred and accurate strategy. For example, the bankruptcy or departure of a supplier in the chain will be categorized under financial risks, while the issue related to waste will be categorized under environmental risks, and problems related to quality standards will be under the operational risk category.

Subgroups of stakeholder risks can also be included in different risk categories. This classification helps identify the most strategically influential stakeholders and the most operationally critical stakeholders. This ensures that risks are managed and prioritized correctly.

Step 2. Risk Analysis: Stakeholder risk-based assessment & evaluation and prioritization

Evaluation and analysis studies are carried out by using various qualitative and quantitative data, including technological ones, within the scope of the probability of risk occurrence, their impact severity, impact areas if they occur, and the duration of the impact. It is natural for companies to lack expertise with every risk management tool and method. Therefore, decisions can be made according to the expertise of the company's employees in the selection of methods. An alternative strategy is to supply expertise, that is, to outsource. If this strategy is chosen, the results of outsourcing should be of the same quality. Here, the company has taken a risk by outsourcing. Another strategy is to invest in training to specialize the people selected from the company's own human resources. It should not lose the personnel it has invested in, otherwise its investments will turn into waste costs. Outsourcing or investing in specializing your own employees carries different risks. No choice yields zero risk. For this reason, companies need to conduct risk analyses and assessments accurately and in a timely manner by choosing the methods and expertise style that align with their budgetary constraints.

In the stakeholder-based risk assessment and evaluation phase, it is essential to develop a strategy for selecting the methods and technologies. The primary reason for this is the high cost of the technological tools and methods selected. The chosen method also creates external resource dependency. For instance, if you are using risk analysis software, you will require its services and updates. Furthermore, system vulnerabilities in the software also create risks. Information leakage, for instance, is another critical company risk. Digital technologies carry inherent risks, including vulnerability to cyberattacks, which can result in the theft of information or system hacking. However, despite the risks posed by cyberattacks, digital technologies have become essential tools due to their ability to provide accurate and efficient results. Therefore, it is essential to develop a strategy for selecting the methods and tools to be used in the risk assessment and evaluation phase.

Risk mapping is the ranking of risks, taking into account their likelihood, impact intensity, impact areas, and impact duration. This ranking is critical given the large number of stakeholders involved. Allocating resources to all of them simultaneously and managing them is extremely difficult. Therefore, the most significant risks affecting the supply chain and related objectives are prioritized, resource allocation is implemented, and the necessary risk management strategies are selected and decided upon for their management. The implementation of risk management strategies begins.

At this stage, implementing multidimensional stakeholder mapping is crucial. The company will need experts for this, as this mapping involves assessing each stakeholder based on criteria such as their potential and strength of influence on the supply chain and company objectives, as well as the stakeholder's criticality and their attitude toward the company (supportive, neutral, opposing, etc.). This allows for the most appropriate allocation of resources and an optimal risk management strategy.

Conducting a risk analysis to understand the relationships among stakeholders is particularly important, as stakeholder networks and communications are evaluated. This analysis will help understand the flow of information within the supply chain, the direction of information flow, potential collaborations and alliances, and potential points of conflict within the supply chain ecosystem. Following this assessment and evaluation, risk profiles are created for each stakeholder. These profiles include stakeholders' risk tolerance and their responses to unexpected events. This allows for the development of strategies to address potential stakeholder impacts. These strategies, if possible, prevent risks before they materialize by taking proactive measures. However, reactive strategies will also be necessary for actual risks. Risk mapping allows for the sequencing of these action plans. All these steps provide a strategic roadmap for managing the complex stakeholder ecosystem and ensuring the sustainable success of the project.

Step 3. Decision-Making on Risk-Handling Strategies: Implementation of risk responses

The final stage of the multifaceted stakeholder risk management process involves the implementation of risk response strategies and the establishment of feedback mechanisms. The act of sharing with stakeholders is of particular importance in ensuring that stakeholder relationships continue to be characterized by trust. This stage is regarded as the implementation of the work undertaken in the first two stages. This approach enables the mitigation of potential risks to the company, thereby minimizing the adverse impact on the supply chain. A fundamental aspect of this comprehensive stage is to remind companies of the importance of stakeholder engagement and to raise awareness. The objective is to encourage companies to develop their organizational capacity and build strong and ongoing relationships with stakeholders. Stakeholder engagement has been identified as a key factor in the effective recognition and management of potential supply chain risk signals.

In the context of risk management and crisis situations, the active involvement of stakeholders is essential. This encompasses not only the exchange of information and feedback but also the active involvement and support of stakeholders at all phases of risk management. In this manner, feedback from multiple perspectives contributes to the development of risk scenarios and risk-handling strategies in a more effective manner. Furthermore, it facilitates the transfer of appropriate risks within the scope of risk management strategies (i.e. take, transfer, share, etc.) to stakeholders who have the capacity to manage that risk. Consequently, the company will be in a position to assume risks within the limits of its risk tolerance. It is evident that the establishment of regular and transparent communication throughout the process is of paramount importance. Such communication, when implemented with transparency and honesty, serves to reinforce trust among stakeholders and facilitate crisis management. This is achieved by preventing misunderstandings in times of uncertainty, thereby ensuring the effective management of crises.

Risks in supply chains can be understood as potential deviations that may result in a loss of value-added activities at various levels. These activities are related to the volume and quality of products at different times and locations. A failure at any level has the capacity to impact numerous activities at other levels. Consequently, risk assessment has become an integral part of the supply chain design process, with a view to safeguarding stable value-added activities. The process of risk assessment entails the identification, evaluation, measurement, and mitigation of risks within the supply chain, with the objective of minimizing unintended consequences (Kumar *et al.*, 2010): disruption, quality-based issues, disruption of production, delay of delivery, etc.

SCRM is a fundamental business process for handling the complexities and uncertainties of modern supply chains, as explained in the SCRM framework. A systematic and holistic approach is key to the effective management of day-to-day operations, managerial and organizational issues, and large-scale, exceptional events. The core goal of SCRM is to reduce vulnerability and ensure business continuity by proactively identifying, assessing, and mitigating risks (Wieland and Wallenburg, 2012).

Step 4. Stakeholder Diversification Strategies: Risk Portfolio

The implementation of risk management strategies in the context of stakeholder diversification is a critical aspect of automotive company operations. For example, automotive companies adopt a supply strategy that involves procuring tires from multiple suppliers, as opposed to relying on a single brand. This necessitates a financial investment to ensure the maintenance of quality and align with the brand strategy. This approach entails the potential risk of passing on costs to the customer; however, it is generally considered a more cost-effective strategy in the long term when compared to the financial implications of a decline in quality. Moreover, the presence of multiple suppliers can confer a competitive advantage on the company. The supplier is cognizant of the absence of a monopoly and, consequently, is motivated to sustain or enhance the quality of their products to maintain their association with the company. The implementation of a supplier diversity strategy necessitates a robust managerial and financial framework. Consequently, the strategic sourcing management (SCRM) process should be meticulously tailored to align with the specific needs and objectives of the company.

Demand forecasts are requested from all sales outlets, including distributors and dealers in each country, in order to assist with inventory management. These forecasts are then submitted to the manufacturer. For the purpose of inventory management, authorized companies in each country and dealers in each city submit their desired inventory quantities to the manufacturer, based on their demand forecast analyses. Vehicle quotas are then allocated on a specific basis, with each country, region, and dealer being allocated a set number. Furthermore, dealers are committed to achieving and maintaining their annual sales targets. The risk is associated with companies that provide inaccurate demand forecasts, resulting in unsold vehicles remaining in inventory. Inventory is a key driver of costs. Should the forecast prove to be at variance with sales figures, dealers may find themselves with excess vehicles. All performance is subject to evaluation by the authorized dealer and the manufacturer. In some cases, due to the manufacturer's decision, dealers may not be able to purchase the desired number of vehicles from the manufacturer, i.e. the amount they believe they can sell. In such circumstances, dealers are compelled to sell the manufacturer's products, which introduces various risks. Performance management is a process that involves a series of interactions between manufacturers, authorized dealers, distributors, vendors, service centers, insurance companies, and finance companies. Errors in one chain can have a domino effect on the others. All companies in the supply chain, that is, stakeholders, are sources of risk (threats and/or opportunities) for each other.

While inventory shortages pose a threat to dealers and consumers, the situation is different for manufacturers. All products manufactured for them have been sold. Additionally, during periods of high demand, manufacturers may increase prices to reflect market conditions. Furthermore, selling vehicles at no or low discounts also translates to increased profits for the manufacturer. Conversely, dealerships are encountering customer dissatisfaction and are exploring alternative options due to challenges in sourcing specific vehicles. Furthermore, high vehicle prices or low discounts mean fewer customers are able to purchase them. To summarize, while a risk may create an opportunity for one stakeholder (the manufacturer), the same risk could pose a threat or harm to other stakeholders (authorized dealers, salespeople, and customers). Similarly, a brand's inability to sell due to a lack of inventory can prompt customers to switch to competitors, resulting in a loss of revenue and a decline in market share.

Companies that succeed in building and participating in strong supply chains will gain a significant competitive advantage in their respective industries. Businesses provide the resources they need to sustain their existence and grow, depending on their supply chains. Each business adapts to one or more supply chains and plays a specific role in each. The pace of change and uncertainty about the future of markets have made it increasingly important for companies to understand the dynamics of the supply chains they participate in and the roles they play. Any disruption in the supply chain can lead to various risks, such as operational and environmental risks. Managing these risks involves understanding, planning, and continuous monitoring and evaluation. This approach enables businesses to be better prepared for potential crises and minimize disruptions in the supply chain. The world economy, which made significant progress toward recovering from the negative effects of the pandemic in 2021, was once again shaken by the Russia–Ukraine war, which broke out at the beginning of 2022.

While increases in energy and food prices, caused by the war, further accelerated inflation—which tended to rise around the world—breaks in international supply and transportation chains created significant difficulties for the business world. In 2022, the automotive industry, challenged by rapidly increasing raw material and energy costs and high exchange rates, also had to manage production bottlenecks, particularly due to supply problems caused by the chip shortage (TOFAŞ, 2022). Semiconductors, for example, are microchips containing billions of tiny transistors, which control electrical current in electronic devices. Their manufacturing process is highly complex and precise, and it can take months to complete a single chip. This process consists of chip design, fabrication, assembly, and testing stages. The industry is divided into various areas of expertise, such as integrated device manufacturers (IDMs) that have their own manufacturing facilities, fabless companies that only design, foundries that specialize in manufacturing, and Outsourced Semiconductor Assembly and Test (OSAT) that perform the final stages. The global chip shortage in recent years has been driven by several factors, including factory closures due to the COVID-19 pandemic, a surge in demand fueled by technologies like AI, and trade tensions between the US and China. This shortage and associated risks in the supply chain, such as natural disasters, cyberattacks, and geopolitical tensions, are of great concern for the future of the semiconductor industry. To manage these complex risks, advanced technology solutions are increasingly being used to enhance transparency and resilience of supply chains (EXIGER, 2025). The supply chain for AI chips is a fundamental component of contemporary innovation. However, the inherent complexity of the system is attributable to its global and interdependent nature. In the context of the mounting demand for AI technologies, companies must identify methodologies for navigating this complexity and adapting to competitive pressures in the market. In the context of heightened geopolitical tensions, stringent regulatory frameworks, and operational risks, a proactive and strategic approach is imperative. Building resilience against major challenges, which are filled with digital transformation, complexity, and volatility, requires companies to invest in better data and risk management tools, diversify their suppliers, and use predictive analytics. Such measures have been demonstrated to facilitate the maintenance of continuity within supply chains, thereby enhancing compliance and operational efficiency. It is evident that a proactive approach to risk management, coupled with a demonstration of adaptability, is instrumental in fostering stakeholder trust and thereby consolidating a firm's position within the dynamic semiconductor value chain. Resilience against such challenges can be enhanced by companies that invest in advanced data and risk management tools, diversify their supplier networks, and harness the power of predictive analytics (Aresu, 2025).

The concept of a supply chain encompasses a series of stakeholders. A disruption in any link in the chain (for example, a power or internet outage, a technological problem such as a software issues, a delay in the supply of raw materials, or a problem in the distribution network) has the potential to disrupt the balance of the entire system and, by extension, other stakeholders. Consequently, risks emerge in the domains of reputation, customer satisfaction and loyalty, the continuity of supplier relationships, the continuity of contracts, and profitability. It is an irrefutable fact that no company can survive in isolation, given that they operate in an environment of interconnected economies. The existence of companies is also contingent upon their stakeholders in the supply chain. This is because every company is directly and indirectly related to other companies within the supply chain and is affected by their activities. It is evident that any interruption in the supply chain has the capacity to exert a detrimental effect on the entire chain. It is imperative to acknowledge that all decisions inherently carry an element of risk. In the context of digital transformation, the process of adapting to change and the decision to adopt digital technologies introduce additional risks. Conversely, maintaining traditional methods and adopting a status quo attitude also carries its own set of risks. The cornerstone of a successful company is the identification, assessment, prioritization, and management of supply chain risks (Sinha *et al.*, 2004).

Achieving maximum customer service availability at minimum cost necessitates the strategic placement of products throughout the distribution network at optimal times and locations. In conclusion, it is evident that SCRM is instrumental in ensuring the alignment and synchronization of collaborating firms. This process consequently enables the optimization of strategic positioning and the augmentation of operational efficiency (Bowersoc *et al.*, 2010).

The objective of SCRM is to formulate strategies aimed at averting adverse scenarios, such as disruptions or quality deterioration, within the supply chain. This endeavor entails a comprehensive and multifaceted approach encompassing both proactive and reactive measures, along with the capacity for prompt execution. The overarching aim is to develop strategies that proactively prevent such undesirable occurrences, thereby ensuring the seamless functioning of the supply chain process. In circumstances where risks escalate into crises, mitigating the repercussions is often more intricate and costly than risk management itself. This is due to the fact that it necessitates swift and cost-effective resolution of crises across various domains, including nominal and financial aspects, while concurrently minimizing the adverse impact on business operations. Consequently, businesses should continuously identify and analyze risk sources and impacts, employing a systematic and commensurate framework. For instance, the airline, rail, nuclear, chemical, and petroleum industries are susceptible to risk. Furthermore, in the event of a crisis materializing within these sectors, there is the potential for significant loss of life and property (Kucuk Yilmaz, 2003). Poor quality or interruptions in the supply system may also reflect in services and products, and additional risks may arise in terms of safety and security.

Businesses rely on their supply chains for the resources necessary for their survival and growth. Each enterprise adapts to one or more supply chains, playing a specific role in each. The accelerating rate of change and the resulting uncertainty surrounding the future of markets have rendered it imperative for companies to comprehend the dynamics of the supply chains in which they are engaged and to recognize their roles. The ability of companies to establish and engage in robust supply chains has been demonstrated to engender a substantial competitive advantage within their respective industries (Hugos, 2003). Reducing the probability of risky operational processes can be achieved through both internal initiatives and collaborative efforts with suppliers. This objective can be realized through a meticulous approach to supplier selection and a systematic enhancement of the underlying processes. Furthermore, the risk can be transferred to insurance companies through various strategies, including transferring inventory responsibility, modifying suppliers' delivery times (e.g. just-in-time deliveries) and customers (make-to-order), or outsourcing supply chain partners. Contracts have been demonstrated to serve as an effective instrument for the transfer of commercial risks (Norrman and Jansson, 2004).

Factors that increase complexity, such as globalization and product diversification, and factors that increase efficiency, such as outsourcing and supplier reduction, are identified as significant developments that drive supply chain risks, thus increasing supply chain vulnerability. These developments could impact dependencies within the supply chain, thereby introducing risks to both the supply and demand sides. It is evident that a broad array of products has the potential to elevate the level of risk involved, thereby generating increased uncertainty within the supply chain (Thun and Hoenig, 2011). Supply chain risk can be defined as adverse changes within a supply chain resulting from triggering events and the potential losses associated with uncertain developments in those characteristics. These losses frequently encompass impacts on the efficiency and effectiveness objectives of the supply chain (Heckmann *et al.*, 2014).

3.4 Supply Chain Risk Sources

SCRM aims to identify potential sources of risk and implement appropriate actions to prevent or contain supply chain vulnerabilities and protect the business from adverse events. Companies across the globe are implementing supply chain management due to its proven results, such as reduced delivery times, improved financial performance, greater customer satisfaction, and increased trust among suppliers (Quesada *et al.*, 2012). SCRM can be defined as the process of identifying and managing risks within a supply chain. This is achieved through a coordinated approach among supply chain members, with the aim of reducing the vulnerability of the supply chain, including stakeholders in its ecosystem (Jüttner *et al.*, 2003).

Business inherently involves many risks. Supply risks essentially arise during the transportation of materials or services necessary for the production of goods or services, such as raw materials, semi-finished goods, or spare parts, from suppliers to the company. Supply risks that companies may face, in addition to logistics-based risks, include issues such as supplier reliability, contractual issues, single or multiple sourcing, and centralized or decentralized resources.

Operational risks have always been a primary risk category within the framework. These are risks that have the potential to affect a company's ability to produce goods and services. These can arise from factors such as production or processing capacity shortages, technological advancements, difficulties adapting to digital transformation, human resource competency issues, and other operational process disruptions. The balance between supply and demand represents a form of market equilibrium. Supply and demand imbalances are among the most critical risks in the supply chain and have been proven to directly impact a company's profitability. Demand and supply issues always carry risks. Achieving a balance between supply and demand is challenging. These risks can include potential issues such as product obsolescence, stock shortages, or excess inventory. In the automotive industry, operating with minimal or no inventory can create opportunities for companies. It reduces inventory management risks and costs. However, if demand increases and supply cannot keep up, customers will not be able to get their cars when they want them. Waiting lists form. Sometimes, cars with the desired specifications are not available. Delays in on-time deliveries occur. All of these factors can lead to reduced customer satisfaction. As risk management consistently emphasizes, risky events present both threats and opportunities. Risk analysis is a crucial process for distinguishing between risks. Furthermore, if risk strategies are not properly defined, opportunities may be missed. Implementing risk management requires developing company capabilities.

The risk sources arising from supply chains are divided into three categories. Firstly, potential environmental risks may be categorized as arising from the interaction between supply chains and the environment. These include accidents (e.g. fire) and socio-political actions (e.g. Changes in regulations or tariffs). The occurrence of protests or terrorist attacks, as well as natural disasters (e.g. earthquakes), may have a significant impact on the affected population. Secondly, the organizational sources of risk must be considered. It is imperative to recognize the significance of adhering to the established parameters inherent to the supply chain, encompassing various contingencies such as labor-related issues (e.g. industrial action) and production uncertainties (e.g. equipment malfunctions). Furthermore, the ramifications of IT system uncertainties must be accorded due consideration. Thirdly, the concept of networked sources of risk is introduced. Such sources are derived from the interactions between organizations within the supply chain. It is possible to attribute any damage caused by suboptimal interaction between organizations throughout the chain to network-related sources of risk (Jüttner *et al.*, 2003):

The supply chain comprises multiple entities, with different layers of suppliers and customers, which are exposed to a multitude of risks at various levels. The increasing sensitivity of supply chains to risk is a consequence of globalization. The occurrence of internal risk factors is frequently attributable to operational discrepancies and coordination inadequacies (e.g. demand, production, and supply risks). External risk factors arise from interactions between the supply chain and its environment (e.g. terrorist attacks, natural disasters, and exchange rate fluctuations). It is evident that these risk factors have the potential to lead to inefficiencies and disruptions within the supply chain, thereby exerting a detrimental effect on overall performance (Kumar *et al.*, 2010). At this point, another risk classification can be made with a focus on the supply of goods and services and quality. It is clear that disruptions in the supply of goods or services, including instances of substandard quality, can result in failing to meet customer requirements in a timely manner. Price volatility has the potential to engender difficulties in transmitting price changes to customers, which may ultimately result in lost profits. Furthermore, delivering a substandard product or service can adversely impact customer satisfaction, which may consequently lead to diminished future revenues or the initiation of financial compensation claims. Moreover, the firm's reputation is susceptible to jeopardy due to concerns that are not inherently associated with the supply chain. For instance, unintentional remarks made by senior executives or disapproval of specific protocols have the potential to negatively impact the organization's reputation (Zsidisin and Ritchie, 2009).

Incoming supply carries various risks. The primary risk is that of business risk, which is associated with financial stability. A further pivotal factor pertains to supplier capacity constraints, which could lead to the unavailability of products or services. Technological advancements in production also pose a significant risk to suppliers. The inability of suppliers to adapt to these changes can have a detrimental effect on costs, product competitiveness in the market, and lead times. Consequently, procurement organizations are required to depend on the competencies of suppliers in order to maintain their own proficiency and efficiency in production processes through the implementation of continuous improvement initiatives. The concept of continuous improvement has been demonstrated to have a significant impact on supplier cost structures, which in turn has been shown to result in cost reductions in the acquiring company's final products or services. The quality of products and services is of paramount importance in such contexts, as substandard goods and services can spread throughout the supply chain and reach the final consumer, exerting considerable detrimental influence on the purchasing organization. Furthermore, the dynamic nature of customer demands renders product design changes as among the risk factors. It is important to note that alterations to products or services may necessitate suppliers making suitable modifications to raw materials or subassemblies. In the event of suppliers failing to implement the aforementioned changes, supply risk is incurred. Finally, natural disasters are also among the critical risks affecting the supply chain. It is an irrefutable fact that companies are often unable to exercise control over the occurrence of disasters such as floods, hurricanes, earthquakes, blizzards, fires, accidents, or diseases. Such disasters, when they occur at suppliers' facilities or during transportation, can have ripple effects throughout the purchasing organization and the entire supply chain (Zsidisin *et al.*, 2000). The high costs of supply chain problems have prompted executives to consider formal SCRM strategies. However, awareness of SCRM is not solely driven by cost considerations. Adapting to new regulations in order to enhance corporate governance is also a significant factor. Increased demand from customers for evidence of risk management procedures (to avoid interruption of supplies), the desire to avoid recurring real losses, and new trading models and logistics activities are among the factors that encourage a review of logistics activities. Furthermore, it is essential to consider the potential risks associated with vulnerable supply chains (Waters, 2007).

Supply chain management is a holistic process that not only integrates an organization's own departments but also encompasses all stakeholders in the chain. In this context, external partners such as suppliers, logistics service providers, third-party businesses, and information systems providers are also involved. Supply chain management encompasses all activities, including raw material and parts supply, production and assembly, warehousing, inventory management, order receiving and processing, multi-channel distribution, customer delivery, and information flow. The coordination of these activities ensures that the process from the procurement of raw materials to the delivery of the final product to the customer is managed effectively and efficiently (Lummus and Vokurka, 1999). It can be expressed as a combination of strategies, policies, and methods applied to identify, evaluate, and manage supply chain risks (Tang, 2006; Jüttner, 2005).

Risk management is often defined as controlling, identifying, and analyzing risks. Unlike traditional risk management, SCRM adopts a cross-company approach that aims to identify and mitigate risks by focusing on the entire supply chain, not just at the company level (Thun and Hoenig, 2011). SCRM is expressed as the management of supply chain risks through coordination or cooperation among supply chain partners to ensure profitability and continuity (Tang, 2006). SCRM enables companies to effectively manage their supply chain, reducing the overall risk level and increasing resilience. In this context, it is critical for businesses to create supply chain risk maps to identify and evaluate potential risk scenarios. However, since the successful implementation and sustainability of the SCRM system can incur significant costs, companies need to lead this initiative at a high level and provide the necessary financial support. An effective TZRY organization should involve experts from different functions, such as procurement, support, and general management. In addition, this structure should be designed to include regular meeting mechanisms with designated participants (Treuner *et al.*, 2014).

SCRM is a management system that must be embraced by, and is the responsibility of, top-level managers and senior decision-makers. It is integral that both managers and employees fully and accurately understand this as a holistic and systematic approach affecting every function, department, employee, and operation within the company. In order to guarantee this level of awareness and understanding, it is essential to implement efforts to establish a risk culture in the preliminary stages of risk management. This is known as the initial step and is a prerequisite for the beginning of the risk management process. To ensure the implementation of SCRM is in accordance with the intended strategy, developing a company-specific risk management guide would be beneficial. However, it is important to note that accessing all information within the organization carries with it a certain degree of risk and may also reduce overall effectiveness. Therefore, it would be appropriate to provide separate risk management framework guides with detailed and comprehensive information to managers and employees as required. It would be advisable to prepare an additional guide for stakeholders, with a view to informing them and ensuring that their trust is gained and maintained. This guide provides concise information on the implementation of SCRM throughout the organization, thereby strengthening the company's reputation by demonstrating mastery of the supply chain process.

Supply chain risks pose significant threats to financial and operational performance, presenting significant challenges to firms and their business partners. Therefore, the ability to mitigate risks from every perspective of the supply chain becomes a strategic requirement for firms. Decision-makers, particularly those involved in business strategy, need effective risk mitigation models to improve overall supply chain profitability, and these models guide efficient decision-making (Daultani *et al.*, 2015).

3.5 Supply Chain Network and Agility

Supply chains face various risks that can arise at different stages. Supply risks include disruptions in the supply of raw materials and products, supplier bankruptcy, or delivery delays. Operational risks can arise from errors in production processes, machine malfunctions, human resource issues, or logistical disruptions. The digitalization of the supply chain introduces cyber risks and creates gaps in the technology–human interface. In addition, given that digital transformation and AI also require changes to employees' skill sets, the risk to human resources remains a priority. Therefore, while automation or a digital supply chain may appear to be a solution in today's industrial environment, it also carries certain risks. Demand risk arises from market fluctuations, inaccurate demand forecasts, or rapid changes in customer needs. Security risks encompass threats such as physical security, cyberattacks, or data breaches. Macro risks consist of factors outside of control, such as economic crises, fluctuations in exchange rates, and natural disasters. Policy risks arise from new regulations, trade restrictions, or geopolitical tensions taken by states. Competitive risks, on the other hand, arise when rival companies develop faster, cheaper, or more innovative solutions. All these elements directly affect the reliability and continuity of the system as sources of risk encountered in supply chains.

SCRM is centered on understanding and enhancing the supply chain. This process involves reducing complexity, simplifying processes, and enhancing reliability. While companies generally demonstrate stronger downstream supply chain awareness, upstream awareness also needs to be increased. Ensuring visibility throughout the supply chain is vital for the early detection of potential risks, thus facilitating timely responses to disruptions. In this context, the establishment of risk management teams and the implementation of procedures in collaboration with customers and suppliers contribute to the creation of a more resilient and sustainable supply chain. The supply chain is a complex structure consisting of nodes and connections. Concrete facilities such as suppliers, factories, and warehouses form "nodes"; the tools that enable physical, informational, and financial flows constitute "connections". The resilience of the supply chain can be determined by identifying critical nodes and connections within the process. The solution to the issue of how to eliminate or reduce risks at these critical points should be identified (Christopher *et al.*, 2011).

Supply chain risk can be defined as exposure to an event that causes a disruption that affects the efficient management of the supply chain network. In companies, the risk management process is often focused on the risk identification phase, but less attention is paid to a holistic approach. Reactive and proactive risk mitigation strategies can be integrated for success. Risk strategies must be compatible with the environment in which the firm operates and competes, both at the general socio-economic level and with respect to the specific environment defined by its customers, suppliers, competitors, potential competitors, and substitute products. Supply chain risks are divided into three main categories: (i) organizational risks arising from within the organization (inventory, process, quality, and management); (ii) network risks arising from interactions between organizations in the network (suppliers and recipients), and (iii) environmental risks arising from external factors (weather, natural disasters, and political or market conditions). In addition, evaluating and including factors such as behavioral perceptions, sustainability considerations, and risk diffusion in risk management can contribute to improving performance (Ghadge *et al.*, 2012).

Supply chain risks are multidimensional internal and external events that can cause disruption of supply chain flow, stoppage or interruption of flows (such as information flow, raw material flow, spare parts flow, product flow, service flow, communication flow, transportation flow, storage flow, and financial flow), and thus cause serious damage to the company in terms of reputation and finance. These losses represent risks that create and/or increase costs in different areas (including financial, reputational, social, and stakeholder relations) by reducing supply chain capacity and negatively affecting its performance (Oliveira *et al.*, 2019; Tran *et al.*, 2018). Since the supply chain is a multi-layered and multi-stakeholder process, events with many and various risk potentials, that is, risk sources, are also many and diverse. In addition, decisions made within the supply chain involve risks in many respects, and unlike conventional commercial decisions, they involve decision nodes that together form a network and contribute to the performance of each member of the network (Ritchie and Brindley, 2007).

The primary goal of SCRM is to ensure that supply chains operate as planned with an uninterrupted flow of materials. In order to support this goal, process design should start with the design of an appropriate supply chain risk strategy, supported by appropriate policies of SCRM. While developing this design, attention should be paid to compliance with laws and regulations. By ensuring that the integration of supply risks with the risk management process is fully and correctly implemented, the necessary resources should be provided with resource allocation. The primary objectives of this framework are to identify and consider guidelines and best practices for optimization in risk management, develop responses to procurement risks in a way that supports corporate goals, implement risk response strategies, and regularly monitor and report the performance of the risk management process. It should also be supported by a good communication and information system (Waters, 2007).

SCRM is a strategic process that aims to enhance the resilience of the supply chain and mitigate potential vulnerabilities. Achieving this objective is dependent on effective stakeholder engagement, which is defined by the presence of trust, transparency, and collaboration among the stakeholders involved.

3.6 Industry Examples

3.6.1 *Ericsson's Proactive Supply Chain Risk Management Approach (VASCSC, 2018; Norman and Jansson, 2004)*

In 2000, a fire at the Philips microchip factory in Albuquerque directly affected Ericsson and Nokia. While Nokia successfully managed the process, Ericsson suffered a loss of $400 million and had to withdraw from the mobile phone market. This experience led Ericsson to initiate a radical transformation in risk management, involving the following:

- a new system for mapping components and products,
- identification of critical suppliers and locations,
- applications such as analyzing the probability and effects of possible accidents.

The main objective of the approach is to reduce the impacts on the supply chain and, especially, ensure business continuity by evaluating risk management measures in a cost-effective manner. In the wake of this critical supplier incident in the supply chain, Ericsson has developed a new proactive framework for risk management. This approach has brought about radical changes not only in processes but also in the organizational structure. Ericsson's crisis paved the way for the company to develop a proactive SCRM model. The key elements of this model are organizational and process transformation, as well as the increasing role of insurance companies and the integration of risk factor into logistics decision-making. With the transformation of the organizational structure in this model, the ultimate goal of which is to establish an optimal risk-prevention balance in the supply chain, Ericsson has integrated the necessary processes and tools by establishing a new structure specific to risk management (VASCSC, 2018).

The company has established a risk management system that is based on the systematic analysis, evaluation, and management of risk sources at all stages of the supply chain. In this context, close cooperation was established with suppliers and certain requirements were expected to be met. It is evident that insurance companies have assumed a pivotal role in this regard, given their growing cognizance of vulnerabilities inherent in contemporary supply chains. Consequently, these entities have embarked on a concerted effort to promote the implementation of sophisticated risk management methodologies. In the context of evaluating logistics solutions, supply chain risks are incorporated into change analyses. This necessitates a comprehensive evaluation of risks in conjunction with conventional logistical criteria such as time, cost, quality, agility, and leanness. The objective is not to eradicate risk entirely but rather to establish an effective level of risk and prevention. A salient finding from this novel approach pertains to the emergent role of insurance companies. It is evident that they are evolving beyond the role of a mere financial safety net; rather, they are assuming a pivotal function as a catalyst for the advancement of SCRM by identifying and addressing the vulnerabilities inherent in contemporary supply chains. Moreover, Ericsson's novel framework underscores the integration of risk into logistics concepts. The company now asserts that supply chain risks must be considered in conjunction with traditional logistics factors, such as time, cost, quality, agility, and efficiency. This will ensure an optimal balance is struck between operational efficiency and resilience (Norman and Jansson, 2004; VASCSC, 2018).

3.6.2 *Fraport's Approach to Supply Chain Risk Management (Fraport AG, 2025)*

Fraport has expressed its support for the German Supply Chain Due Diligence Act (*Lieferkettensorgfaltspflichtengesetz*), legislation which, upon its entry into force on 1 January 2023, will prioritize the protection of human rights and environmental risks in supply chains. Since 2013, the company has established a Supplier Code of Conduct for its suppliers and emphasized that it is publicly available. Furthermore, the company has demonstrated a firm commitment to international norms, including the United Nations Global Compact, the International Labour Organization's (ILO) Core Labour Standards, the Organisation for Economic Co-operation and Development's (OECD) Multinational Enterprises Guidelines, and the Paris Climate Agreement.

Fraport employs a systematic approach to risk management within its supply chain, utilizing an integrated risk management system (RMS). The monitoring of human rights and environmental risk obligations is achieved through the implementation of both annual and *ad hoc* analyses, which are integrated into the supplier selection process. In the event of non-conformity, the supplier is requested to take corrective action. Should these measures prove ineffective, the employment relationship may be terminated.

The company has an electronic whistleblowing system that allows all stakeholders, including employees and suppliers, to report violations of human rights or environmental regulations. The system under discussion guarantees privacy and anonymity. Incoming reports are subject to rigorous evaluation, and investigations are initiated when deemed necessary. The complainant is apprised of the process and appropriate actions are taken. While the report, prepared at the conclusion of the process, is disseminated to the relevant parties in accordance with the principle of confidentiality, measures are being planned to prevent similar errors in the future.

Fraport has a robust compliance management system that encompasses all group companies. The implementation of this system is a mandatory requirement for all employees and managers, in accordance with the prevailing internal culture. Its application is subject to regular monitoring, conducted within the framework of internal audits. This process involves updating policy statements and providing ESG reporting. Fraport transparently presents these commitments and processes to the public through publications such as the non-financial declaration, ESG Factbook, and EMAS-verified environmental declaration.

3.6.3 *TAV Airport Hotel İzmir Supply Chain Risk Management* (*TAV Airport Hotel İzmir, 2024*)

TAV Airport Hotel Izmir, a subsidiary of TAV Airports Holding, seeks to mitigate risks in supply chain processes while enhancing its service quality in accordance with its sustainability policies. The business possesses an extensive supply chain network that is directly related to both airport and hospitality operations. The TAV Airport Hotel Izmir has established a paradigm that integrates environmental awareness, ethical principles, and operational continuity in the domain of SCRM. Its emphasis on local and sustainable sourcing has been demonstrated to mitigate environmental risks while concurrently supporting social sustainability by contributing to the regional economy. The BTA Purchasing Directorate is responsible for the procurement of goods and services for all TAV units through the central system. The structure under discussion has been designed to address the requirements in the categories of direct materials, indirect materials and services, and investments. It is anticipated that this will result in cost advantages and quality continuity with long-term central purchasing contracts. Suppliers are subject to analysis through the medium of the Supplier Interview and Evaluation Form, following which they are included in the cooperative process. This approach optimizes stock tracking, thereby enhancing operational efficiency and ensuring continuity in product distribution. Within the scope of SCRM, environmental and social risks, ethical and compliance risks, operational risks, and stakeholder communication are considered to be of key importance. By collaborating with suppliers who demonstrate sensitivity to biodiversity issues, TAV is able to mitigate the environmental impacts of its business operations. This is achieved through a collaborative process that examines the company's environmental and social risks. As of 2024, all shell eggs have started to be sourced from non-cage sources, with local suppliers being prioritized. Consequently, the number of suppliers increased from 9 in 2023 to 17 in 2024, 11 of which were local suppliers. Within the scope of ethics and compliance risks, TAV conducts third-party assessments within the framework of its Ethics and Compliance Policy and requests suppliers to comply with business ethics and environmental legislation. In terms of operational risks, the centralized purchasing structure reduces the risks of price fluctuations and supply continuity. At the same time, the alternative supplier network increases resilience against supply disruptions. Stakeholder communication is provided through regular supplier visits, digital channels, and printed publications; cooperation is maintained through continuous information exchange, order management, and strategic decision-making processes (TAV Airport Hotel İzmir, 2024) (see Fig. 3.5).

3.6.4 *CİSCO Cisco Supply Chain Risk Management*

Cisco Systems is a global leader in technology, specializing in telecommunications and networking hardware. Due to its extensive supplier network and global operations, the company is highly vulnerable to supply chain disruptions. To address this, Cisco has adopted a proactive approach to risk management, aiming to identify, minimize, and respond effectively to potential threats. Cisco has transformed SCRM into a core corporate value and competitive differentiator. By combining proactive risk

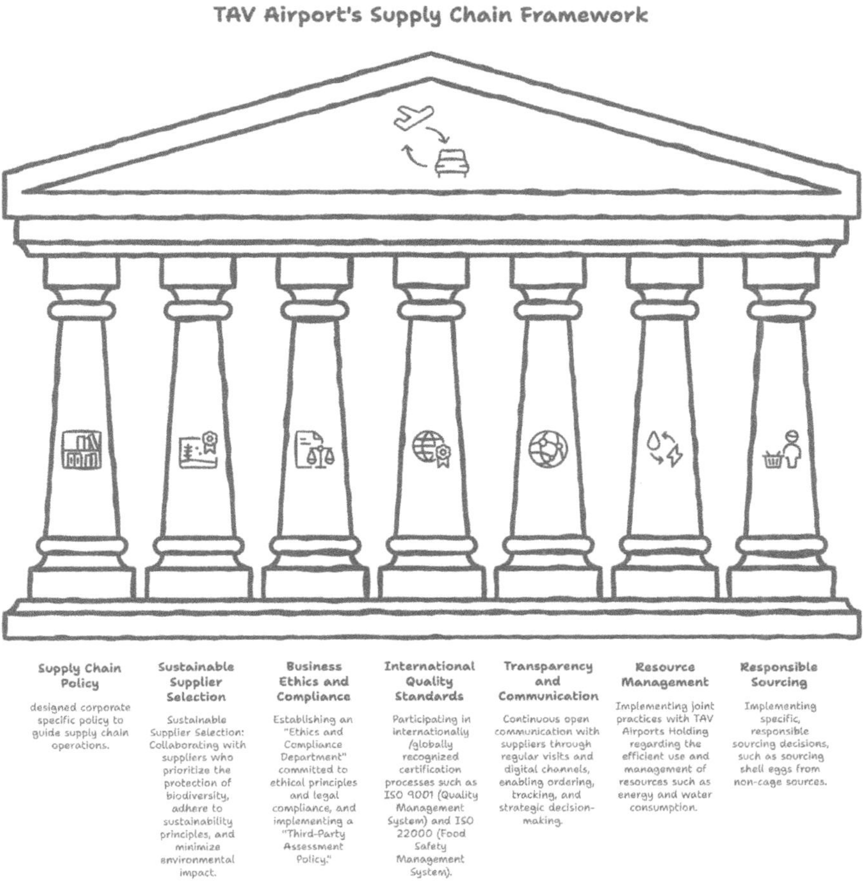

Fig. 3.5. TAV Airport İzmir supply chain risk management framework: Components of the TAV Airport Izmir supply chain risk management concept.

Source: The original design is by the authors; Napkin AI was used for visualization purposes only. https://app.napkin.ai/page/CgoiCHByb2Qtb25lEiwKBFBhZ2UaJGNkNjU2ZGE4LWZiNGItNDc0Mi1hMTU1LTBmZTViZGI3MzAxNA.

identification, cyber resilience, and innovative visibility tools, the company ensures business continuity and enhances its global supply chain robustness (CISCO, 2025; Massachusetts Institute of Technology (MIT) Center for Transportation & Logistics, 2025).

Cisco recognizes risk management as both a strategic asset and a form of insurance. As part of the company's Product Durability and Risk

Mitigation program, early risk assessments are conducted prior to production in order to identify single-source components. Furthermore, it requires its critical suppliers to submit and regularly test these plans against its Business Continuity Plans (BCPs). Finally, it provides real-time monitoring of outsourced production, ensuring immediate detection of any defects and preventing quality control overrides (CISCO, 2025; Munson *et al.*, 2014; Massachusetts Institute of Technology (MIT) Center for Transportation & Logistics, 2025; Conway *et al.*, 2025) as follows:

- **De-risking:** The company has adopted the concept of "de-risking" its supply chain and products in advance. This involves identifying alternative components during the product development phase and utilizing multiple production sites.
- **Real-time visibility:** By providing real-time visibility into outsourced manufacturing processes, it prevents skipped quality issues or testing requirements.
- **Business continuity plans:** BCPs **are regularly requested and tested from critical suppliers**. In this way, the company manages to ensure business continuity on a global scale by minimizing supply chain disruptions.

Supply chain risks can arise from both internal and external sources (Massachusetts Institute of Technology (MIT) Centre for Transportation & Logistics, 2025; Munson *et al.*, 2014):

- **Internal risks:** These arise from the pursuit of efficiencies within the supply chain. It can be controlled by administrative measures such as process optimization and monitoring of key nodes (Massachusetts Institute of Technology (MIT) Centre for Transportation & Logistics, 2025; Munson *et al.*, 2014).
- **External risks:** These arise from the company's exposure to its external environment. Natural disasters, economic uncertainties, political events, and cyber threats are among these risks (Massachusetts Institute of Technology (MIT) Centre for Transportation & Logistics, 2025; Munson *et al.*, 2014).

Cisco's risk management process is based on four key steps: the identification of risk, its assessment, the mitigation of risk, and continuous monitoring. The company facilitates this process through real-time data collection, integrated systems, and transparent communication with its suppliers as follows (CISCO, 2025):

i. **Risk identification:** Identifying potential internal and external risks, such as natural disasters, political instability, and logistical disruptions.
ii. **Risk assessment:** Analyzing and prioritizing the likelihood and potential impacts of identified risks.
iii. **Risk mitigation:** Identifying alternative suppliers and taking preventive measures, such as managing inventory for critical components.
iv. **Continuous monitoring:** Continuous monitoring and updating of risks in the supply chain.

This process is supported by real-time data collection, integrated systems, and transparent communication with suppliers (CISCO, 2025). (CISCO, 2025) see Fig. 3.6.

The risk management strategies based on resilience, cybersecurity, and quality management are discussed as follows (CISCO, 2025; Munson *et al.*, 2014):

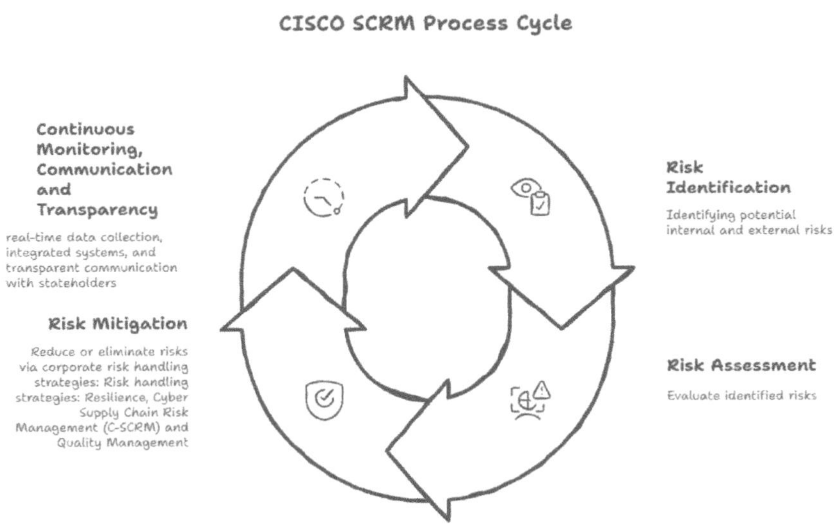

Fig. 3.6. CISCO SCRM process cycle.

Source: The original design is by the authors; Napkin AI was used for visualization purposes only. https://app.napkin.ai/page/CgoiCHByb2Qtb25lEiwKBFBhZ2UaJDliOTYyZTg3LWZjYzUtNDU0Yi1hN2EyLTcwZTIzNTY3Y2Q0ZQ.

- **Resilience:** Cisco's dedicated SCRM team was established in the aftermath of Hurricane Katrina in 2005. This team is regarded as a pivotal investment, as it empowers the company to respond methodically to significant events and thoroughly evaluate their financial ramifications. The team's primary objective is to minimize vulnerabilities before a disruption occurs, thereby ensuring that suppliers can meet their committed recovery times.
- **Cyber supply chain risk management (C-SCRM):** For Cisco, C-SCRM is an integral part of the supply chain. This management approach focuses on specific risks, such as counterfeit or tainted products, malicious software, and the misuse of intellectual property. The company has evolved its security role from "limiting damage" to "enabling business". In order to achieve this objective, it is necessary to integrate security requirements with physical security requirements across the supplier network and throughout the entire product lifecycle.
- **Quality management:** Despite utilizing a 100% outsourced manufacturing model, Cisco ensures product quality through innovative methods. The company utilizes a proprietary software system that provides real-time visibility into the production processes of its outsourced manufacturers. This system transmits live production data to headquarters, enabling immediate detection of component-level defects and preventing suppliers from bypassing testing requirements before shipment.

3.6.5 *Volvo Group ERM and Supply Chain* (*Volvo Group, 2023, 2025*)

The Volvo Group's Supply Partner Code of Conduct provides a comprehensive framework for managing risks in the supply chain. The company requires its suppliers to comply with legislation, as well as demonstrate environmental, social, and ethical responsibility. From an ERM perspective, this code of conduct is designed to ensure that legal, operational, reputational, environmental, and social risks are proactively addressed. Suppliers are obliged to comply with all applicable regulations, manage necessary licenses and permits transparently, and apply stricter standards when there is a conflict between local legislation and Volvo standards. This approach is intended to minimize legal and compliance risks.

The Volvo Group employs a comprehensive risk management strategy that is monitored and managed through various business units, trucking divisions, and group functions. This process is supported by a centralized ERM reporting process, which is a systematic and structured framework for reporting and reviewing identified risks, risk assessments, and mitigation measures. The Volvo Group's risk management process categorizes risks into four main groups: macro and market-related, operational, compliance, and financial.

In terms of reputational risks, Volvo adopts a zero-tolerance policy with regard to human rights abuses such as child labor, forced labor, discrimination, and violence. The provision of safe, healthy, and fair working conditions is widely recognized as a fundamental element in the management of social risks. The evaluation of environmental risks is conducted within the context of sustainable resource utilization, biodiversity conservation, water and waste management, and climate change mitigation. Volvo has set expectations for its suppliers to track and report Scope 1, 2, and 3 emissions and develop strategies that align with net-zero targets in the long term.

A critical dimension of SCRM is the responsible sourcing of raw materials. It is imperative to prevent the use of minerals derived from conflict zones and ensure transparency through tools such as the Cobalt Reporting Template (CRT) and Conflict Minerals Reporting Template (CMRT). This encompasses not only direct suppliers but also their network of sub-suppliers. Furthermore, the company has a zero-tolerance policy for ethical risks such as bribery, corruption, conflicts of interest, and unfair competition. Privacy, information security, and data protection represent further significant components of risk management within the context of business ethics.

In the context of operational risks, occupational health and safety is a priority. Volvo requests that its suppliers conduct risk analyses, train employees on occupational safety, and implement contingency plans. The framework also encompasses the fundamental needs of employees, including housing, hygiene, meals, and rest. In order to effectively manage these risk areas, Volvo expects suppliers to establish effective management systems, conduct periodic reporting, be open to audits, and adopt continuous improvement processes.

Volvo's approach is strong from an ERM perspective. The risk categories are extensive, encompassing social, environmental, ethical, and climate-focused risks, all of which are clearly defined. Furthermore, both mandatory requirements and expectations for improvement are presented, thus creating opportunities for suppliers to develop. Concrete targets, such as net-zero emissions, make risk management measurable. However, there are some challenges in implementation. It can be challenging to thoroughly assess the risks present within the sub-supplier network. For small-scale suppliers, meeting environmental and ethical requirements can incur significant costs. Furthermore, regulatory variations across different countries can complicate the implementation of standards. Within the context of the supply chain, the Volvo Group expects its supply partners to adhere to the same standards. The Supply Partners Code of Conduct establishes sustainability requirements and expectations for the Volvo Group's supply network. In this context, supply partners are required to implement a continuous risk management process to identify, prevent, mitigate, and take responsibility for risks and impacts on climate, resources, people, business ethics, and compliance. Supply partners must proactively address any risk of breaches that may occur within their own facilities or supply networks. These risk management efforts should comply with international standards, such as those set by the OECD and the UN. Volvo's approach allows the company to integrate its own internal risk management with its supply chain, creating a broader scope of risk (Volvo Group, 2023, 2025).

3.6.6 *Tüpraş Supply Chain and Risk Management (Tüpraş, 2024)*

Tüpraş recognizes supply chain management as a fundamental aspect of its operations. The company's primary objective is to ensure a reliable and uninterrupted supply of crude oil and other raw materials and to distribute its refined products to the market in a consistent and secure manner. In order to ensure operational continuity, the company places great emphasis on optimizing logistics processes and managing costs. Effective management of these processes is part of Tüpraş's corporate risk management approach. The company's risk management process is overseen by its risk management committee, which comprises members of the board of directors. The company's integrated system is used to manage all of its risks. The risk management committee's remit is to diagnose and manage risks that may threaten the existence and sustainability of the company.

Tüpraş adheres to the ISO 31000 Risk Management Standard, utilizing its Corporate Risk Directorate to oversee risk management processes.

There are eight different categories of risk, which are monitored as follows:

- technical safety and environmental risks,
- financial risks,
- commercial risks,
- operational risks,
- strategic risks,
- compliance and legal risks,
- reputational risks,
- climate-related/environmental risks.

Tüpraş's comprehensive risk management approach is aimed at maintaining operational resilience and sustainability by taking proactive measures against potential disruptions in the supply chain.

3.6.7 *TOFAŞ—Supply Chain Risk Management Practices*

TOFAŞ is committed to creating a supply chain that is financially strong, operationally eco-friendly, and reliable in terms of production quality and continuity. The company, which has pioneered localization efforts in the Turkish automotive industry since its founding and attaches great importance to reducing foreign dependency, procures an average of 75% of the parts it buys, excluding engines and transmissions, from domestic suppliers. Its strategic goal is to increase the domestic rate in direct material supply to 90% by 2030. TOFAŞ considers the supply chain not only as a logistics process but also as an important part of sustainability and corporate development. In this direction, it contributes to the continuous development of its suppliers, supports the dissemination of organizational excellence, integrates sustainability culture into its value chain, and implements practices to increase the efficiency of its suppliers. In 2022, the total budget size of its procurement activities reached 3 billion euros, and TOFAŞ cooperates with more than 3,000 suppliers and purchases directly from 152 material suppliers operating in 14 cities of Turkey. The main products purchased by the company include formed sheet metal parts, forged and cast machined parts, mechanical and electromechanical parts, electrical installations, plastic and rubber injection products, seats, door panels, glass, glove boxes, bumpers, exhausts, chemicals, interior and exterior trim parts, and fasteners. In addition, the company conducts service and industrial procurement activities that support production continuity; this includes investment, contracting, services, training and consultancy, software, and machinery and consumable purchases. TOFAŞ adopts a multifaceted risk management approach against operational, financial, environmental, and quality risks that may be encountered in all these processes; it minimizes risks through supply chain diversification, increased domestic supplier capacity, integration of sustainability criteria, and supplier development programs. Thanks to this approach, the company ensures production continuity and at the same time leads the strengthening of domestic suppliers in the Turkish automotive industry (TOFAŞ, 2022).

The TOFAŞ SCRM-based targets are as follows (TOFAŞ, 2024):

- **Localization and reducing foreign dependency:** Tofaş attaches great importance to localization and reducing foreign dependency in the Turkish automotive industry. With the exception of engines and transmissions, the company sources an average of 70% of the parts it purchases from domestic suppliers. As its 2030 target, the company aims to increase the domestic supply rate of direct materials to 90%.
- **Supplier development:** Tofaş is committed to the continuous development of its suppliers, who play a vital role in the value chain. This commitment is driven by the desire to achieve organizational excellence and cultivate a culture of sustainability.
- **Global competitiveness:** Thanks to its strong position in Stellantis, Tofaş aims to act as a bridge in the development of suppliers in Turkey.
- **Supply chain commitment:** The company is committed to creating a financially strong, operationally eco-friendly, and reliable supply chain in terms of production quality and continuity.
- **Supplier diversity:** In parallel with developments in automotive technologies, it increases supply chain diversity. The company has bolstered its competitiveness in this field by strategically integrating companies specializing in the development and production of advanced components, particularly those tailored for electric vehicle technologies, into its supply chain. Tofaş collaborates with over 3,000 suppliers in its procurement processes and purchases from 155 domestic direct

material suppliers across 14 cities in Turkey. Included in the new projects are 347 international suppliers, bringing the total number of direct material suppliers to 502.

- **Project management:** Securing annual factory capacity allocated for overseas sales through take-or-pay export agreements with Stellantis helps manage a significant portion of Tofaş's commercial risks. These agreements are designed to safeguard the company against potential financial risks, including costs, profitability, exchange rates, and foreign market fluctuations.

References

Aresu, E. (2025, February 26). Navigating supply chain risk in AI chips. The New Stack. https://thenewstack.io/navigating-supply-chain-risk-in-ai-chips/. Accessed at September 1, 2025.

BCarm. (2025, September). Supply chain fragility. BCarm Business Continuity & Risk Management. https://www.bcarm.co.uk/insights-and-news/business-continuity/supply-chain-fragility/.

Bowersoc, D. J., Closs, D. J., and Cooper, M. B. (2010). *Supply Chian Logistics Management.* McGraw-Hill/Irwin, New York.

Christopher, M. (2011). *Logistics & Supply Chain Management.* Pearson Education Limited, Edinburgh Gate.

CISCO. (2025). What is supply chain risk management (SCRM)? Cisco Systems, Inc. https://www.cisco.com/site/us/en/learn/topics/security/what-is-supply-chain-risk-management-scrm.html.

Conway, E., Luu, N., and Shaffer, E. (2025, July). Best practices in cyber supply chain risk management Cisco® managing supply chain risks end-to-end. U.S. Resilience Project. https://www.cisco.com/c/dam/en_us/about/doing_business/trust-center/docs/cyber-supply-chain-risk-management.pdf.

Daultani, Y., Kumar, S., Vaidya, O. S., and Tiwari, M. K. (2015). A supply chain network equilibrium model for operational and opportunism risk mitigation. *International Journal of Production Research*, 53(18), 5685–5715. http://dx.doi.org/10.1080/00207543.2015.1056325.

Diabat, A., Govindan, K., and Panicker, V. V. (2012). Supply chain risk management and its mitigation in a food industry. *International Journal of Production Research*, 50(11), 3039–3050. https://doi.org/10.1080/00207543.2011.588619.

EXIGER. (2025, January 02). Chip challenges: Semiconductors and supply chain risks. https://www.exiger.com/perspectives/chip-challenges-semiconductors-and-supply-chain-risks. Accessed September 1, 2025.

EXIGER. (2025, January 30). Winter storms: A lesson in supply chain fragility and the need for visibility. EXIGER: www.exiger.com. https://www.exiger.com/perspectives/winter-storms-a-lesson-in-supply-chain-fragility-and-the-need-for-visibility/.

Fraport AG. (2025, September 08). Risk management, responsibility in supply chain, supply chain due diligience act. fraport.com. https://www.fraport.com/en/our-group/responsibility/supply-chain-due-diligence-act.html. Accessed September 01, 2025.

Gallagher. (2025, September 15). From lab to launch: Strategies for overcoming supply chain fragility. Gallagher. https://www.ajg.com/-/media/files/gallagher/us/news-and-insights/2025/how-to-overcome-supply-chain-fragility.pdf.

GEP. (2025, September 15). 5 Ways to reduce supply chain fragility. GEP: gep.com. https://www.gep.com/blog/strategy/5-ways-to-reduce-supply-chain-fragility.

Ghadge, A., Dani, S., and Kalawsky, R. (2012). Supply chain risk management: Present and future scope. *The International Journal of Logistics Management*, 23(3), 313–339.

Harland, C., Brenchley, R., and Walker, H. (2003). Risk in supply networks. *Journal of Purchasing & Supply Management*, 9(2), 51–62. https://doi.org/10.1016/S1478-4092(03)00004-9.

Harper, L. (2024, July 22). Airline leaders expect supply-chain challenges to persist for years. Flight Global. https://www.flightglobal.com/airlines/airline-leaders-expect-supply-chain-challenges-to-persist-for-years/159271.article.

Heckmann, I., Comes, T., and Nickel, S. (2014). A critical review on supply chain risk—definition, measure and modeling. *The International Journal of Management Science*, 52, 119–132. http://dx.doi.org/10.1016/j.omega.2014.10.004.

Hugos, M. (2003). *Essentials of Supply Chain Management.* John Wiley & Sons, Inc., New Jersey.

Jüttner, U. (2005). Supply chain risk management: Understanding the business requirements from a practitioner perspective. *The International Journal of Logistics*, 16(1), 120–141.

Jüttner, U., Peck, H., and Christopher, M. (2003). Supply chain risk management: Outlining an agenda for future research. *International Journal of Logistics: Research and Applications*, 6(4), 197–210. https://doi.org/10.1080/13675560310001627016.

KPMG. (2024, July). Global supply chain fragility: Five trends and their impact on the global economy. kpmg.com. https://kpmg.com/us/en/articles/2024/2024-supply-chain-update.html.

Kucuk Yilmaz, A. (2003). *Risk Management from a Safety Perspective in Aviation and Case Studies of Its Implementation in Aviation Organizations.* Anadolu Üniversitesi, Sivil Havacılık Yönetimi Anabilim Dalı. Eskişehir: Anadolu University, Social Science Institute, Civil Aviation Department, Master Program.

Kumar, S. K., Tiwari, M., and Babiceanu, R. F. (2010). Minimisation of supply chain cost with embedded risk using computational intelligence approaches. *International Journal of Production Research*, 48(13), 3717–3739. http://dx.doi.org/10.1080/00207540902893425.

Lummus, R. R. and Vokurka, R. J. (1999). Defining supply chain management: A historical perspective and practical guidelines. *Industrial Management & Data Systems*, 99(1), 11–17.

Massachusetts Institute of Technology (MIT) Center for Transportation & Logistics. (2025). Cisco Systems, Inc.: Supply chain risk management. https://ctl.mit.edu/sites/ctl.mit.edu/. https://ctl.mit.edu/sites/ctl.mit.edu/files/attachments/tab%207a%20Cisco%20Case.pdf.

Munson, C., Sáenz, M. J., and Revilla, E. (2014). *The Supply Chain Management Casebook*. Upper Saddle River, NJ: Pearson Education, Inc. https://ptgmedia.pearsoncmg.com/images/9780133757446/samplepages/0133757447.pdf.

Norrman, A. and Jansson, U. (2004). Ericsson's proactive supply chain risk management approach after a serious sub-supplier accident. *International Journal of Physical Distribution & Logistics Management*, 34(5), 434–456. https://doi.org/10.1108/09600030410545463.

Oliveira, J., Jin, M., Lima, R., Kobza, J., and Montevechi, J. (2019). The role of simulation and optimization methods in supply chain risk management: Performance and review standpoints. *Simulation Modelling Practice and Theory*, 92, 17–44. https://doi.org/10.1016/j.simpat.2018.11.007.

Payne, T. (2025, March 21). Build supply chain resilience to arrive at an antifragile state. GARTNER: gartner.com. https://www.gartner.com/en/articles/supply-chain-resilience.

Quesada, H., Gazo, R., and Sanchez, S. (2012). Critical factors affecting supply chain management: A case study in the US pallet industry. In Groznik, A. and Xiong, Y. (eds.), *Pathways to Supply Chain Excellence*. InTech, Croatia, pp. 33–56.

Ritchie, B. and Brindley, C. (2007). An emergent framework for supply chain risk management and performance measurement. *Journal of the Operational Research Society*, 58(11), 1398–1411.

Ross, D. F. (2008). *The Intimate Supply Chain Leveraging the Supply Chain to Manage the Customer Experience.* Taylor & Francis Group, Boca Raton; Auerbach Publications, New York. https://doi.org/10.1201/9781420064988.

Sinha, P. R., Whitman, L. E., and Malzahn, D. (2004). Methodology to mitigate supplier risk in an aerospace supply chain. *Supply Chain Management*, 9(2), 154–168. https://doi.org/10.1108/13598540410527051.

Sustainability Directory. (2024). Supply chain fragility. Sustainability Directory: https://sustainability-directory.com/. https://esg.sustainability-directory.com/term/supply-chain-fragility/.

Tang, C. S. (2006). Perspectives in supply chain risk management. *International Journal of Production Economics*, 103(2), 451–488. https://doi.org/10.1016/j.ijpe.2005.12.006.

TAV Airport Hotel İzmir. (2024). 2023 Sustainability Report. izmirairport.com. https://tavairporthotels.com.tr/UserFiles/files/2-TAV_AIRPORT_HOTEL_SURDURULEBILIRLIK_RAPORU_2023.pdf.

Thun, J.-H. and Hoenig, D. (2011). An empirical analysis of supply chain risk management in the German automotive industry. *International Journal Production Economics*, 131(1), 242–249. https://doi.org/10.1016/j.ijpe.2009.10.010.

TOFAŞ. (2024). Tofaş 2024 Annual Report. https://www.tofas.com.tr/. https://www.tofas.com.tr/YatirimciIliskileri/FaaliyetRaporlari/Documents/tofas-turk-otomobil-fabrikasi-as-2024-faaliyet-raporu.pdf.

Tran, T. H., Dobrovnik, M., and Kummer, S. (2018). Supply chain risk assessment: A content analysis-based literature review. *International Journal of Logistics Systems and Management*, 31(1), 1–30.

Treuner, F., Hübner, D., Baur, S., and Wagner, S. M. (2014). A survey of disruptions in aviation and aerospace supply chains and recommendations for increasing resilience. *Supply Chain Management III*, 7–12. https://scm.ethz.ch/content/dam/ethz/special-interest/mtec/chair-of-logistics-mgmt-dam/documents/practitioner-articles/Treuner%20etal%202014%20A%20survey%20of%20disruptions%20in%20aviation%20and%20aerospace%20supply%20chain.pdf.

Turkish Airlines. (2025). Star Alliance. Turkish Airlines. https://www.turkishairlines.com/en-int/press-room/about-us/star-alliance/. Accessed at August 31, 2025.

TÜPRAŞ. (2024). Tüpraş 2024 Integrated Annual Report. tupras.com. https://www.tupras.com.tr/assets/uploads/entegre-faaliyet/tupras-2024-entegre-faaliyet-raporu.pdf.

Vikram A. Sarabhai Community Science Centre (VASCSC). (2018, September 01). Ericson's proactive supply chain risk management, opp. Gujarat University. Vikram A. Sarabhai Community Science Centre (VASCSC). https://vascsc.org/case_study/ericssons-proactive-supply-chain-risk-management/. Accessed September 01, 2025.

Volvo Group. (2023). Volvo group supply partner code of conduct edition 3. volvogroup.com. https://www.volvogroup.com/content/dam/volvo-group/markets/master/suppliers/our-supplier-requirements/Volvo-Group-Supply-Partner-Code-of-Conduct-edition3-2023.pdf.

Volvo Group. (2025, September). Risk and uncertainties. https://www.volvogroup.com/. https://www.volvogroup.com/en/investors/risk-and-uncertainties.html.

Waters, D. (2007). *Supply Chain Risk Management: Vulnerability and Resilience in Logistics*. London, UK: Kogan Page Limited.

Wieland, A. and Wallenburg, C. M. (2012). Dealing with supply chain risks linking risk management practices and strategies to performance. *International Journal of Physical Distribution & Logistics Management*, 42(10), 887–905.

Zsidisin, G. A. and Ritchie, B. (2009). Supply chain risk management—developments, issues and challenges. In Zsidisin, G. A. and Ritchie, B. (eds.), *Supply Chain Risk: A Handbook of Assessment, Management, and Performance* (pp. 1–11). New York, NY: Springer.

Zsidisin, G. A., Panelli, A., and Upton, R. (2000). Purchasing organization involvement in risk assessments, contingency plans, and risk management: An exploratory study. *Supply Chain Management: An International Journal*, 5(4), 187–197. https://doi.org/10.1108/13598540010347307.

Chapter 4

Kaizen-Based Supply Chain Risk Management Strategy: Lean and Agile

"Supply sustains business, people, and progress".
"Supply drives us—and our industries".
"No supply, no life;
the core of us and our industries".
—My son, M. Efe Yilmaz (M.E.Y.)

4.1 Kaizen, SCRM, and Organizational Behavior and Culture

The most crucial need in today's business and life is to be lean and agile. We must use our resources efficiently, sufficiently, and execute with speed, accuracy, and optimal results. Failure to maintain our supply chain is an existential risk. Our resilience and continuity are a direct result of effective supply. Supply chains are the core of our operations and the foundation of our success.

We, as humans, are transforming digitally at a much slower pace than technology. Therefore, we need to streamline our environment, processes, work, and supply chains, while also making them more agile and, most importantly, implementing holistic risk management. Otherwise, it will become impossible for us to keep up with the times. It is an approach that focuses not only on processes but also on the development of organizational behavior and human resources.

Supply chain risk management's (SCRM) approach to risk management and lean thinking offers a system that enables the realization of both the organization's overall potential and the potential of each individual employee, simplifying the learning and working process by removing unnecessary barriers and interruptions, and creating equal opportunities among participants. The combination of lean management and digitalization to optimize processes will enable participants to enter the labor market more quickly and effectively. This is because lean management is a necessity in today's world. Everything is becoming increasingly complex, and the momentum of digital transformation is also hindering the comprehensibility of this complexity.

SCRM also provides practitioners with organizational behavior transformation, and thanks to SCRM, they will have the opportunity to learn not only green procurement and supply chain techniques but also the most efficient and systematic ways to achieve sustainability. The lean management structure, which is basically based on the systematic elimination of waste, also makes it possible to implement an approach that coincides with the Sustainable Development Goals by integrating it with organizational behavior. Thanks to this approach, both concrete operational outputs will be achieved in supply chains, and strategic value will be added to the execution process, resulting in an efficient and quality-oriented SCRM model. At this point, SCRM makes a difference not only in the result but also in all stages of the process.

Risk is part of every business, from pandemics to cyber threats and supply chain disruptions. The risks facing organizations are real, and there is increasing demand for qualified and skilled risk professionals who can help improve organizational resilience in an ever-evolving risk landscape (IRM, 2025). Failure to maintain our supply chain presents an existential risk. Our current resilience and continued existence are a direct result of our ability to supply. Supply chains are the foundation of our operations and the very core of our existence.

The environmentally focused lean integration within the scope of SCRM is supported by the Total Productive Maintenance (TPM) approach, one of the cornerstones of lean production. TPM applications represent an approach that supports the goals of extending equipment life and preventing unplanned downtime. The TPM approach contributes to reducing energy and resource consumption while also minimizing waste by increasing production efficiency. Therefore, SCRM strengthens the direct impact of lean management on environmental sustainability while ensuring that environmentally friendly transformation is supported by concrete results.

Digitalization in SCRM is positioned not only as a technological transformation but also as a strategic tool to streamline processes and increase efficiency. Taking into account the lean and agile management approach, SCRM supports objectives such as reducing waste, reducing process complexity and cycle times, strengthening data-driven decision-making, and implementing real-time monitoring and guidance systems using digital skills. The SCRM framework based on enterprise risk management (ERM) offers the opportunity to merge digitalization and lean production, bringing these two axes of transformation into a holistic and synchronized structure. This powerful integration will increase quality, sustainability, and agility across all processes, from training to production, thus contributing concretely to the digital, environmentally friendly, and agile transformation capabilities of industries and the regions in which they operate, thereby increasing resilience.

The SCRM model will increase its impact by making processes agile based on risk management and simultaneously streamlining all elements that hinder agility. By comparing and evaluating organizational processes implemented in different industries, the best risk management practices can be approached. In this way, collaboration will generate value not only strategically but also operationally. Therefore, the lean management approach in the supply chain will increase process efficiency by supporting collaboration, accelerating information flow, and reducing barriers to performance development.

4.2 Holistic SCRM and Stakeholder Engagement and Relationship

SCRM is built on collaborations and naturally supports strategies for establishing and developing them. Because each stakeholder affects the other, each stakeholder represents a source of risk for the other. This cooperation will ensure that lean transformation is built on a common knowledge base and internalized by stakeholders at all levels, becoming an integral part of the organizational culture. Each country and industry have different levels of maturity in terms of lean practices. By seizing these differences as opportunities, SCRM can encourage the cross-border transfer of best practices. Thus, by taking advantage of the strengths of each country or industry, it will contribute to the rapid spread of risk and lean management practices in supply chains on a global scale and to make them more efficient. For example, this process can create a common body of knowledge across Europe and support the continuity of a lean culture. This quality-oriented structure aims to go beyond training processes to provide not only theoretical knowledge transfer but also long-term benefits to participants and the sector by reinforcing a culture of continuous improvement.

Establishing risk awareness, understanding, and culture among stakeholders is critical from the moment an enterprise risk management (ERM) framework is developed. Risk awareness in the public sector is particularly strong at the board and senior management levels. However, at the operational level, risk awareness tends to focus more on specific issues such as health, safety, or data privacy (KPMG, 2019).

Engaging and collaborative relationships built on trust with suppliers and stakeholders are critical for effective risk management, as this increases collaboration and communication about common risks and challenges in the supply chain. Building strong relationships enables companies to develop risk mitigation strategies and enhance the overall resilience of the supply chain. To optimize this process, regular communication channels must be established, such as workshops and joint risk assessment meetings, thereby facilitating the sharing of critical information. Involving suppliers in risk assessment processes helps identify weaknesses and promotes a culture of transparency and trust. Furthermore, using technology-enabled shared platforms for reporting and analyzing risks strengthens collaboration. When these initiatives are prioritized, risk management efforts become aligned with suppliers and stakeholders, enabling a more proactive approach and preventing potential disruptions (DataGuard, 2024).

Stakeholder engagement helps identify and prioritize potential sources of supply chain disruptions, such as natural disasters, political instability, cyberattacks, or quality issues. Consulting stakeholders provides insights into their needs, expectations, and how they may be affected by different scenarios. Feedback can be used to assess the likelihood and impact of risks and prioritize those requiring more attention. Engagement also supports the development and communication of contingency plans—such as switching suppliers, increasing inventory, or modifying delivery methods—ensuring they are realistic, feasible, and aligned with stakeholder capabilities. Regular communication builds trust and collaboration, enabling information sharing, coordinated actions, and joint problem-solving, which strengthen supply chain resilience. Additionally, involving stakeholders allows organizations to learn from disruptions, identify root causes, gather suggestions and best practices, and improve risk management processes while acknowledging contributions and achievements (LinkedIn, 2025).

Within the scope of SCRM, enterprise-wide risk management and lean management principles play a critical role in shaping processes, particularly in threat mitigation, error prevention, process monitoring, capacity building, and continuous improvement. This approach also supports the simplification of complex processes that arise with digitalization and the more effective management of these processes. Lean management, which is integrated with digital transformation, eliminates unnecessary or excessive steps, repetitions, unnecessary resource use, and waste in operational processes. In addition, it helps to use resources more efficiently by clarifying the critical tasks that personnel should focus on first in terms of human resources and organizational culture, as well as jobs and their descriptions.

SCRM, which creates a shared risk culture involving stakeholders by influencing organizational and individual culture, can encourage both leaders and employees to share their green awareness and reflect this awareness to internal and external stakeholders. The continuous improvement mindset provided by lean culture not only fosters individual skill development but also strengthens the learning cycle within teams. In this way, knowledge sharing becomes more effective, and organizational learning can become more widespread. This increases the agility and resilience of organizations. Thus, by integrating lean management principles into the supply chain and corporate risk, it will be possible to contribute to the formation of an organizational culture that will lay the foundation for sustainable efficiency and long-term success, while also ensuring process efficiency.

Strengthening stakeholder relationships plays a crucial role in building a resilient supply chain, as supply chains are also stakeholder chains. Companies identify and analyze risk-generating events with the potential to impact their supply chains, utilizing the information and collaboration they receive from stakeholders. They then manage these risks by formulating risk strategies aligned with their objectives. Stakeholder relationships and collaboration are crucial during times of crisis. Involving stakeholders in both the development and implementation of supply chain management is crucial for all stakeholders to overcome the crisis with minimal damage and even transform it into an opportunity through collaborative solutions. Collaboration and engagement with stakeholders also foster trust and collaboration, which in turn foster trust-based and interconnected supply chains. Stakeholder relationships are also fundamental to empowering managers and employees to manage supply chain risks. As is well known, every supplier depends on other suppliers for survival. We, the people, regardless of sector or industry, depend on suppliers for our survival.

By adopting the SCRM culture, organizational capacity development is possible in line with the following objectives:

- **Prevention of waste of resources:** Minimizing waste by increasing the efficient use of resources,
- **Elimination of unnecessary and/or steps in the organizational hierarchy and also in the processes:** Increasing operational efficiency by identifying and eliminating unnecessary steps in the processes,
- **Reducing non-value-added workload:** Minimizing inefficient workloads and focusing only on value-added activities,
- **Empowering personnel with risk, decision-making, and problem-solving culture:** Effective handling of difficulties in processes by developing risk management-based and lean thinking and problem-solving skills of personnel.

This approach will support green and digital transformation processes not only as a technological transformation but also as one that strengthens organizational efficiency. Adopting a lean culture will be an effective tool in achieving digitalization and environmental sustainability goals by strengthening the problem-solving competencies of employees.

This is important for SCRM to create a more sustainable and efficient workforce by supporting digital and green transformation not only as a technological approach but also with the transformation of organizational culture.

As a result, in today's complex risk landscape, organizations must look beyond first-tier buyer-supplier relationships and consider how multiple risk categories intersect across the supply chain. A network-level perspective highlights how events can ripple across borders, amplifying downstream issues. Supplier-level risks include operational, financial, reputational, and structural challenges, while natural disasters, geopolitical tensions, and fiscal risks occur at regional or national levels. Additionally, industry-wide risks, such as emerging technologies, must also be considered. Higher-level risks can trigger regulatory pressures, including international trade barriers, sanctions, embargoes, or tariffs. Companies may also proactively adjust suppliers to protect their reputation or meet ESG commitments, for example, by disengaging from suppliers involved in political conflicts or human rights violations. According to Aon's Executive Risk Survey (2022) (AON, 2022), confident leaders view this complex risk interplay as an opportunity rather than a threat. They proactively prepare for, finance, and respond to unplanned events and volatile supplier performance by leveraging deeper insights into how and where risks affect the supply chain (AON, 2025).

4.3 Supplier Network and Interrelationships

There are often multiple suppliers in the supply chain. In addition, the storage of products in the supply chain requires consideration of stock management and stock risks. Warehousing and inventory are separate cost items and play an active role in achieving supply chain targets. Managerial applications such as Just-in-Time have been developed with the aim of eliminating these costs. Stock management encompasses the provision of suitable warehouse conditions, the mitigation of risks during storage and handling, and the continuous monitoring and optimization of inventory levels. It means reducing costs through inventory reduction, simplified processes, and reduced inventory-scoped risks. However, working with less stock also presents different risks. A zero-risk system does not currently exist. At this point, businesses can make their risk choices by answering questions about which risks can be taken and transferred (and which need to be taken and managed). Although stock reductions make the business more agile in terms of warehouse management, they also make it fragile in responding to demand fluctuations. Therefore, for the success of the lean-based supply chain, it is necessary to develop risk analysis and assessment capacity with a focus on SCRM. Companies implement either agile or lean or a lean–agile integration according to their priorities for optimal risk management implementation.

Supply and demand are no longer the sole drivers of the market. Consumer behaviors and economic movements are changing daily, so manufacturers and shippers alike are forced to find ways to keep up. Supply chains need to consider fluctuating market dynamics. Today's customers are both digital and global. This means they have access to just about every product and company right at their fingertips. This boosts competition in a way that was never possible in the past. This competition creates a need for companies to innovate with respect to their products and how they deliver them to consumers quickly and efficiently.

Supply chains form the basis of global trade and economic activity. It promotes prosperity, especially for developing countries and small businesses, by enabling goods and services to move easily across borders. Effective supply chains should not only be limited to logistical processes but should also include financial factors. In this context, supply chain finance (SCF) helps businesses reduce financing costs, increase efficiency, optimize capital flow, and manage risks (Taifa and Nzowa, 2025). Additionally, the worldwide web has enabled trends to quickly pop up and then disappear just as rapidly; consumer preferences are changing at an unprecedented pace, and companies need to maintain flexibility and adaptability in response.

4.4 Kaizen Philosophy: Continuous Improvement

The turbulent business environment that emerged in the 21st century created a new scenario for the competitive development of companies. In this market, where consumer expectations for high product quality, low prices, and easy availability come to the fore, companies must use the best management practices, strategies, and tools to survive and compete successfully. In this context, the Kaizen strategy stands out as an effective method to increase performance and improve organizational and working environments. It is an important tool for changing workplace culture, methods, and work experience. From an innovation perspective, Kaizen is designed as a collection of small, independent, and incremental process innovations adopted by employees, teams, and leaders. The expected effects and ease of use of Kaizen influence the willingness of companies to integrate it into their operations.

Kaizen contributes to leaders developing strategic vision, increasing their ability to adapt to change, and strengthening their problem-solving skills. A culture of continuous improvement enables leaders to better observe and manage their business processes and achieve long-term goals in small steps. Openness to change allows them to see innovation as an opportunity rather than a threat and increases internal flexibility by spreading a common culture among employees. Additionally, Kaizen supports leaders in analyzing the root causes of problems, generating radical solutions, and fostering a culture of data-driven decision-making, fostering effective management across the organization (Trex, 2024):

There are several major aircraft manufacturers that have achieved significant improvements in their operations by effectively implementing Kaizen practices. These include (Aeroplane Tech, 2024):

- **Boeing:** Boeing adopted continuous improvement techniques that resulted in streamlined production processes. The company saw increases in output and quality by involving employees at all levels.
- **Airbus:** Airbus incorporated Kaizen practices into the A350 production line and focused on reducing assembly time. It used cross-functional teams to identify areas for improvement. This collaborative effort not only increased productivity but also fostered a culture of innovation and teamwork.
- **Lockheed Martin:** Lockheed Martin also demonstrates the success of Kaizen practices in aircraft production. The company achieved significant cost savings by utilizing value stream mapping and waste reduction strategies. Continuous feedback loops established within teams ensured that improvements were not only implemented but also sustained over time.

The Kaizen approach promotes constant improvement and the participation of all employees in identifying opportunities for improvement and waste elimination. For the aerospace and maritime industries, this means increasing operational efficiency, ensuring faster adaptation to market changes, and implementing sustainable solutions. The Kaizen Institute helps companies in these sectors become more competitive and resilient (Kaizen Institute, 2025).

Kaizen transforms strategic management in businesses, supporting long-term success. A culture of continuous improvement enables leaders and teams to build a stronger organization. This approach increases customer satisfaction while reducing costs and maintaining competitiveness. Employee motivation and productivity are supported by continuous training, contributing to the sustainability of the business. Furthermore, by fostering innovative thinking, Kaizen enables businesses to adapt to changing market conditions and secure sustainable growth (Trex, 2024).

The expected effects of Kaizen and its ease of use influence companies' willingness to integrate it into their operations. This method has gained popularity not only in the manufacturing sector but also in the service sector and has spread to many countries through multinational companies. Considering the opportunities it offers for continuous improvement and the benefits it provides, it is surprising that despite being a simple method, Kaizen has a high implementation rate and is widespread across almost all continents, yet the results obtained are not satisfactory or at the expected level (Janjić *et al.*, 2019).

Kaizen promotes a multifaceted approach that has a significant impact on leadership and organization. It assists leaders in developing a strategic vision and enables them to achieve long-term goals through small, continuous steps. It also encourages openness to change, facilitating the adaptation of leaders and employees to innovations and increasing organizational flexibility. It strengthens problem-solving skills, enabling them to analyze the root causes of problems, produce lasting solutions, and reinforce a data-driven decision-making culture. Kaizen increases efficiency and effectiveness by continuously improving work processes, encouraging employee participation to boost motivation and commitment. Furthermore, it contributes to the development of a culture of continuous learning and innovation within the organization and supports both environmental and economic sustainability by optimizing resource use (Almehareb and Graham-Jones, 2011; Trex, 2024; Janjić *et al.*, 2019).

The growing demand for regional air transport and rising customer expectations are compelling the aviation industry to produce more efficient, environmentally friendly, and low-cost aircraft. However, as the supply chain—including material, component, and assembly suppliers—is already operating at full capacity, simply increasing operations is not sufficient. This is where Kaizen comes in, promoting continuous improvement in production and maintenance processes, enabling increased efficiency in existing processes and the most effective use of new technologies. Advanced technologies such as data analytics, robotic systems, and 3D printing can be used to increase the efficiency of the supply chain and reduce bottlenecks in processes. Teams that embrace the Kaizen culture can reduce stock levels and optimize resource utilization by ensuring that each stage runs smoothly. In summary, the Kaizen approach is a critical tool for increasing the efficiency of production and MRO processes in the aviation sector by supporting flexibility, transparency, and continuous improvement in the supply chain (Niwa, 2009).

The Kaizen approach in aircraft manufacturing focuses on incremental and effective changes that enhance production methods and employee participation. This approach fosters a culture of continuous improvement, encouraging every employee to generate ideas for streamlining operations and eliminate inefficiencies. The collaborative nature of Kaizen develops problem-solving skills across the organization, strengthens communication between teams, and creates an environment where standard operating procedures are regularly reviewed and improved. The processes play a critical role in aligning operational efficiency in the sector with the stringent demands of quality and safety standards, while also encouraging innovation and strengthening the overall production process (Aeroplane Tech, 2024).

The increasing competition and stringent regulations in the aviation and maritime sectors necessitate improvements in operational efficiency and sustainability. Key challenges encountered in optimizing critical processes include reducing maintenance time, utilizing production areas effectively, eliminating bottlenecks, and improving control over production process variables. In this context, continuous improvement methodologies such as Kaizen, Lean, and Six Sigma ensure that supply chain processes become more flexible, faster, and more efficient. Thanks to Kaizen applications, maintenance time has been reduced, bottlenecks on the production line have been eliminated, space utilization has been optimized, and quality control processes have been strengthened. Furthermore, cost savings have been achieved by reducing waste and non-quality costs, while process consistency and efficiency have increased. All these gains demonstrate that Kaizen plays a critical role in increasing operational efficiency, cost reduction, and flexibility in supply chain and production processes (Kaizen Institute, 2025).

4.5 Enterprise Risk Management: For Building Resilient and Agile Supply Chains

Modern supply chains have grown increasingly fragile due to efficiency-driven strategies such as global sourcing, just-in-time fulfillment, and reduced inventories, which heighten vulnerability to disruptions. To build resilience and agility, businesses must take a proactive approach. First, risks should be quantified using data analytics and forecasting to assess financial impacts, align macro-level exposures to industry-specific events, and identify opportunities to strengthen risk policies. Second, organizations need to prioritize critical contracts, customers, and products based on the probability, impact, and detectability of risks, and implement risk mitigation and financial transfer strategies to safeguard essential operations. Third, understanding both direct suppliers and their upstream partners is crucial; cross-functional collaboration among risk, finance, and supply chain teams can model scenarios, identify vulnerabilities, and inform re-engineering and contractual risk management. Finally, breaking down internal silos by integrating supply chain, procurement, insurance, risk management, and finance functions—supported by external advisors—enables a coordinated strategy that mitigates volatility and optimizes costs, ensuring a more resilient and agile supply chain (AON, 2025).

Traditional supply chain models remain vulnerable in the face of uncertainty, whereas supply chain agility provides organizations with flexibility, resilience, and the ability to leverage risks as opportunities. Agility refers to the capacity to adapt to shocks such as labor or raw material shortages, demand fluctuations, logistical failures, extreme weather, geopolitical risks, and pandemics.

The lean supply chain focuses on cost and inventory optimization, prioritizing predictability but risking missed business opportunities during sudden demand spikes (Lakshman, 2024).

Conventional/traditional supply chain models remain vulnerable to uncertainty, whereas the agility inherent in SCRM provides companies with flexibility, resilience, and the ability to transform risks into opportunities. Agility refers to the capacity to adapt to shocks such as labor and raw material shortages, demand fluctuations, logistical disruptions, extreme weather conditions, geopolitical risks, and pandemics. Lean supply chains increase predictability through cost and inventory optimization but carry the risk of missing opportunities during sudden surges in demand. In contrast, agile supply chains (ASCs) leverage data-driven strategies and advanced technologies to quickly respond to unexpected disruptions while sustainably meeting customer demands. Recent events such as the COVID-19 pandemic, natural disasters, and geopolitical conflicts have highlighted the critical importance of supply chain agility. The agile approach not only helps businesses survive by increasing resilience, enabling timely risk management, minimizing the impact of crises, and encouraging organizational learning but also strengthens their competitive advantages (adopted from Lakshman, 2024).

A lean supply chain emphasizes efficiency, cost reduction, and waste elimination by producing large volumes at the lowest possible cost. It relies on long-term planning and predictability, and it is best suited for stable-demand products such as food or toiletries (Redwood Logistics, 2023).

Global supply chains are becoming increasingly complex, and fluctuations in demand are leaving companies facing serious risks in terms of inventory management; while stock shortages can bring operations to a standstill, overstocking can tie up capital and negatively impact profitability. Although the lean supply chain approach focuses on reducing costs and excess stock, its inflexible structure has proven inadequate in adapting to sudden changes such as the pandemic. In contrast, the ASC offers flexibility and resilience, enabling real-time data-driven decision-making, responding quickly to sudden changes in demand, and maintaining customer service levels. The agile approach is supported by principles such as end-to-end collaboration, data-driven management, responsive systems and analytics, risk management, multi-source supply design, and process ownership. As a result, supply chains become more resilient to disruptions, crises are addressed swiftly, market share is increased, and a competitive advantage is gained; moreover, strategic planning and decision-making processes are strengthened through real-time visibility (Resilinc Editorial Team, 2023).

4.6 Lean Supply Chain Model

A lean supply chain is a management approach that seeks to minimize waste and maximize value creation across the entire supply chain. Its purpose is to streamline operations, cut costs, enhance quality, and ultimately elevate customer satisfaction by operating at peak efficiency SAP Taulia (SAP Taulia, 2025).

Lean supply chain management can be defined as the application of lean principles and practices across the supply chain with the goal of eliminating waste, reducing costs, and creating value for both organizations and customers. It emphasizes the continuous flow of goods, services, and technology without unnecessary activities that add no value, while strengthening collaboration with suppliers and customers to enhance long-term strategies. By improving operational efficiency, flexibility, and quality, lean supply chain management not only increases competitiveness but also supports environmental sustainability through waste reduction. Ultimately, it represents a multidimensional strategy that integrates cost efficiency, process improvement, and customer responsiveness to optimize resources and deliver superior performance across organizational operations.

According to the lean supply management philosophy, the "seven rights" (7Rs), which are the main objectives, can be defined as follows (Helmold, 2020):

i. **Right product:** The right product is one that fully meets the specifications and requirements of the customer requesting it. Products must have the correct dimensions, order, material, color, and other specified characteristics.
ii. **Right quality:** Right quality means clearly defining all quality requirements and taking the necessary improvement measures to achieve optimal quality levels.
iii. **Right time:** Right time means that ordered products must be delivered to the buyer on time, neither too early nor too late.
iv. **Right quantity:** Right quantity means placing a specific order quantity determined in line with internal and customer demands. Organizations must correctly communicate customer and company demands to their supply networks.
v. **Right location:** The right location refers to where the products are needed. In this context, it is closely related to the delivery time of the products. The delivery time of a product includes the process up to the physical delivery of the products or services to the ordering party.
vi. **Right people:** The meaning of right people expands the current definition of the five rights in line with the modern and lean philosophy of the new supply management paradigm. Suppliers in global markets must have the right salespeople, project managers, and operators who can meet the desired criteria. In particular, project managers must have sufficient language skills, and operators must be properly trained to produce quality parts. Human resources are playing an increasingly critical role in the changing and globalized world of trade.
vii. **Right cost:** Any product must have the right cost level; otherwise, it will not be in demand and will not be purchased.

Lean-based initiatives such as just-in-time, continuous improvement, and supplier collaboration work in harmony with green approaches such as recycling, pollution prevention, and ISO 14001 certification to increase operational efficiency while also supporting sustainability goals. Lean practices facilitate the adoption of green strategies and, when integrated with green initiatives, create synergy by strengthening lean systems, thereby leading to improvements in supply chain efficiency, reverse logistics, and corporate outputs. However, due to insufficient financial resources, technological capacity limitations, and a lack of environmental expertise, lean and green management practices often face the risk of remaining limited and informal. In this regard, for the supply chain to achieve its targeted performance indicators, it is necessary to implement SCRM by comprehensively covering ERM with an agile approach (Rodrigues *et al.*, 2020).

Lean supply chain management is an approach that aims to increase efficiency and customer value by reducing waste in the supply chain. Based on lean manufacturing principles, this model aims to reduce costs by simplifying processes and to deliver the needed product at the right time and in the right quantity (Seattle University, 2024).

Lean supply chain practices enhance efficiency by minimizing inventories and streamlining processes, yet these same features render the system more vulnerable to disruptions. The heavy reliance on single sourcing, limited buffer stocks, and reduced redundancy may amplify the impact of demand fluctuations, supplier failures, or logistical delays, leading to cascading effects across the production system. Moreover, insufficient supplier integration and inadequate information sharing exacerbate risks, as misalignment and a lack of trust between partners can undermine the intended benefits of lean principles. Consequently, the successful implementation of lean supply chains requires proactive risk identification, the development of alternative sourcing strategies, and the establishment of continuous improvement mechanisms to balance efficiency with resilience (Jurado, 2013).

A lean supply chain, as a strategy focused on efficiency and cost reduction, relies on a limited but effective supplier base, reduces storage costs through low stock levels, and continuously ensures product standards through strict quality control. This approach, which sits at one end of the supply chain strategy spectrum, represents the predictability and efficiency that lean brings, while the ASC, at the other end, emphasizes responsiveness and resilience (SAP TAulia, 2025).

4.7 The Agile Supply Chain Risk Management Model

Agile SCRM is a best practice approach that combines these five SCRM strategies. Agile SCRM takes an end-to-end view of the supply chain, with a focus on efficient collaboration, robust planning, and rapid, effective decision-making. This approach is not an add-on; it is fully integrated with the management systems, organizational structures, and operating practices of the business. That means that the whole organization is involved, from senior leadership to the front line (Venne, 2023).

An ASC, in contrast, prioritizes flexibility and quick responses to market changes. It uses postponement—delaying final production until demand is clearer—and is ideal for fast-changing or customizable products such as fashion. ASCs depend on strong supplier collaboration and reduce inventory holding by producing closer to actual demand (Redwood Logistics, 2023).

ASCs should be developed specifically for the company. It is especially important to establish a balance of risk appetite level of senior decision-makers that is compatible with the company's risk tolerance. Senior management works with ERM to determine the risk appetite that aligns with the organization's strategic goals. This appetite varies depending on the type of organization: For example, life-saving medical device manufacturers have almost no tolerance for disruption in critical component supply; large commodity suppliers with production facilities on a global scale can tolerate periodic outages at individual sites (Venne, 2023).

An ASC aims to adapt quickly to fluctuations in demand or changes in market conditions by focusing on speed, flexibility, and responsiveness. Particularly effective in sectors where demand is unpredictable or product life cycles are short, this approach integrates real-time demand forecasting with inventory visibility, leveraging automation and analytics to bring products to market more quickly. It also enhances resilience through supplier redundancy; however, this approach may require sacrificing a certain degree of efficiency (SAP Tauila, 2025).

Integrating agility with flexibility, responsiveness, and quick adaptation into both functions and processes in supply chains is vital to manage related risks in view of aims and objectives. Business leaders should focus on becoming more agile in their supply chains to achieve improvements. Furthermore, integrating new technologies into their infrastructure can yield truly effective results (Spencer, 2024).

The ASC model is a flexibility-focused approach that emerged as a response to the competitive and volatile nature of the business environment. Agility is the ability to perceive changes in the environment and respond to them with appropriate capabilities. The ASC approach seeks to turn these changes into advantages by responding to unforeseen market changes with rapid delivery and flexible delivery times. It aims to solve unexpected problems using new technologies, methods, and techniques. Therefore, using an ASC in the early stages of the product life cycle (introduction and growth) of innovative products is appropriate for ensuring high internal performance and customer satisfaction. ASC is effective in dynamic markets that require diversity, speed, and a customer focus (Banihashemi, 2011).

Modern lean supply chains leverage advanced tools and technologies such as real-time data analytics, cloud-based warehouse management systems, and automated logistics solutions incorporating the Internet of Things (IoT), and RFID tracking solutions. These innovations enhance visibility through the entire process, streamline operations, and support continuous improvement practices, making lean principles more achievable and effective in today's fast-paced business environment (Seattle University, 2024).

To adapt to the evolving supply chain landscape, companies typically rely on two main models: the lean supply chain and the agile supply chain, each addressing market fluctuations in different ways. However, many organizations are increasingly adopting a lean–agile hybrid strategy to achieve smoother operations. This hybrid approach enables the production of small, customized quantities by pre-building certain components, thereby balancing forecasting with real-time data and ultimately reducing overall risk (Redwood Logistics, 2023).

4.8 Optimum Solution: RAgilean Supply Chain Risk Management Model

The Resilient Agile and Lean (RAgilean) approach is a combination of lean and agile strategies and offers an ideal solution for businesses that face both constant and fluctuating demand in mixed product portfolios or within the same supply chain. In this model, the decoupling point is strategically positioned, ensuring that processes are managed in a "lean" manner up to the point where product differentiation begins and in an "agile" manner after that point. For example, while the basic components of a product are pre-produced in an efficient and cost-effective manner, flexibility is achieved by finalizing the product when the customer orders it. This hybrid structure is particularly suitable for supply chains where both trendy items and standard products are contained within the same system. The RAgilean strategy makes it possible for businesses to consider both cost and customer satisfaction at the same time as product and market diversity increases (Ambe, 2010).

Lean, agile, and SCRM tools are interconnected and interrelated. However, these relationships are quite complex; using one tool may increase risk, while using another may decrease it. Therefore, using several tools simultaneously can make the situation quite complex. Therefore, the first task is to systematize knowledge about supply chain concepts, strategies, and tools, and only then attempt integration and subsequently implement the risk management process and steps. Supply chains and supply chain management primarily change and evolve under competitive pressures. Generally, the current activities of supply chain management aim to reduce costs using tools of lean management (the concept of lean management) and/or achieve a higher service level with greater flexibility (the concept of agile management) (Konecka, 2021).

The RAgilean supply chain model is a kind of corporate-wide risk management strategy for integrating lean management, which aims to reduce environmental impacts and optimize resource utilization while ensuring the effectiveness and efficiency of processes and operational activities, and agile management approaches that support maneuverability and risk management in a digital transformation environment (Fig. 4.1).

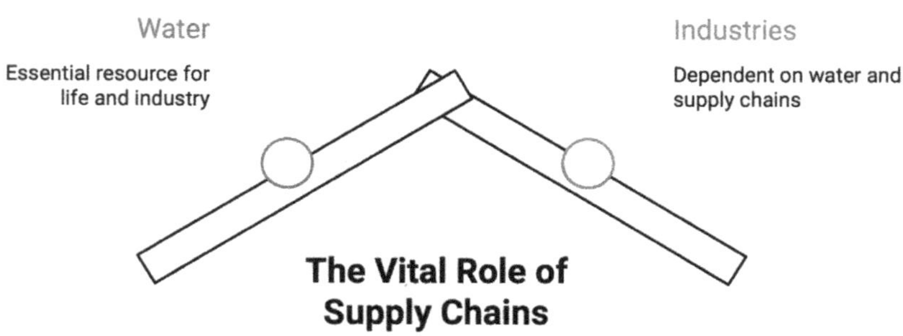

Fig. 4.1. Water of industries: The vital role of supply chains.

Source: The original design is by the authors; Napkin AI was used for visualization purposes only.

To manage risks, companies need flexibility and the continuous development of their supply chain networks, organizational capabilities, and competencies. Accessing and acquiring resources is becoming increasingly difficult for companies. Even without resource constraints, preventing waste should be an ethical mission for companies. However, agility and standardization are at odds with each other. In this context, we posit that leanness represents an effort to refine the environment that will support agility and resilience. In other words, the goal is to achieve optimal financial, environmental, and social outcomes in the management of all administrative functions and operational activities related to the supply chain.

Of course, achieving supply chain optimization is challenging. An ERM-based approach is essential for achieving supply chain optimization. In the age of digital transformation and AI, identifying risks and predicting their impacts has become increasingly difficult. Time to manage risks has become even shorter. While technology is rapidly transforming and evolving, humans cannot adapt to it at the same pace. Digitalization and AI are currently ahead of us. Managing stock effectively requires identifying and addressing gaps in warehouse conditions, mitigating risks during handling and transit, and continuously monitoring inventory levels to achieve strategic reductions.

References

Aeroplane Tech. (2024, June 25). Enhancing aircraft efficiency through effective Kaizen practices. Aeroplane Tech. https://aeroplanetech.com/kaizen-practices/?utm_source=chatgpt.com#Understanding_Kaizen_Practices_in_Aircraft_Manufacturing.

Al-Shebawi, H. K. M. and Al-Yasiri, A. H. H. (2017). The role of lean supply chain management activities in supporting logistical excellence: An analytical study of opinions of a sample of administrative leaders in General Company for Pharmaceutical Industry and Medical Supplies in Samarra. *Al-Qadisiyah Journal for Administrative and Economic Sciences (QJAE)*. https://qu.edu.iq/journalade/index.php/Al-QJAES/index.

Ambe, I. M. (2010). Agile supply chain: Strategy for competitive advantage. *Journal of Global Strategic Management*, 4(1), 5–17. https://doi.org/10.20460/JGSM.2010415835.

AON. (2022, October). Making better decisions in uncertain times Aon's 2022 executive risk survey. https://www.aon.com/getmedia/683e7940-86d0-4fee-9b78-0b6330458d80/aon-2022-executive-risk-survey-report.pdf.

AON. (2025, September 08). 4 ways to build resilient and agile supply chains. AON. https://www.aon.com/en/insights/articles/4-ways-to-build-resilient-and-agile-supply-chains.

Banihashemi, S. A. (2011, September). Improving supply chain performance: The strategic integration of lean and agile supply chain. *African Journal of Business Management*, 5(17), 7557–7563. Article Number - 1083CDF16812. https://doi.org/10.5897/AJBM11.596.

DataGuard. (2024, August 20). Supply chain risk assessment: A critical tool for business resilience. DataGuard Insights. https://www.dataguard.com/blog/supply-chain-risk-assessment/.

Helmold, M. (2020). *Lean Management and Kaizen: Fundamentals from Cases and Examples in Operations and Supply Chain Management.* Springer Nature Switzerland AG, Cham.

Institute of Risk Management (IRM). (2025, September 08). International certificate in enterprise risk management. Institute of Risk Management (IRM). https://www.theirm.org/qualifications/international-certificate-in-enterprise-risk-management/?utm_adgroup=&utm_network=Searchg&utm_matchtype=b&utm_device=c&utm_placement=&utm_location=1012763&utm_Audience=kwd-619213488653&utm_campaignid=20813896526&utm_a. Acccessed September 08, 2025.

Janjić, V., Bogicevic, J. R., and Krstić, B. (2019). Kaizen as a global business philosophy for continuous improvement of business performance. *Ekonomika*, 65(2), 13–25. https://doi.org/10.5937/ekonomika1902013J.

Jurado, P. J. M (2013). *Lean management: State-of-the-art and success factors in the adoption process. Evidence from the aerospace sector*. Tesis doctoral. Universidad de Jaén. https://ruja.ujaen.es/items/16083c7f-d852-436f-8639-892c5974aa8a.

Kaizen Institute. (2025, September 08). Maintenance and quality: How to overcome the challenges in the aerospace sector? Kaizen Institute. https://kaizen.com/insights/maintenance-quality-aerospace-maritime/. Accessed September 08, 2025.

Konecka, S. (2021, May). Lean and agile supply chain management concept in the aspect of risk management. *Logforum*, 6(4), 23–31. https://www.researchgate.net/publication/351852988_Lean_and_agile_supply_chain_management_concept_in_the_aspect_of_risk_management.

KPMG. (2019). Enhanced Risk Management the Journey to ERM 2.0, a Guide for the Public Sector in Singapore. KPMG Services Pte. Ltd., Singapore. https://assets.kpmg.com/content/dam/kpmg/sg/pdf/2019/08/the-journey-to-erm-2.pdf.

Lakshman, R. (2024, August 02). Agile supply chain: Strategies and benefits of building a flexible and responsive supply chain. PandoAI. https://pando.ai/blogs/benefits-of-building-a-resilient-supply-chain. Accessed at September 09, 2025.

Linkedin. (2025, September 09). How can stakeholder engagement help you manage supply chain disruptions? Linkedin. https://www.linkedin.com/advice/1/how-can-stakeholder-engagement-help-you-manage-0iqvf.

Niwa, T. (2009, June 11). Kaizen and changing mindsets in aircraft manufacturing. Spectra Mitsubishi Heavy Industries, Ltd. https://spectra.mhi.com/kaizen-and-changing-mindsets-in-aircraft-manufacturing. Accessed September 08, 2025.

Redwood Logistics. (2023, August 24). Should you use a lean or agile supply chain? Redwood Logistics. https://www.redwoodlogistics.com/insights/use-lean-agile-supply-chain

Resilinc Editorial Team. (2023, June 05). Agile supply chain characteristics & resiliency. Resilinc. https://resilinc.ai/blog/combine-agile-supply-chain-concepts-with-resiliency-for-world-class-supply-chain-management-results/.

Rodrigues, H. S., Alves, W., and Silva, A. (2020). The impact of lean and green practices on logistics performance: A structural equation modelling. *Production*, 30, e20190072. https://doi.org/10.1590/0103-6513.20190072.

SAP Tauila. (2025, September 08). What is a lean supply chain, Glossary. SAP Tauila. https://taulia.com/glossary/what-is-a-lean-supply-chain/.

Seattle University. (2024, May 29). What is lean supply chain management and how does it work? https://www.seattleu.edu/business/online/albers/blog/what-is-lean-supply-chain-management-and-how-does-it-work. Accessed September 08, 2025.

Spencer, B. (2024, September 05). Agile supply chain strategies for modern organizations. Fresh Consulting. https://www.freshconsulting.com/insights/blog/agile-supply-chain-strategies/.

Taifa, I. W. and Nzowa, J. S. (2025). Implementing supply chain management 4.0: Potential driving forces and strategies from an empirical study of pharmaceutical industries. *Engineering Reports*, 7, e70190. https://doi.org/https://doi.org/10.1002/eng2.70190.

Trex. (2024, November 11). *Kaizen'in Liderlik ve Çalışan Katılımı Üzerindeki Etkileri*. Trex. https://trex.com.tr/tr/blog/kaizenin-liderlik-ve-calisan-katilimi-uzerindeki-etkileri?utm_source=chatgpt.com.

Venne, U. (2023). 5 agile supply chain risk management strategies: From reactive to proactive. Everstream. https://www.everstream.ai/articles/5-agile-supply-chain-risk-management-strategies. Accessed September 08, 2025.

Chapter 5

Digital Risks and Supply Chain Resilience: From Fragility to Empowerment

5.1 Digital Risks and Supply Chain

Enterprise risk management (ERM) is a management system that enables one to monitor current conditions, to act flexibly and agilely when necessary, and to adapt and, if possible, become maneuverable by developing and foreseeing potential future scenarios. This describes the basic and vital need for companies and, indeed, for all organizations. Risk management provides reasonable assurance of meeting this vital requirement, seizing opportunities, and eliminating or mitigating negative effects of threats on the company. Based on these critical issues, keeping pace with technological transformation is also a current need for supply chain management.

Supply chains now incorporate digital and virtual technologies in their operations and management, enabling optimized risk management and enhanced visibility across the supply chain. Integrating virtual and real supply chain systems or backup systems is also evident to manage risk. As in aviation, manual emergency systems are activated when an unmanageable malfunction or error occurs in the electronic system. For instance, portable oxygen systems are utilized in situations where cabin air conditioning and oxygen systems are not viable options. In the event of a cabin pressure drop, when the pressure falls below the specified tolerance level during flight, the relevant systems are designed to open automatically. In the event of a malfunction or unavailability of the automatic systems, the oxygen masks can be opened manually via the panel.

In the supply chain, manual systems may be required to continue during periods of vulnerability or disruption to digital systems or in the event of interruptions to data and power systems, such as the internet and electricity, which are essential for the operation of digital technologies. Systems that can be used interchangeably under normal conditions and in emergencies play a vital role in reducing downtime and continuing operations.

Departure control systems are an example of such technology and are generally used in computer check-in procedures for passenger tickets and baggage in air transportation. Air tags for passengers' boarding passes and baggage are generated using the data entered digitally into the system. Simultaneously, electronic records are maintained of passengers and their baggage. In instances where this is not feasible, manual check-in procedures are implemented. The check-in process is conducted manually using pre-prepared flight documents, with no reliance on digital technologies or computer support. Passenger and baggage records are maintained through the use of manually prepared documents. Manual check-in is only applicable in instances where system installation is not feasible or is deemed particularly beneficial (DGCA, 2013, 2025). Manual systems that are critical for survival and needed for handling some difficult conditions will continue to be an element of fully digitalized systems. At this point, regardless of how artificial intelligence (AI) and digital transformation evolve, there will always be a place for people and a continued need for them. In the digital transformation environment, the need for companies to increase their compliance and flexibility is also relevant for implementing risk management. This is because supply chains are also transforming to incorporate virtual or digital elements, either completely or partially. If processes and their scopes are changing, management functions and approaches must develop their capacity accordingly. Digital transformation is vital to the day-to-day operations of businesses in terms of global development and customer needs.

Supply chain processes are being redesigned to incorporate digital technology and flexible automation, with the goal of eliminating redundant activities and processes. Key supply chain processes are digitally driven, providing visibility and traceability to address issues at their source. Supply chain processes are carried out autonomously wherever possible. Key supply chain actors are always on the lookout for opportunities to leverage and apply technology to make incremental improvements in performance and adapt to changes in demand (MacCarthy and

Ivanov, 2022). The current approach to transport organization in existing supply chains leads to negative impacts such as heavy traffic, reduced travel safety, and increased emissions of pollutants. Increased traffic congestion reduces the average technical speed of vehicles, extending delivery times and potentially leading to customer dissatisfaction and even cancellation of some orders. In the long run, this causes companies to unwittingly move toward worse financial results and reduced competitiveness. A lean and agile digital supply chain (DSC) can provide significant advantages in overcoming these problems (Hajdul and Mindur, 2015).

DSCs present certain risks alongside their benefits. These risk areas can be directly defined as "security and trust issues" and "environmental uncertainty" (such as demand, supply, and technology). These risks need to be managed. The adoption of advanced technologies (such as AI, the Internet of Things (IoT), and blockchain) creates increased cybersecurity risks. These risks include a breach of the supplier's system that could compromise sensitive research data or proprietary manufacturing features, as well as lead to the leakage of counterfeit materials into the supply chain. This can pose significant financial and reputational risks while putting intellectual property and product integrity at risk (Ba Awain *et al.*, 2024).

All key supply chain actors use strong digital connections at all levels of operations, resulting in improved productivity and service levels and reduced costs. Organizations with digitally transformed supply chains leverage traditional forecasting techniques with vast market intelligence and consumer analytics to anticipate demand changes. This allows for more effective positioning and distribution of inventory. As a result, warehouse capabilities become fully automated (MacCarthy and Ivanov, 2022).

5.2 Corporate Infrastructure: Digitalization, Risk Culture, and Communication

"Is Corporate Risk Culture Ready for Digitalization?"

Supply chain risk management (SCRM) considers the company and human resources represent one of the riskiest areas. Human manageability is a multifaceted issue, and the risks that human(s) can create are many and varied. Digitalization and AI have a direct impact on individuals and organizations, introducing changes to various areas of business, including work models, communication tools, and business processes. Organizational culture has a significant impact on attitudes and behaviors regarding risk management. Therefore, it is especially necessary to structure organizational culture as a risk culture for risk management efforts to achieve their goals. As individual and managerial risk perceptions are also one of the factors that affect risk attitudes and strategies, organizational behavior and culture are always within the scope of SCRM.

Digital transformation is a critical process in supply chain management that integrates modern technologies to mitigate risks and optimize processes. This integration not only enhances operational efficiency but also strengthens ERM strategies. Digital tools can also identify potential weaknesses in the supply chain, enabling data-driven measures to proactively prevent future disruptions. This capability allows companies to better protect themselves against market fluctuations, high inflation, and recession risks. By continuously monitoring processes and generating automated alerts when anomalies are detected, administrators can deploy recovery plans in a timely manner to prevent potential disruptions. In this context, digitalization lays the foundation for creating a risk management culture and promotes transparency and collaboration among all stakeholders. As a result, a DSC transforms into an efficient, sustainable, and resilient structure that is resistant to unexpected challenges, enhancing the organization's competitiveness (Kessler, 2023). A DSC is a digital ecosystem that integrates customers, manufacturers, suppliers, and distributors on a global scale in real time and at high speed. At the core of this structure are IoT devices such as space sensors, inventory tracking systems, and production systems. While DSC facilitates the spread of IoT technology, it also creates new areas susceptible to cyberattacks (Boyson *et al.*, 2022).

SCRM is a process that includes a series of repeatable and verifiable steps that systematically address the risks an organization may encounter while achieving its main goals. When implementing SCRM, the steps involved are typically designed within a company-specific risk management framework, encompassing the identification, evaluation, response, communication, and monitoring of risks. A comprehensive risk management approach is founded on a thorough examination of an organization's internal and external context. This enables the organization to clearly state its objectives and define internal and external parameters that will impact risk management. A key element of this process is to comprehend the risk culture, risk tolerance, and risk appetite (i.e. the willingness to accept adverse events) of the company. These elements determine the organization's openness to opportunities that are aligned with its strategic objectives. An organization's risk tolerance may differ according to its culture and changing internal and external conditions. Determining this tolerance can be achieved through consultation with relevant parties or by assessing stakeholders' responses to varying levels of risk. This approach enables risk management to achieve both a strategic and comprehensive focus. Risk culture, which is an integral component of integrated risk management, pertains to the attitudes and behaviors associated with risk management within an organization. This distinction is pivotal in determining whether risk is perceived as a mere reporting obligation or as an integral component of effective decision-making. It also demonstrates whether the organization adopts a risk-averse or opportunity-inclusive perspective and whether risk management is implemented at all levels (Treasury Board of Canada Secretariat Organization, 2001).

Digitalized SCRM is a vital part of any business's ongoing efforts to be both profitable and sustainable. It assists companies in identifying and addressing environmental and social risks within their supply chains, including issues related to environmental impact, waste, energy use, and labor practices. For instance, the implementation of technologies capable of tracking energy usage can result in substantial carbon emissions reductions. Furthermore, SCRM can assist companies in promoting circular economy principles by reducing waste. A full assessment of risk is key to enabling companies to make decisions that align with their goals and values (McGrath and Jonker, 2023).

The COVID-19 pandemic and global trade tensions have shown that supply chains need to be reconsidered in both digitalization and risk management dimensions. One of the most important requirements that stands out in this process is that companies have full visibility into their supply chains. For this purpose, a holistic mapping is required, covering not only the first- and second-tier suppliers but also distribution centers, logistics networks, and transport points. In this way, fragile points within the chain will be identified and managed more effectively. Digitalization stands out as a fundamental element that increases the resilience of supply chains. Technologies such as automation, next-generation process technologies, continuous flow production methods, and additive manufacturing (3D printing) both increase efficiency in companies' production processes and reduce dependence on global suppliers. In this way, it becomes possible to establish smaller, digitalized, and interconnected production networks instead of structures that traditionally rely on large-scale, centralized facilities; flexibility is provided by geographical diversity (Shih, 2020).

5.2.1 *Risk Communication and Corporate Infrastructure*

Effective communication is always difficult, and the companies and individuals who can achieve it are limited. Speaking the same language does not mean good communication. Communication is limited to the perceptions, understandings, and understandings of the people who communicate and are established. No matter how perfectly the message is prepared, the message reaches the other party in different ways. Because individuals perceive information through their own filters, the original message can never be perceived exactly as it is. In addition, environmental factors also affect communication. Culture also affects communication and shapes the framework of perception and understanding. The dynamics, sensitivities, values, attitudes, and behaviors of each culture differ. Understanding cultural characteristics of communication and tailoring the risk culture accordingly are among the basic requirements for establishing and maintaining it. Today, the supply chain ecosystem has begun to evolve due to the impact of digital transformation and AI. Why is this important? Efforts to prevent the fragility of the supply chain are based on healthy, timely, and transparent communication among stakeholders (both internal and external). Transmission is everything. Where there is no communication, the probability of all negative risks increases. For this reason, it is difficult to manage human factor or human resource risk, or "communication risk". Communication in a digital environment has different characteristics and challenges than in a non-digital environment. To achieve SCRM as targeted, it is essential to establish the company's risk culture and communication infrastructure.

Risk communication is an integral part of decision-making processes. This process involves the timely transfer and reporting of risk information to the relevant organizational levels. This approach enables stakeholders who may be affected by these risks to understand the basis on which decisions are made and the rationale behind the required actions. It also ensures that individuals have enough information to contribute to the decision-making process in an informed way. It facilitates the reuse of existing risk information across different processes (e.g. planning, auditing, and resource allocation) without requiring multiple assessments of the same risks (Treasury Board of Canada Secretariat Organization, 2001).

As an important detail, risk communication is carried out with both internal and external stakeholders (Treasury Board of Canada Secretariat Organization, 2001):

(a) ***Internal:*** *It ensures that risk information is conveyed to employees in different units of the organization in a meaningful and useful way.*
(b) ***External:*** *Involves communicating with clients and stakeholders who may be influenced by the organization's decisions and actions.*

Tools such as risk registers, dashboards, and risk profiles can be used to facilitate systematic, stakeholder-wide risk communication. These tools enable routine and effective communication by revealing the connections between different units, programs, and projects within the organization. Organizations can provide clear guidance in the risk management process on the following issues (Treasury Board of Canada Secretariat Organization, 2001):

- ***What Information*****:** *What information needs to be communicated at different stages of the process?*
- ***To whom*****:** *Who is the target audience of the information (management, employees, external stakeholders, etc.)?*
- ***How*****:** *In what ways will the information be conveyed to the target audience?*

5.2.2 *Risk Leadership for Building a Risk Culture*

Active risk leadership of senior management plays a vital role in creating a supportive risk culture. Senior executives must take a visible role in promoting risk management and knowledge sharing. The extent to which leaders adopt integrated risk management principles establishes a cultural tone for the entire organization. In order to engage senior management, it is necessary to follow this procedure (Treasury Board of Canada Secretariat Organization, 2001):

- It should be ensured that risks and responses to them reflect the priorities of management.
- By providing assurance that operational risks are adequately managed, management can be freed up to focus on the organization's main risks.
- Managerial decision-making can be facilitated by showing the links between operational risks and main risks.

- Risk management should be part of the agendas of management meetings and committees.
- Risk management can be linked to the performance agreements of senior executives.

The effective integration of advanced technologies into manufacturing is enabled by the interplay between innovation, supply chain optimization, and risk leadership. This synergy is a fundamental factor for fostering industrial environments that are resilient, agile, and sustainable in the face of dynamic global challenges. The rapid development of digitalization and technology poses various risks to businesses. At this juncture, the significance of robust risk leadership becomes paramount. Effective risk leadership enables businesses to anticipate potential threats and turn these threats into opportunities, enhancing resilience and operational efficiency (Flouris *et al.*, 2025). Due to the current economic conditions (high inflation, energy costs, etc.), cybersecurity is losing priority, especially in small businesses and aid organizations. This leads to a relaxation of basic cybersecurity measures and difficulties in detecting cyberattacks. The decline in the number of reported attacks since 2020 may be explained by the weakening detection capacity of small-scale organizations rather than the actual decrease in attacks. This illustrates the importance of continuous improvement in cybersecurity and the development of an organizational risk culture. In addition, strong communication between technical teams, employees, and boards of directors stands out as a critical requirement for employees to report suspicious activities and to establish a culture of awareness (Johns and Ell, 2023). In supply chains across industries, the complexity of technological integration and the existence of global networks interact, introducing new risks. In this environment of low awareness but high-risk interactivity, the need for risk leaders is vital to maintaining trust with stakeholders, developing strategies for risks, and at the same time in the process of making supply chains agile.

We are focused on enhancing the agility and resilience of supply chains, and to that end, it is essential to empower leaders. Leaders can successfully manage the accelerated change in the digitalized and AI-influenced supply chain ecosystem and develop risk strategies. These leaders are also instrumental in fostering a clear attitude and behavior among other employees in this environment. In this regard, leaders should assume the role of risk leaders, with efforts focused on enhancing risk management capacity in areas such as supply chain, digital procurement risks, and risk strategies.

The implementation of a supply chain within an organizational framework necessitates the integration of digital technologies and the establishment of an AI-driven risk culture infrastructure. This initiative entails the appointment of a risk leader who is proficient in the domain of risk management. To become a competent risk leader, it is essential to develop individual capacity in terms of certain characteristics. The following categories are generally recognized as encompassing these features:

a. **Integration capability:** The risk leadership role requires the ability to integrate risk management and supply chain management and to implement them across the organization. The ability to integrate means being able to see all the parts and to bring them together with each other. It is challenging to see the bigger picture and even more challenging to visualize it.
b. **Learning ability:** The ability to use digital and AI technologies to improve risk management performance.
c. **Ability to use and deploy new working models:** The risk leader should have the ability to direct and motivate human resources with the same effectiveness even if they work under different models, including on-site (office), remote, and hybrid working models. The ability to connect with employees using digital tools without perceiving the time-space difference and the ability to influence people, that is, to motivate them in terms of performance, in this increasingly complex social environment is one of the most critical needs of today.
d. **Digital and transactional capability:** The risk leader should have the ability to learn digital skills and transform the employees and the work environment in line with the goals and the changing conditions of the day by using digital technologies.
e. **Ability to share leadership and distribute it when necessary:** The risk leader must have the ability to share and distribute leadership in order to reach the elements of the supply chain on time, as the concept of time and space has disappeared in the supply chain ecosystem, which is under the influence of digital transformation and AI, and every element of the chain, including its stakeholders, is changing with high momentum. But first of all, in order to share and distribute, it is necessary to have the competence to establish a team of leaders.

f. **Multiculturalism and multifaceted communication ability:** In the global supply ecosystem, the ability to direct, negotiate, and communicate with diverse stakeholders in terms of both culture and language is decisive. Openness and sensitivity to different cultures, effective communication, and negotiation skills with different stakeholders in the supply chain have always been important in achieving goals and will always remain important as long as people are involved.

In addition to these, analytical competence and decision-making skills, strategic and visionary thinking, and projection skills, the ability to see opportunities as well as threats, the ability to develop strategies to seize opportunities, and the ability to convince stakeholders that opportunities should be seized are also among the necessary skills. Supply chains are the most important component of the business world. For this reason, it needs leaders who can manage and direct these main topics in order to mitigate its vulnerability and become agile. Supply chains will provide the opportunity to be competitive thanks to the leader. Selecting stakeholders is a strategic issue. The degree of communication and transparency to be established with stakeholders is also a strategic issue. The opportunity created by each stakeholder is different. Risk leaders can analyze the holistic picture of all stakeholders, as well as the individual picture of each stakeholder and their impact on the supply chain, both individually and interactively.

One of the key roles of risk leaders in risk management is to establish and maintain a reasonable balance between risk appetite and the company's risk tolerance. Risk tolerance can be raised through institutional capacity building.

Risk tolerance covers the amount of risk that the company can bear or overcome. The company determines the risk portfolio it wants to take in proportion to these tolerance limits. At this point, risk leadership and support are decisive for increasing risk tolerance and achieving a risk appetite (the willingness of the top leaders/decision-makers to take risks). It is critical that senior management also support the leader's efforts because it will be possible to both understand and increase risk tolerance through communication between employees and managers. Risk tolerance and appetite should also be included in the training programs to be organized to create a risk culture. Risk management consists of elements that support each other through its infrastructure and process.

5.3 From Fragility to Empowerment: Building a Resilient Supply Chain Risk Management

Supply chain risk management emphasizes a comprehensive, strategic, updated, and strengthened management system for the supply chain according to the conditions of the day and also shaped by experience. With SCRM, we express a framework and philosophy (way of thinking and understanding) that will guide decisions. The risks and sources of risk (events) that have the potential to affect businesses are no longer solely "internal financial and labour concerns"; they consist of multi-layered, interconnected, and rapidly changing systemic events.

Companies work with many suppliers while producing their products and/or services and fulfilling their managerial functions. For example, an airport operator can receive services from external sources in matters such as ground handling providers, maintenance and repair services, power systems, ticketing, check-in, boarding, cargo handling, security services, and these suppliers are a source of risk for input, process, and output stages for both the airport (i.e. the supplier company) and other suppliers. At the same time, the company's suppliers are competitors of each other. This duality requires that risks be managed in a multifaceted and interactive manner.

The supply chain is actually a network of stakeholders, so much so that it is created by complex, multiple, and interactive stakeholders who simultaneously affect each other. This stakeholder network consists of many diverse stakeholder communities and includes those who are directly or indirectly involved at any point in the process of meeting customer demand. From this point of view, it is necessary to manage stakeholder relations risks in the supply chain on an institutional basis.

The customer portfolio in the supply chain is also wide. The relationships among these stakeholders can include both commitment and dependency. Stakeholders often interact with each other in both ways, including through risk management and advice regarding technological systems, software, materials, space, transportation, information, and finances: this means that stakeholders are potential sources of risk for each other. Both numerous and diverse customers constitute the customer base of the supply chain. As can be understood from the stakeholder and customer portfolio, supply chain stakeholders include all manufacturers and suppliers—including raw materials and spare parts—as well as logistics companies, transporters, warehouses, retailers, and even buyers of final products and services. The supply chain encompasses all functions within an organization, such as a manufacturer, involved in receiving and meeting a customer demand. These functions include, but are not limited to, new product development, marketing, operations, distribution, finance, and customer service (Chopra and Meindl, 2013). It is not enough to simply identify the risks faced by businesses from a supply chain and holistic perspective. Modeling the integrated effects of potential risks and their interactions with each other and developing scenarios increases/strengthens the maneuverability of businesses to be agile and resilient.

As seen in current news, cyberattacks have the potential to affect all technology-intensive businesses. Although technology-intensive operations support speed and flexibility, as well as perfection in achieving goals, cyberattacks indicate that the same level of threat potential can be activated. Exploiting the vulnerabilities of technology giants can leave both public and private companies vulnerable to cyberattacks for a short or long time. As a result, the likelihood of threats with high impact increases. A lack of resilience directly impacts the supply chain's capacity for sustainable operations.

These stakeholders are sources of opportunity for perceiving, understanding, and interpreting risk sources and events that may arise from these risk sources. At this point, digitalization provides great convenience for quickly and accurately obtaining data for supply chain management functions and operations, analyzing that data in a multifaceted and comparative manner, creating scenarios, identifying risks, and evaluating their correlations. This means a supportive environment for accurate and timely decision-making in all areas related to supply chain operations, such as location, vehicles, stock, and logistics, within the scope of supply chain management.

In supply chain management, information is the basis of all decisions in the supply chain system. It refers to the link between all activities and operations within a supply chain. To the extent that this connection is strong (i.e. the data is accurate, timely, and complete), companies in a supply chain will each be able to make sound decisions regarding their operations. This will also tend to maximize supply chain profitability. This is how stock markets and other free markets work, and supply chains share similar dynamics (Hugos, 2003). The supply chain plays a decisive role in companies' timely and effective access to the market. Therefore, the supply chain is vital to accessing and sometimes entering markets.

SCRM is a key component of a complete sustainability strategy. Having contingency plans for potential disruptions helps companies prevent situations that create waste and allows them to maintain their pursuit of sustainability goals even amid unexpected changes. A thorough risk management program can bolster a company's reputation for corporate responsibility, which can be critical to its brand image (McGrath and Jonker, 2023). SCRM is not only at the core of strategic decision-making processes; it is also closely associated with managing and mitigating potential risks. Effective management of the chain depends on the implementation of correctly developed risk mitigation strategies and the successful implementation of the decisions made.

Location choices within the supply chain also have the potential to affect strategies because locations (country, country neighbors, region, etc.) determine resources and access conditions to those resources. It emphasizes the need to think long-term regarding resource risk management. For example, due to labor costs and environmental concerns, establishing the supply chain and production in the Middle East can later develop production expertise there and then create competitors for the company. Today, China is the best global example of this.

In the current business climate, it is crucial for global companies to reevaluate their manufacturing strategies in China. The ongoing challenges caused by the pandemic and the evolving geopolitical landscape have brought to light the inherent risks associated with long-distance supply chains and geographic concentration. For example, companies may need to reconsider their China-based manufacturing networks to improve supply chain resilience. This process involves more than simply leaving China; it also entails diversifying supplier networks and spreading production locations across different regions through strategies such as "China + N (alternative countries or locations)". The "China + N" strategy places a strong emphasis on the development and management of sourcing portfolios. It refers to the establishment of production and supply structures for global companies in one or more other countries, instead of concentrating their production and supply networks only in China. As a risk-handling strategy, it aims to diversify, strengthen resilience, and enhance flexibility within the scope of "China + N". Therefore, the production network will be protected against any potential threats posed by a single geographic location. Furthermore, it will increase its capacity to resist possible environmental disasters, laws and regulations (such as customs tariffs and taxes imposed by countries) with a durable and strong structure that can be adapted flexibly. By diversifying risk, companies can participate in new supply chain markets, easily adapt to new markets, and efficiently shift production to different locations based on the advantages and disadvantages of each location. This enhances their overall capacity (developed from Chenneveau *et al.*, 2023).

In terms of risk management, environmental and geopolitical developments in the supply chain ecosystem, supply–demand imbalances caused by sources, such as pandemics or natural disasters, supply shocks, and economic nationalism triggered by trade wars, have led companies to reconsider their supply strategies. In this context, it is critical to identify, classify, and manage potential risks in the ecosystem with their sources, that is, SCRM, by making use of digital transformation. In order to maintain a risk-based approach to procurement, it is recommended that companies categorize their suppliers into low-, medium-, and high-risk groups and conduct a thorough analysis based on the following criteria (Shih, 2020):

- income loss effect,
- recovery times of production facilities,
- availability of alternative sources.

Supply chain risks can arise from any internal or external event with the potential to disrupt the flow of materials from the initial supplier to the final customer. These risks can have cascading consequences, such as delivery delays, cost increases, production stoppages, or damage to business partnerships, and can seriously impact a company's financial performance. The company is exposed to many different internal risks, including controllable operational disruptions. Such disruptions can take the form of late deliveries, inaccurate forecasts, inventory management issues, human errors, or information system failures. External risks, on the other hand, are events beyond the company's control, such as earthquakes, floods, wars, terrorist attacks, epidemics, price fluctuations, or supplier problems. While external risks can create large-scale, unpredictable impacts, internal risks are more frequently encountered threats that can be mitigated through management measures. Therefore, it is critical for managers to design their operations with resilience, flexibility, and a balance between cost and risk, recognizing that risks cannot be completely eliminated (Waters, 2007).

In the common language of risk, location and location selection in supply chain management, whether digital or real, is critical as a strategic determinant for supply chain management functions and operations to be carried out in line with company goals. For this reason, the decisions taken regarding the activities within the scope of each stage of the supply chain process affect the results. If a virtual supply chain is to be preferred, the software used for this should be considered a risk of technological resource dependency. If the supply company does not have expertise in software development, there will be a dependency on the company from which the software is purchased, as the software will be purchased by outsourcing. Even if the software is outsourced, there will be a need for technological expertise and competence to operate the software and use it for procurement. In addition, the company's infrastructure, including the internet and technological tools, must be ready to use this technology. Otherwise, technological risks will pose a threat to the company.

Digital transformation is not confined to technological systems. It is important to note that changes to systems can have a significant impact on various aspects of society, including social life, the economy, and the environment. The aforementioned effects have consequences for both social life and the working world, in terms of individuals and society as a whole, including financial implications.

Digitalization is creating increasingly interconnected systems. Interconnected systems also increase vulnerability. Prior to the advent of digitalization, the risk portfolio was already extensive and varied, though more predictable. Digital transformation increases the momentum of change but also reduces dominance. While the concepts of time and space are rendered obsolete by technological advances, the loss of any digital technology, whether intentional or not, creates a communication gap. In the event of a cyberattack, there is a possibility that our electricity supply could be interrupted, resulting in a loss of power to heating, communication, and internet systems, including vehicles. This is a simple example of highly interconnected systems. While the example is straightforward, its implications have the potential to present significant challenges that could hinder our progress.

For instance, the most prevalent and concerning risk today is the risk of cyberattacks. A significant number of cybersecurity scenarios, involving individuals, companies, and even countries, have been adapted for film and television, such as Robert De Niro's *Zero Day* (details can be seen from the following web page link: https://www.hollywoodreporter.com/tv/tv-reviews/zero-day-review-robert-de-niro-netflix-1236141441/).

Developing risk scenarios supports a proactive approach and strengthens a company's preparedness for potential events (event = risk source) and its resilience and resistance to their disruptive effects. Therefore, incorporating risk scenario development into risk identification within the supply chain risk management process is an important detail. That's why we presented the series *Zero Day* as an example. Regardless of the show's overall performance and the series' plot, interpreting the series' events from an SCRM perspective can be a good example of developing risk scenarios. In the risk scenario we developed, cyberattacks can have direct or indirect and potentially devastating effects on today's complex and global supply chains. Recent cyberattacks across various sectors serve as evidence of this. Digitalization and digital technologies have the potential to create a cascading effect. When widespread power outages we experience more frequently today, access issues with digital platforms, and check-in issues occur simultaneously, the resulting chaos can cause crises far more damaging than anticipated. It's often said that "chains are only as strong as their weak links". From a supply chain perspective, supply chains are affected by their weaknesses. Even if a company has and implements excellent internal risk management, if one of its stakeholders or business partners fails to manage its risks, the company will also be affected. Because today's supply chains increasingly utilize digital systems and software, particularly in managing operational processes and activities, this is a sign of the digital dependency of supply chains.

In the contemporary business world, supply chains are heavily dependent on digital systems and software for the effective management of operational processes. Let's continue with our example. In the event of a cyberattack disrupting or even collapsing the power grid, it is estimated that factories would shut down, warehouses would be affected and products requiring a cold chain would be spoiled. Consequently, supply chain distribution would also be partially or completely disrupted.

Supply chains make use of a variety of transportation networks, including air, land, sea, and rail. In the event of a disruption in one of these modes, the disruption can be mitigated or prevented by transferring to other modes. However, a simultaneous cyberattack will prevent the supply chain from progressing. This will prevent products from reaching factories or retail locations from suppliers. Supply chains that operate under a Just-in-Time model, based on a zero-inventory principle and a lean management philosophy, are particularly vulnerable to such disruptions. For instance, in the automotive sector, vehicles may not be delivered to authorized dealers and then to customers. Digital risks have gone beyond being a mere sub-area of information technologies.

The cyberattack likely targets the most vulnerable points in the chain through various suppliers and systems. One of the most crucial issues in SCRM is excessive dependence on critical suppliers. The chip crisis during the COVID-19 pandemic era has not yet been fully resolved. Because chip manufacturers are few in number and creating a sector in the chip industry is difficult, increasing their numbers is unlikely in the near future. Developed countries, having failed to be visionary in shifting their manufacturing economies to the Chinese market, failed to grasp the knowledge and skills they were migrating and created risks for themselves.

For suppliers, if companies rely on a single provider of critical software or systems for their chain operations, activities, and even risk management systems, a cyberattack targeting that provider can disrupt all operations. This is due to the fact that companies' reliance on a single software or system creates a significant vulnerability.

SCRM, when based on accurate and timely information communication, can provide reasonable assurance of achieving objectives. However, in order to identify risk sources, it is essential that stakeholders establish effective and transparent communication with each other. Trust is another vital requirement. In the event of disruption to the flow of information within an information system by cyberattacks, this can create fragility in the supply chain. Errors in decision-making are invariably attributable to communication problems. In the event of cyberattacks disrupting communication, this can result in incorrectly or inadequately made decisions or even the failure to make any decisions at all.

Although risk scenarios attempt to understand potential risks and their consequences, there will always be unknowns (unshared information, malicious individuals, etc.), and unimaginable scenarios will eventually materialize. One strategy that can be useful in this regard is diversification. Working with different suppliers simultaneously, such as creating a risk portfolio, to manage the risk of single-source dependency. Does this fundamentally solve the problem? Of course not. But it does create options, and this is vital. To manage risks, one must understand the alternatives and make decisions to choose the best among them. Because every choice means giving up another alternative, proper analysis must be performed. The manual systems, digital systems, or power sources mentioned at the beginning of this section should be ready for use when attacked; this is another risk management strategy. Risk management strategies are developed to eliminate or mitigate the effects of threats. Furthermore, the social tensions that cyberattacks can create must be managed. A person or community in crisis is one of the most difficult factors to manage. A risk leader is essential for managing people who deviate from the norm. Ultimately, even if a TV series does not generate much box office revenue, this does not diminish the importance of these scenarios for SCRM. Risk leaders distinguish themselves not only with their leadership skills but also with their ability to develop scenarios and possess a visionary perspective.

The development of comprehensive, sustainable, and holistic SCRM strategies is an essential prerequisite for all companies. The following strategies are considered to be the most significant. As can be seen, the objective of implementing these strategies is to ensure the most effective risk strategies are both company-wide and holistic:

- **Diversification:** The objective is to ensure that spreading/extension production activities are distributed across different geographies, without being dependent on a single country or region. To mitigate the risk of concentration in a single geography, it is recommended that the supplier and production network be spread across different countries ("China plus one" strategy) (Shih, 2020; developed from Chenneveau *et al.,* 2023).
- **Integration and optimization:** The goal of digital supply chains is to seamlessly integrate the system for peak performance, breaking down barriers. The integration of new technologies creates an intelligent and value-driven network that can handle large volumes of data, enabling broader collaboration and faster responses (Ba Awain *et al.*, 2024).
- **Resilience:** The creation of a more resilient structure is vital to protect against potential disruptions, such as natural disasters or tariff changes (developed from Chenneveau *et al.*, 2023).
- **Flexibility:** It is vital that the company adapt more quickly to new markets and shift production to different locations according to changing conditions (developed from Chenneveau *et al.*, 2023).
- **Regional production:** The objective is to enhance/improve production capacity in geographic areas that are near the markets where the final products are consumed (Shih, 2020).
- **Creating intermediate stock:** Maintaining safety stocks for critical products when alternative sources are not available (Shih, 2020).

- **Efficiency and speed:** Digitalization increases efficiency and effectiveness by affecting every stage of the process, such as procurement, operations management, delivery, and service. Real-time inventory management offers benefits such as speed, flexibility, transparency, innovation, and scalability (Ba Awain *et al.*, 2024).
- **Corporate capacity-building:** In order to meet the risks of digital transformation, the company's corporate and supply chain capacity should be developed in accordance with the situational approach (human resources training, digital technology investments, increasing digital skills and competence, developing risk management competence, etc.).
- **Digital infrastructure investment, security investment, and digital literacy:** This term refers to the process of preparing for the implementation of digital SCRM through technology-based hardware and software investments. It also includes the establishment of contracts with relevant parties. At the same time, it is important to invest in security measures against cyberattacks and strengthen the company in this respect.

The internalization of digital transformation by companies on a corporate scale, and the progress levels of organizations in these processes and their content at the levels also differ. The need for adequate maturity and integration in risk management becomes even more evident with this differentiation. What is at stake here is maturity in terms of risk management and digital transformation, the level of integrating digital technologies within the scope of organizations' strategic goals, harmonizing all processes, including organizational behavior and the organization's risk culture, leadership style, functions and processes, technical (digital literacy) and non-technical skills (the ability to relate digital skills to their behavior), control and audit mechanisms, and human resources, within the scope of transformation (Peter *et al.*, 2020). It does not seem possible to completely abandon globalization in the future of supply chains. However, it has become a necessity for companies to establish more flexible and transparent structures by using digitalization opportunities and, at the same time, adopting diversified, balanced, and resilient strategies in risk management to achieve sustainable competitive advantage (Shih, 2020).

Digital transformation, which supports the maturity level of risk management, plays a critical role in the effective and high-performance implementation of risk management in the supply chain by leveraging digital technologies and artificial intelligence. Therefore, it is crucial that digital transformation be fully and accurately perceived and internalized by companies—for decision-makers, employees, and even stakeholders across the entire supply ecosystem. Today, maturity levels in both digitalization and risk management are at the forefront of leaders' agendas. This is because the maturity level required for effective and holistic enterprise risk management is directly linked to and interacts with a company's digital transformation process, influencing and even being influenced by each other. Risk management, which complements digital transformation, must be integrated with the company's strategy and objectives and made the basis of decision-making.

At this point, enterprise risk management is essentially a direct integration of organizational behavior, leadership style, management functions and systems, employee technical and non-technical skills, controls, audit, and reporting functions within the framework of risk culture. As can be seen, risk management affects and transforms every element of the company.

Will the globalized supply chain ecosystem revert to a more local approach? This seems unlikely. Local applications will remain very limited in scope and geographic area. However, it should be noted that the impact of this aspect of the digitalized and globalized business ecosystem will be felt even in local environments. From a situational perspective, companies need to learn and develop their implementation capacity in risk management that supports maneuverability in the digital, global, and volatile environment. Otherwise, it will be impossible to establish flexible, resilient, and transparent digitally supported supply chains needed today and tomorrow.

SCRM strengthens companies' competitive positions. Therefore, emphasis should be placed on holistic and systematic risk management system efforts that include stakeholders, with frameworks designed and shaped specifically for the company.

5.4 Cyber Risks in Supply Chains: Transformed and Emerging Risks

In today's business world, organizations rely heavily on their suppliers for the supply of products, systems, and services. However, the complex and broad nature of supply chains allows cybersecurity vulnerabilities to emerge, persist, or be exploited at any point in the chain. This makes it difficult to determine whether adequate protection is provided across the entire supply chain.

The World Economic Forum identifies supply chain interdependencies as a leading factor in the increasing complexity of cyberspace in 2025. Named the top ecosystem cyber risk, supply chain vulnerabilities are the primary barrier to cyber resilience for 54% of large organizations. Companies must proactively manage supply chain risks. In order to ensure the success of this proactive approach, it is essential to focus on strengthening the weakest links in the supply ecosystem. This can be achieved by increasing visibility throughout the supply chain, enhancing its resilience, collaborating with stakeholders, developing employee capacity to deal with cyber risks, and adhering to regulations related to digitalization and AI. In addition, business continuity planning and supporting small partners are steps to strengthen the cyber resilience of the entire ecosystem (Tuteja, 2025). This digital transformation brings with it a range of security challenges, including open attacks such as ransomware, which disrupt operations, and covert attacks such as state-sponsored cyber espionage and phishing. Such threats have the potential to result in considerable financial losses, theft of intellectual property, and significant operational disruption (Boyson *et al.*, 2022).

There has been a marked increase in cyberattacks caused by vulnerabilities in supply chains in recent years. These attacks have the potential to have a significant impact on affected organizations, their supply chains, and their customers, with costly and long-lasting consequences. However, the 2022 Security Breaches Survey indicates that only 13% of businesses assess the risks posed by their direct suppliers, compared to 7% for the broader supply chain. Despite awareness of these challenges, the complex and dispersed nature of the supply chain makes it difficult to understand how suppliers manage and maintain their cybersecurity. Organizations with limited resources, in particular, face challenges such as insufficient understanding of cybersecurity risks in the supply chain, insufficient investment to mitigate these risks, limited visibility into the supply chain, and a lack of tools and expertise necessary to assess suppliers' cybersecurity levels. Furthermore, the absence of clarity regarding the security practices being requested from suppliers is a substantial concern, as illustrated by the following issues (National Cyber Security Centre, 2022):

- ***Cyber Inequity:*** *While large organizations are increasing their cybersecurity investments, small and medium-sized enterprises (SMEs) are* *often left behind due to a lack of resources. This leaves the entire supply chain vulnerable through its weakest link. The solution is support for SMEs, cross-sectoral cooperation, and the dissemination of cybersecurity training.*

- ***Limited Visibility in the Supply Chain:*** *As supply chains become more complex, it becomes difficult for organizations to monitor the security level and maturity of all their suppliers. This expands the potential attack surface and makes it difficult to achieve third-party compliance. The solution is to establish stronger regulations and mechanisms to increase transparency.*
- ***Third-Party Software Vulnerabilities:*** *New software included in the supply chain can introduce new vulnerabilities, especially through open-source codes or third-party components. Integrating AI tools quickly but without security assessments also increases this risk. The solution is through secure coding practices, regular testing, independent audits, and the adoption of AI safety frameworks.*
- ***Dependency on Critical Providers:*** *An overreliance on a small number of large cloud and software providers poses a systemic risk. A failure or hack on one of these providers can set off a chain reaction that affects the entire ecosystem. The solution is to create effective business continuity plans, alternative providers, and a resilient IT architecture.*
- ***Geopolitical Implications:*** *Geopolitical tensions weaken supply chains through trade constraints, supplier changes, and a shortage of skilled labor. Additionally, conflicts between states can cause cyberattacks to become more sophisticated. The solution is continuous monitoring of geopolitical risks, supplier diversification, and the adoption of flexible business strategies.*

The following news item reveals what can happen to different industries in the event of only a minor cyberattack.

It was reported that, as a result of a cyberattack on Collins Aerospace's Muse software, a total of 29 flights were canceled at London Heathrow, Brussels, and Berlin on Saturday, 20 September, from 11:30 am. The cyberattack disrupted the electronic check-in and baggage processing systems, resulting in long queues and significant delays for airport customers. While the airline RTX confirmed a "cyber-related outage", the disruptions continued into Sunday. According to Cirium flight data, there were more cancelations on Sunday than Saturday; Brussels

Airport alone canceled 44 outbound flights and requested the cancelation of half of its scheduled flights through Monday at the request of Eurocontrol. The incident demonstrated the aviation industry's critical reliance on digital systems and its vulnerability to cyberattacks (Siebold *et al.*, 2025; Davies, 2025). The disruptions at European airports are being blamed on a cyberattack targeting a third-party provider of check-in and boarding systems. According to the report, aviation firm Collins Aerospace confirmed that its MUSE software, used by many European airports, suffered a ransomware-related disruption. This impacted electronic check-in and baggage drop operations, particularly at airports in Brussels, Berlin, and London (Heathrow). However, the firm stated that the issue could be mitigated through manual check-in operations. Collins Aerospace stated that it is actively working to resolve the issue as quickly as possible (DW, 2025).

5.5 Cyber Security Risk Management Framework for Supply Chains

Cybersecurity risks spread through supply chains are still a major source of problems, especially for SMEs. For the first time, the majority of large businesses report taking actions to review cyber risks from their suppliers. In contrast, SMEs' awareness of this area remains low, and several factors may play a role in making progress in this area, such as customer pressure and auditor feedback, which may encourage companies to review their supply chain risks. The most common practices in organizations' approaches to identifying and managing cyber risks are the use of security monitoring tools and risk assessments. While medium- and large-sized enterprises adopt these methods more intensively, the application rate in small enterprises and non-governmental organizations is quite limited. Awareness-raising training and threat intelligence activities for employees remain generally low, while a more systematic approach is observed in sectors such as finance, insurance, healthcare, and IT. In terms of audit activities, it is seen that only a limited number of organizations conduct cybersecurity vulnerability audits, while large enterprises create a stronger assurance mechanism by using internal and external audits together (Johns and Ell, 2023).

High supply chain costs have prompted managers to consider formal strategies to mitigate risk. However, awareness is also being driven by regulations aimed at improving corporate governance. Customer demands for risk management proof and the desire to avoid losses are among the factors stimulating the reexamination of logistics activities and the potential losses that could arise from vulnerable supply chains (Waters, 2007).

Supply chain risks can be examined under four main headings: external, economic and financial, operational, and natural and environmental risks. Although organizations try to reduce these risks through contracts and agreements, it is not possible to eliminate them completely. Global risks can arise from geopolitical developments such as political instability, wars, and trade restrictions, leading to cost increases and supply disruptions. External risks include strategic risk which arises from both external and internal sources. Operational risks arise from production problems, equipment failures, labor shortages, production delays, and human errors in internal processes; therefore, it is important to establish backup strategies for critical parts. Natural risks are caused by environmental factors such as earthquakes, floods, and epidemics and can disrupt the entire supply chain; therefore, business continuity plans and alternative supplier models play a critical role. Financial and economic risks, on the other hand, arise from macroeconomic factors such as demand fluctuations, inflation, exchange rate changes, and recession, making the cost–price balance difficult. Also, this category includes supplier bankruptcy-based risks. In addition, trade disputes, sanctions, and regulatory changes in the digital transformation supply chain ecosystem are a separate category of geopolitical risks. These risks have strategic as well as economic effects. Again, cyber risks in this ecosystem include data breaches, ransomware, and interruptions related to information technology (IT) systems. Therefore, supply chain managers can gain a competitive advantage with accurate risk assessments, effective mitigation strategies, flexible supplier relationships, and comprehensive continuity plans, knowing that they cannot completely eliminate risks (Gordon, 2024; SAP, 2025).

Other potential risks include quality failures, theft of intellectual property, and shifts in customer demand through sourcing and manufacturing. As many supply chains depend on multilayered supplier networks, risks can emerge from within the ecosystem. These risks can often go undetected until it is too late (SAP, 2025). See Fig. 5.1.

SCRM covers all processes of the supply chain, from production to the end user of products or services. During these processes, potential events in different areas that may affect the supply chain are a source of risk, and these potential risks are examined under different categories.

Fig. 5.1. Supply chain risk classification.

Sources: Developed from Gordon (2024) and SAP (2025). Napkin AI was used for visualization purposes only.

Companies can create risk categories according to their own frameworks. There is no single prescription style or standard categorization. Here, supply chain risks are classified under six categories: operational, natural, economic, geopolitical, cyber, and other, within the scope of the SCRM framework. This categorization is useful for administrative convenience and resource usage savings and provides the ability to manage risks within the scope of risk groups at the same time. As it is known, companies have hundreds of risks within the scope of the supply chain, and it will not be possible to manage them simultaneously without categorizing them. Time is also limited for companies, and 24/7 time unfortunately cannot be increased. The sub-risks within the scope of the risk categories are exemplified as follows (see Fig. 5.1):

a. **Operational risks:** This category includes disruptions in the day-to-day operations of the supply chain. Interruptions in production or supply processes, logistical errors, or unexpected breakdowns fall into this group.
b. **Natural risks:** Events beyond human control, such as natural disasters (earthquakes, floods, storms, etc.) or epidemics, directly affect the supply chain.

c. **Economic risks:** Factors such as financial fluctuations, currency changes, inflation, interest rate hikes, or economic crises can negatively impact costs and profitability.
d. **Geopolitical risks:** Geopolitical events such as political instability, wars, embargoes, or trade disputes can lead to major disruptions in global supply chains.
e. **Cyber risks:** With the widespread use of technology, threats such as cyberattacks, data theft, or system crashes can halt all operations of the supply chain.
f. **Other risks:** This category includes risks that fall outside the above headings and remain significant. Risks such as product quality issues, intellectual property theft, or sudden shifts in customer demands are evaluated in this section.

Strategies should be developed to implement risk management frameworks that support company objectives. These strategies should be developed at various levels, from the corporate to the operational and tactical levels, while considering the supply chain ecosystem. In light of the constantly evolving digital landscape, the risks associated with the ecosystem are also subject to change and increase. Therefore, designing a flexible risk management system that is amenable to development and updating is essential for the sustainability of risk management. Furthermore, achieving the desired level of risk management performance depends on senior management ownership and shared responsibility with all employees. This objective can only be achieved by incorporating the philosophy of "everyone is a risk manager" into the risk culture. Risk management is a sophisticated system that considers both internal (originating within the company) and external (originating from external) events and stakeholders within the supply chain ecosystem. It should be noted that low complexity can also occur in stable or unchanged economic, social, and environmental conditions, although such circumstances are generally very rare. In the context of digital transformation, the interconnected nature of complexity and risk is a growing concern. This results in a more complex and multifaceted supply chain, necessitating a comprehensive and intensive supply chain risk management system. Therefore, it is imperative that a holistic, company-wide risk management system be designed (see Fig. 5.2).

Fig. 5.2. Supply chain risk management strategies.

Source: The original design is by the authors; Napkin AI was used for visualization purposes only. https://app.napkin.ai/page/CgoiCHByb2Qtb25lEiwKBFBhZ2UaJDFhOTIyNWM0LTJmOWYtNGI5ZS1iNjBjLTY5YmJkMzcwZjFjNg, August 26, 2025.

When both industries and sectors related to organizations in these sectors are examined, it is seen that they have many and, at the same time, various supply chain systems due to the systems and subsystems within their scope. Since the national and international conditions and industrial requirements of enterprises (organizations) are different, they have different obligations and compliance issues related to laws and regulations.

The national and international laws and regulations that industries have to comply with, according to the products and services they produce and also according to the locations, are also many and different. It is especially important to design supply chain systems by taking into account internal and external environmental conditions in terms of managing supply chain risks.

If cybersecurity and SCRM are not considered together, it creates very serious security vulnerabilities by increasing the risks in terms of cost, disruption, breakage, and reputation loss in the following areas through weak suppliers (Karimi *et al.*, 2024):

(a) **Transition from physically oriented supply chains to digitalization:** The efficiency of physically oriented supply chains is being enhanced by digitalization, but this comes with a caveat: increased vulnerability to cyber threats.
(b) **Risk of cyberattacks:** The development of the cybercrime-as-a-service market on the dark web has enabled attackers to infiltrate systems through vulnerabilities, with smaller and resource-constrained suppliers being particularly targeted.
(c) **Supplier and third-party dependency:** Large companies typically have numerous suppliers, which can create a complex network of access points for potential attackers.
(d) **Cost impact:** It has been determined that data breaches resulting from partner involvement are approximately 12% more costly than other data breaches.
(e) **The companies' approach to security risk management:** According to the global survey conducted by IBM, IBV, and Microsoft, only 30% of companies prioritize a secure and connected ecosystem in their supply chain operations.
(f) **Management issues in integrating cyber risks with supply chain risk management:** It is evident that companies that manage cyber risk and supply chain risk concurrently encounter a reduced number of disruptions. However, most organizations experience loss of visibility and negative operational outcomes due to a siloed approach and poor security practices.

5.6 Digital Supply Chain Challenges and Cybersecurity Risk Management Strategies

Potential events that could impact a company's ability and capacity to achieve all strategic and operational objectives across its supply chains are identified and analyzed throughout the ecosystem through risk management. It is a fundamental principle that risks and opportunities are interconnected. Consequently, companies, decision-makers, and leaders must be cognizant of this fact. This enhanced awareness has a profound impact on their approach to risk perception and management. The assumption of calculated risks, in accordance with the company's risk tolerance, is vital for the successful execution of corporate strategies. It is essential to emphasize that the development and establishment of a risk culture is pivotal in ensuring that all employees are cognizant of the strategic direction of risk management. This, in turn, enables them to effectively identify and manage both risks and opportunities, thereby contributing to the achievement of company goals.

A primary challenge is the interdependency of risk, which can result in cascading effects, leading to widespread supply chain disruptions with increased severity. For instance, a cyberattack on a logistics provider has the potential to result in delays to material deliveries, production halts, and lost sales (SAP, 2025). The European Union Agency for Cybersecurity (ENISA) has noted that there are key challenges in supply chain cybersecurity, as outlined in its comprehensive report, "Good Practices for Supply Chain Cyber Security". The challenges include a lack of common terminology, the inability of current best practices to eliminate all risks, such as hidden backdoors in hardware, and the difficulty of preventing individual state-sponsored attacks. These challenges pose significant issues for organizations. Furthermore, a lack of information sharing between member states on newly discovered vulnerabilities, such as "zero-day" exploits, and inadequate testing and assurance processes in the procurement of critical infrastructure equipment also pose serious risks. In order to solve these problems, the following measures are recommended: the creation of common terminology, cooperation with intelligence services at the national level, increased information sharing and the establishment of industry-based common testing platforms (ENISA, 2023).

The supply chain dimension in this list should also be analyzed and evaluated in detail within the scope of sub-risk areas (assessment and evaluation risk analysis). The digital surface of companies is expanding rapidly, which creates serious cyber risks and challenges in the supply chain (including third and fourth parties). Potential risk strategy recommendations with their associated challenges for cyber risks in the supply chain are presented as follows (Bank of America, 2025; ENISA, 2023):

i. **Vendor management:** It is essential to identify critical suppliers, and cybersecurity standards, risk acceptance criteria, breach notification protocols, and insurance terms should be included in contracts. It is also necessary to address fourth-party risks.

ii. **Terminology confusion:** The lack of common terminology in the realm of supply chain cybersecurity (Bank of America, 2025) leads to confusion and comparison challenges between approaches (ENISA, 2023).
iii. **Limitations of good practices:** Current cybersecurity best practices cannot eliminate all supply chain risks, especially hidden vulnerabilities such as backdoors in hardware, which may not be detected by traditional testing (ENISA, 2023).
iv. **State-sponsored attacks:** Sophisticated and high-resource state-sponsored cyberattacks pose risks that are difficult for individual organizations to manage and may need to be managed at the national level with the involvement of intelligence services (ENISA, 2023).
v. **Lack of information sharing:** The lack of information sharing among member states about newly discovered vulnerabilities, such as zero-day vulnerabilities, increases the risk of these vulnerabilities being exploited by malicious groups (ENISA, 2023).
vi. **Lack of testing and assurance:** Inadequate testing and assurance processes in the procurement of equipment for critical infrastructure jeopardize the security of services critical to society. This may require the creation of industry-based, common testing platforms (ENISA, 2023).
vii. **Continuous audit:** It is recommended that suppliers' security processes be subject to regular review and that updates and patches be duly implemented (Bank of America, 2025).
viii. **Digital assets:** IoT devices, software, data storage methods, and external resources used are potential vulnerabilities; they should be included in the risk assessment (Bank of America, 2025).
ix. **Post-breach process:** Forensic analysis (a detailed technical investigation to collect and examine digital evidence after a cyber incident and restore the security of the system) should be performed; otherwise, there is a risk of ransomware or other attacks being repeated (Bank of America, 2025).

This means that supply chain security encompasses a multifaceted, multi-layered spectrum of challenges, including all risks, such as cyber. These challenges encompass a broad portfolio of risks, such as operational, environmental, digital, and cultural contractual agreements, including those related to contracts, stakeholder relationships, and international collaborations. Managing this portfolio requires integration techniques and tools that combine quantitative and qualitative analysis, as well as a strategic approach and multi-criteria decision-making.

Security is not limited to a company's internal systems. Given the importance of cybersecurity in today's business landscape, it is essential that companies implement robust and systematic management processes to protect their interests and maintain operational efficiency. Should this not be the case, there is a possibility that said stakeholders may pose a threat to the company. While auditing can help mitigate a significant portion of risk, even existing best practices may be inadequate against sophisticated threats such as state-sponsored attacks or subtle vulnerabilities like hidden backdoors in hardware. This means there is always a residual risk. In addition, this finding emphasizes the importance of effective information sharing within the supply ecosystem, as well as the necessity for processes that are designed to address deficiencies on a continuous basis, thus continuously improving the system's capacity. In essence, regardless of the quality of supply chain design, inadequate information sharing and digital process testing can lead to risks that require attention at various levels, including the sectoral and national levels. Cybersecurity is such a complex issue that publishing policies and standards alone is insufficient. In fact, effective risk management involves much more than adhering to standards and guidelines. Therefore, establishing a risk culture and developing competency capacity related to digital technologies are essential for risk management.

Supply chain risks constitute one of the weakest points of cybersecurity. Research results reveal that only a small proportion of organizations regularly assess close suppliers and even fewer evaluate the vast supply chain. Although large-scale enterprises are taking more steps in this area, obstacles such as a lack of resources, difficulty accessing information, and a lack of prioritization make it difficult to effectively manage supplier risks. Differences are observed according to the level of institutional maturity: while some large organizations take a systematic approach with contractual obligations, accreditation requirements, and regular supplier meetings, smaller organizations often resort to informal and project-based methods. The analysis indicates that cyber risks must be addressed not only through internal measures but also via a comprehensive and sustainable management framework (Johns and Ell, 2023).

The implementation of cyber risk-based handling strategies requires the creation of a preparedness plan and the subsequent execution of these plans by command structures under the leadership of the leader. It is recommended that supply chain maps be created. It is imperative to have a comprehensive understanding of how risks interact with each other. It is imperative that risk management strategies are developed in accordance with these principles. The selection of suppliers is the first of the risk management strategies, and cyber insurance, which is also a risk transfer strategy, should be ensured to cover supply chain disruptions and supplier-related breaches. It is also recommended that safety and security standards be included in contracts with critical suppliers and that processes be monitored and kept under surveillance. In line with the risk culture, all employees should be made aware of cyber risks, monitoring, and response processes in relation to employee awareness and competence (Bank of America, 2025).

In light of the current digital landscape, it is crucial to recognize the potential for cyber threat actors to exploit vulnerabilities in supply chains for malicious activities. Organizations need to implement robust cyber SCRM strategies to ensure operational resilience in the face of cyber threats. This strategy is based on the identification, assessment, and mitigation of risks arising from the global and distributed nature of information and communication technology (ICT) product and service supply chains (Government of Canada (GC) the Canadian Centre for Cyber Security, 2022).

Managing risks in the cyber supply chain is not only a technical issue but also requires a holistic approach to organizational risk leadership, assessing potential incidents and incident-related risks across the supply chain, strategic planning, and taking proactive measures. An effective risk management approach involves a multi-stage process for assessing cyber supply chain risk (Government of Canada (GC) the Canadian Centre for Cyber Security, 2022):

i. **Determining the sensitivity of technology**
   This step involves assessing the sensitivity of a product or service based on technological and contextual factors. Leaders must understand the potential impact of a compromise on data confidentiality, integrity, and availability, and how attractive the system is to threat actors. Its strategic positioning within critical infrastructure networks or its integration with emerging technologies such as AI can further enhance its precision.

ii. **Assessing supplier trust**
It is the responsibility of the leadership team to establish a sufficient level of trust. In order to do so, they must consider a number of factors, including the supplier's business practices, their cybersecurity policies, and their compliance with international standards. It is important to note that elements such as foreign ownership, control, and influence (FOCI) and geopolitical context are crucial risk indicators when assessing a supplier's credibility. This assessment empowers risk leadership to make informed decisions when selecting suppliers.

iii. **Determining the distribution**
The final step involves evaluating risk exposure within the context of the organization's current cybersecurity posture. It is the responsibility of leadership to decide whether the risk from a particular supplier is acceptable, whether stronger mitigation measures are required, or whether an alternative technology or supplier should be chosen. This phase involves a review of the organization's capabilities in risk mitigation and incident management.

Cyber supply chain risk management (C-SCRM) has emerged as a critical discipline in response to these risks. C-SCRM's primary objective is to deliver comprehensive protection by integrating methodologies from cybersecurity, supply chain management, and enterprise risk management. In the United States, the National Institute of Standards and Technology's (NIST) Cybersecurity Framework has become the global de facto standard for C-SCRM, guiding strategies in this field (Boyson *et al.*, 2022). The increasing interconnectedness, globalization, and digitalization of supply chains have resulted in a concomitant rise in the complexity and urgency of risk management. An effective strategy for managing customer relationships has been shown to have a number of benefits for companies. Firstly, it can be used to mitigate the impact of potential disruptions. Secondly, it can be used to increase a company's agility and competitive edge. Organizations that prioritize SCRM are frequently better positioned to maintain customer satisfaction, ensure consistent revenue streams, and meet compliance demands. It is a fundamental principle of supply chain management that risk management is a core competency for achieving success in this field (SAP, 2025).

The challenges of the supply chain, both in the digital transformation and AI environment, as well as in its nature and operations, reveal that security risks in the supply chain are also critical. However, it is understood that managing cyber risks, which are among the supply chain risks, is much more than a problem that can be overcome only through technical solutions. Cyber risks are multifaceted, and the potential risks and severity of impact of each aspect are also different. This means that cyber risks are an issue that extends beyond any manager or even beyond the boundaries of the company. This feature reveals that managing stakeholder relations is vital. The level of knowledge about the sources of cyber risks is highly limited. The level of competence and expertise of companies in managing these risks is still in the development stage. Although cybersecurity regulations have been established for cyberattacks in industries, it would not be wrong to say that it is still at an early stage. Management success cannot be mentioned without a common language in risk management. A common language has not yet been developed in terms of cyber risks. This means that communication is still weak. The sources of cyberattacks are not yet fully known, and some of them may remain unknown. It is not possible to overcome cyberattacks without establishing high-level and trust-based cooperation between countries and stakeholders. Internal controls and audits mean the infrastructure for the performance of risk management and the appropriate establishment and implementation in terms of targets. Therefore, if there is not enough maturity regarding internal and/or external auditing, this will create gaps in the management of cyber risks.

It is not possible to manage the risks in this digital transformation environment with a siloed or traditional supply chain management. For this reason, the capacity of the supply chain should be improved, and a company-wide implementation phase should be started as a part of SCRM. With SCRM, collaborations can be developed, frameworks can be established, and a stakeholder-wide management covering the entire supply chain system will be possible.

5.7 Industry Case Samples

5.7.1 *CISCO Cybersecurity SCRM (C-SCRM) "2011 Japan Earthquake and Tsunami Crisis" (NIST, 2025; Conway et al., 2025)*

For Cisco, C-SCRM is an integral part of the supply chain. This form of management focuses on specific risks, such as counterfeit or corrupted products, malware, and misuse of intellectual property (National Institute of Standards and Technology, 2025). The company has transformed its security roles from "limiting damage" to "strengthening the business". Cybersecurity requirements are integrated with physical security requirements throughout the supplier network and product lifecycle. The company evaluates supplier reliability by incorporating industry guidelines such as the National Institute of Standards and Technology (NIST) standards and internationally recognized certifications such as Common Criteria into its processes for cyber risk management (NIST, 2025; Conway *et al.*, 2025).

Cisco's risk management approach has evolved from reactive business continuity planning, implemented in 2004, to a more proactive model. This transformation has been accelerated by lessons learned, particularly from events such as Hurricane Katrina in 2005 (Massachusetts Institute of Technology (MIT) Centre for Transportation & Logistics, 2025; CISCO, 2025; Munson *et al.*, 2014).

The earthquake and tsunami in Japan in March 2011 was one of the largest disruptions in modern history for Cisco's supply chain (Munson *et al.*, 2014). Cisco had approximately 250 tier-one (tier-1) suppliers located in Japan, many of which were single-source suppliers for highly engineered components. Through predetermined crisis management protocols, the company was able to determine whether all suppliers were affected within 12 hours of the incident. A "war room" was set up to quickly identify affected suppliers and orders. It is estimated that Cisco has hardly lost any revenue thanks to this quick response. This unfortunate incident proved the importance of Cisco's proactive resilience management approach (Massachusetts Institute of Technology (MIT) Centre for Transportation & Logistics, 2025; Munson *et al.*, 2014).

5.7.2 *Jaguar Land Rover: Cyberattack and Threats on Their Supply Chain*

On 1 September, 2025, Jaguar Land Rover (JLR) was forced to halt its production lines due to a major cyberattack. The company took the proactive step of shutting down its computer networks to safeguard them; however, vehicle production also came to a halt due to the reliance on automated processes in production and supply chains. The company has factories in Solihull, Halewood, and Wolverhampton in the UK. These were closed for approximately two weeks, which incurred a cost of

£5–10 million per day for JLR, amounting to a total expenditure of £50–100 million. The recent cyberattack on JLR has had a significant impact on the company and its extensive supply chain, which employs tens of thousands of individuals. The production halt at JLR poses a threat not only to the company itself but also to the wider supply chain. Should the crisis persist, it is likely that bankruptcies and job losses will ensue. It is anticipated that JLR's supply chain will be the most impacted by this incident (Leggett, 2025):

- Approximately 250,000 people are employed within JLR's supply chain.
- It is evident that a significant number of small- and medium-sized suppliers encountered a sudden and unexpected interruption to their revenue streams, a situation that can be attributed to their reliance on JLR.
- Some companies will go bankrupt, while others have started to lay off workers. According to industry experts, several companies will face insolvency, with a consequent reduction in staffing levels.
- One supplier has already made half of its workers redundant; others are keeping their employees waiting at home. It is evident that the repercussions of the economic downturn have already begun to be felt by several suppliers within the sector. Indeed, one supplier has already made the decision to lay off half of its workforce, while others have adopted a policy of keeping their employees waiting at home.

This poses a serious risk to both the permanent workforce and temporary workers. Companies whose cash flow has been cut are expected to turn to mass layoffs. Unions and experts are calling on the government to launch a furlough scheme. Thus, while the salaries of the workers are paid with the support of the state, the companies will be able to survive. JLR, along with the National Centre for Cyber Security, continues to investigate the effects of the attack. The company also admitted that some data may have been stolen (Leggett, 2025).

The Unite union drew attention to the threat posed by JLR's production pause due to the cyberattack in the supply chain and called on the government for a short-time working allowance program similar to the one implemented during the COVID-19 period. The union emphasized that the layoffs started in small- and medium-sized supplier companies, especially from JLR's own employees, and that the financial resilience of these companies was limited. As JLR is a company that produces around 1,000 vehicles a day worldwide, the production halt results in losses of £5–10 million every day; total losses to date are in the range of £65–130 million. While the company acknowledged in a statement on September 10 that some data was affected by the attack, uncertainty is growing for the future of tens of thousands of workers in the supply chain (Unite the Union, 2025).

When this issue, which started with cyberattacks and is expanding its sphere of influence, is analyzed in terms of the risk of "dependency on a single customer" and the risk of structural fragility created by the cyberattack in the supply chain, the following results help us understand the root cause of the risk responsible for the current crises faced by JLR stakeholders, especially those in the supply chain (Smart Business Recovery, 2025):

(a) **Dependence on a single customer can cut off the revenue stream overnight.** Suppliers who depend heavily on a large customer such as JLR lose all their orders as soon as production stops. This means a direct risk of bankruptcy, especially for SMEs.
(b) **The high investment requirement adds to the financial burden.** Automotive suppliers often must invest in custom machinery, molds, and manufacturing processes for each and every customer. When production is cut, the cost of these investments remains constant, and credit and financing obligations place a heavy debt burden on companies.
(c) **Cash flow fragility quickly creates a crisis.** When orders stop, salaries, rent, energy, and loan payments resume. Companies whose income flow is cut resort to borrowing to survive. However, this can lead to a rapid increase in debt, a loss of investor confidence, and bankruptcy within a very short time.
(d) **Lack of diversification creates a major weakness.** Loyalty to a single customer provides apparent stability but destroys durability. Orders from smaller but more diverse customers can act as a "survival buffer" in large customer-driven shocks.
(e) **Cyberattacks are also a serious threat to SMEs.** In the UK, an SME is hacked every 19 seconds, which is more than 4,500 attacks per day. In other words, the attacks are not only directed at giants like JLR but also at smaller companies in the supply chain.

(f) **Cybersecurity is a matter of business continuity.** An attack directly collapses not only computer systems but also the capacity to do business. Therefore, cybersecurity investments are not merely an "IT expense" but a strategic security shield that can prevent bankruptcy.

A full understanding of the areas affected and to be affected by the risk of cyberattacks is necessary to manage this crisis. Some of the risk areas and impacts are as follows (Yalçın, 2025):

- **Duration of the crisis and production situation:** JLR factories are expected to remain closed until at least September 17 due to the crisis, which has entered its third week. This gives the date and duration details in addition to the emphasis on previous news that there will only be a pause for weeks.
- **Daily financial loss:** The company's daily loss is stated as £5–10 million; total loss is in the range of £50–100 million. There was an estimate of loss in previous summaries, but in this news, approximate values were given in TL and dollars and a striking expression such as "500 million TL loss every day" was used.
- **Quantity in layoffs:** Previously, only some suppliers were reported to have made layoffs; this article cites an example: Qualplast (which is a second- or third-tier supplier to JLR, Nissan, Aston Martin, Lotus, Bentley, Toyota, and Honda; see details on the company web page at https://www.qualplast.com/) laid off 40 employees (50%).
- **Gap between permanent staff and temporary workers:** Employees at a supplier in the West Midlands do not expect to return to work until 29 September; hundreds are at home. It is clearly emphasized that temporary workers will be the first to be laid off, and permanent personnel are also at risk.
- **Government and union reaction:** The Unite union stresses that thousands of workers are at risk of losing their jobs and reiterates its demand for a salary-supported furlough. Business and Trade Secretary Chris Bryant states that they are in daily contact and working toward a solution. Previous news reports included a call for the government, but this news includes official statements and union emphasis together.
- **Emphasis on the long-lasting impact of the crisis:** Some suppliers state that even if they have other work on hand, there is a serious need for restructuring due to the crisis that will last for weeks.

JLR had to stop its production lines after a cyberattack on September 1, and its factories are expected to be closed for three weeks. While the company is losing £5–10 million per day and £50–100 million in total, approximately 250,000 people in the supply chain are at risk of serious job loss. Small- and medium-sized suppliers experienced a sudden and significant reduction in revenue due to their reliance on a primary large customer. The combination of high fixed costs and significant credit obligations increased the likelihood of insolvency. Some firms are making redundancies, while others are planning to allow staff to work from home in order to make up for unworked hours. Temporary workers are the primary risk group. The cyberattack has a direct impact on JLR and SMEs in the supply chain. In the UK, an SME is hacked every 19 seconds, posing a serious threat to business continuity. While trade unions are demanding that the government ensure workers' wages are protected by implementing a furlough scheme, some suppliers are being forced to make restructuring plans due to the weeks-long crisis. This demonstrates the vulnerability of supply chains when they are reliant on a single customer and vulnerable to cyberattacks (Yalçın, 2025; Leggett, 2025; Smart Business Recovery, 2025).

The JLR case is also important for recognizing how a crisis in a large customer can rapidly increase the widespread impact of risk throughout the supply chain. In terms of resource dependency, combined with the risk of single customer dependency and cybersecurity vulnerabilities, SMEs can face the threat of layoffs and bankruptcy in a very short time. It strongly underlines the need to consider the effects of the interactions of these risks.

Cyberattacks, as a source of risk for a supply chain ecosystem, have high potential to impact a wide range of categories. The JLR case is a complex issue that tests the resilience of companies in several ways. Given the fact that cyberattacks have the potential to impact production, as well as data leakage and data security risks, they directly affect not only the company but also its stakeholders. As demonstrated in the JLR case, the companies in the supply chain are subject to the consequences of this risk to a greater extent than the most affected company. In the current business climate, cyberattacks have become a prevalent risk. The results indicate that the business continuity of stakeholders, particularly those in the supply chain sector, is facing significant challenges.

These case studies provide an understanding of the degree to which the threats facing modern supply chains differ from traditional supply chains. Unlike natural risks, digital risks do not have geographical boundaries. For this reason, they include the digital resilience of companies, as well as their geographical and political resilience, and redundancy for digital systems, within the scope of risk management.

The Cisco crisis actually points to the benefits of building a risk portfolio because in the case of Cisco, it has shown the potential risks associated with relying on single-source suppliers can create, especially for critical and valuable components.

In addition to physical components, software systems also create weak points or gaps in supply chains. The software in question here may not only be a software system purchased by the company; it may also involve large-scale software or a cloud data service with sharing points. This situation emphasizes that the detection of vulnerabilities that create fragility in digital systems, backup systems that can be used when the main systems are not working, as in physical systems, and data backup should all become essential parts of the processes.

References

Bank of America. (2025). Meeting the challenges of digital supply chain security. Bank of America Corporation: business.bofa.com. https://business.bofa.com/en-us/content/digital-supply-chain-security.html.

Chenneveau, D., Cheung, E., Le Deu, F., and Zhan, D. (2023, August 23). Supply chain resilience—in China and everywhere else: How can overseas multinationals balance the benefits and risks of keeping their existing China manufacturing strategies? McKinsey & Company: https://www.mckinsey.com. https://www.mckinsey.com/capabilities/operations/our-insights/operations-blog/supply-chain-resilience-in-china-and-everywhere-else.

Chopra, S. and Meindl, P. (2013). *Supply Chain Management- Strategy, Planning, and Operation*, (5th ed.). Upper Saddle River, NJ: Pearson.

Conway, E., Luu, N., and Shaffer, E. (2025, July). Best practices in cyber supply chain risk management Cisco® managing supply chain risks end-to-end. U.S. Resilience Project. https://www.cisco.com/c/dam/en_us/about/doing_business/trust-center/docs/cyber-supply-chain-risk-management.pdf.

Davies, A. (2025, September 21). Heathrow warns of second day of disruption after cyber-attack. BBC. https://www.bbc.com/news/articles/cwy88857llno.

Deutsche Welle (DW). (2025). European airports disruption due to ransomware — EU agency. Deutsche Welle (DW). https://www.dw.com/en/european-airports-disruption-due-to-ransomware-eu-agency/a-74073365.

Directorate General of Civil Aviation (DGCA). (2013). Passenger Services, Publications of the General Directorate of Civil Aviation, Publication Type: Technical Publication NO: HAD/T-20. Directorate General of Civil Aviation

DGCA: shgm.gov.tr. https://web.shgm.gov.tr/documents/sivilhavacilik/files/pdf/kurumsal/yayinlar/yolcu_hizmetleri_06.02.2014.pdf.

European Union Agency for Cybersecurity (ENISA). (2023, June). Good practices for supply chain cybersecurity. European Union Agency for Cybersecurity (ENISA). https://www.enisa.europa.eu/sites/default/files/publications/Good%20Practices%20for%20Supply%20Chain%20Cybersecurity.pdf. Retrieved September 2025.

Flouris, T., Kucuk Yilmaz, A., and Malagas, K. (2025). *Innovative Risk Leadership in Aviation: Industry Insights and Cases*. https://doi.org/10.4324/9781003513636. Routhledge, UK, Chapter 9.

Gordon, R. (2024, February 05). What are the various risks in supply chain management? American Public University. https://www.apu.apus.edu/area-of-study/business-and-management/resources/what-are-the-various-risks-in-supply-chain-management/.

Hugos, M. (2003). *Essentials of Supply Chain Management.* John Wiley & Sons, Inc., New Jersey.

Karimi, K., Campos, F., Drummond, B., and Parham, G. (2024, May 24). All supply chains are digital. IBM Home Technology and Security, CIO. https://www.ibm.com/thought-leadership/institute-business-value/en-us/report/supply-chain-cybersecurity.

Kessler, J. (2023, March 28). Digital transformation in the supply chain [supply chain risk management]. NeuroSYS S. https://neurosys.com/blog/digital-transformation-in-the-supply-chain-supply-chain-risk-management.

Leggett, T. (2025, September 13). Some JLR suppliers 'face bankruptcy' due to hack crisis. BBC: bbc.com. https://www.bbc.com/news/articles/czdjn0lv64ro.

McGrath, A. and Jonker, A. (2023, December 2). What is supply chain risk management (SCRM)? IBM. https://www.ibm.com/think/topics/supply-chain-risk-management.

Munson, C., Sáenz, M. J., and Revilla, E. (2014). *The Supply Chain Management Casebook*. New York, NY: Pearson Education. https://ptgmedia.pearsoncmg.com/images/9780133757446/samplepages/0133757447.pdf.

National Cyber Security Centre. (2022, October 12). How to assess and gain confidence in your supply chain cyber security. National Cyber Security Centre:ncsc.gov.uk/.https://www.ncsc.gov.uk/collection/assess-supply-chain-cyber-security/understanding-the-threat.

National Institute of Standards and Technology (NIST). (2025). Best practices in cyber supply chain risk management: Cisco. U.S. Resilience Project. National Institute of Standards and Technology (NIST) https://www.cisco.com/c/dam/en_us/about/doing_business/trust-center/docs/cyber-supply-chain-risk-management.pdf.

Peter, M. K., Kraft, C., and Lindeque, J. (2020). Strategic action fields of digital transformation. *Journal of Strategy and Management*, 13(1), 160–180. https://doi.org/10.1108/JSMA-05-2019-0070.

SAP. (2025, August 01). Supply chain risk management. SAP: sap.com. https://www.sap.com/turkey/resources/supply-chain-risk-management.

Shahzad, K., Imran, F., and Butt, A. (2025). Digital transformation and changes in organizational structure. *Research-Technology Management*, 68(3), 25–40. https://doi.org/10.1080/08956308.2025.2465706.

Shih, W. C. (2020, September–October). Global supply chains in a post-pandemic world. *Harvard Business Review Magazine*. https://hbr.org/2020/09/global-supply-chains-in-a-post-pandemic-world.

Siebold, S., Steitz, C., and Muvija, M. (2025, September 19). European airports snarled by cyberattack, disruption to stretch into Sunday. Reuters. https://www.reuters.com/en/cyberattack-causes-flight-delays-cancellations-brussels-airport-2025-09-20/.

Smart Business Recovery. (2025, September 15). The ripple effect of a cyber attack: Lessons from Jaguar Land Rover's supply chain disruption. Smart Business Recovery: https://www.smartbusinessrecovery.co.uk. https://www.smartbusinessrecovery.co.uk/news/102/137/The-Ripple-Effect-of-a-Cyber-Attack-Lessons-from-Jaguar-Land-Rovers-Supply-Chain-Disruption.

Treasury Board of Canada Secretariat Organization. (2001). Guide to integrated risk management. Treasury Board of Canada Secretariat Treasury Board of Canada Secretariat Organization Risk Management Guide to Integrated Risk Management: Canada.ca. https://www.canada.ca/en/treasury-board-secretariat/corporate/risk-management/guide-integrated-risk-management.html.

Tuteja, A. (2025, January 31). Supply chains and transportation 5 risk factors from supply chain interdependencies in a complex cybersecurity landscape. World Economic Forum: weforum.org. https://www.weforum.org/stories/2025/01/5-risk-factors-supply-chain-interdependencies-cybersecurity/.

Unite the Union. (2025, September). JLR supply chain workers impacted by cyberattack must receive government support, says Unite. https://www.unitetheunion.org/news-events/news/2025/september/jlr-supply-chain-workers-impacted-by-cyberattack-must-receive-government-support-says-unite.

Waters, D. (2007). *Supply Chain Risk Management: Vulnerability and Resilience in Logistics*. London, UK: Kogan Page Limited.

Yalçın, U. C. (2025, September 15). Lüks otomotiv devinde üretim üç haftadır felç, tedarikçiler iflasın eşiğinde: 250 bin kişinin işi risk altında. sozcu.com.tr. https://www.sozcu.com.tr/amp/luks-otomotiv-devinde-kriz-devam-ediyor-250-bin-kisinin-isi-risk-altinda-p227938.

Chapter 6

Enterprise Risk Management Framework Design: Drive Corporate Value

6.1 Create and Add Value via Optimization in Decision-Making

Dynamic and agile enterprise risk management (ERM) requires the establishment of a strategic decision-making process tailored to the company, which addresses all managerial functions together with the allocation and use of corporate resources within companies. This decision-making process takes into account the interactions between all managerial and operational units within the organization, both internally and externally. Traditional business models and even silo-based risk management approaches fail to consider this interaction and the interrelationship between risks and are therefore insufficient in achieving the desired outcome in terms of holistic risk management.

The effort to eliminate all sources of risk is neither logical, nor necessary, nor possible. Even when risks are managed, the focus should not be on eliminating and/or removing risks, as risks will still remain, but rather on managing their effects in line with corporate objectives. This is also the perspective of corporate risk management. Furthermore, risks are often multifaceted, meaning their effects manifest in multiple areas. A more important detail is that risks do not only affect activities related to managerial functions and operations. Risks also influence each other, playing a modifying role in their effects. Unfortunately, it is not very common for risks to cancel each other out. More often, risks trigger each other's effects. For example, health risks also bring about economic risks. In fact, every risk has an economic dimension, i.e. a cost. From this perspective, it would not be wrong to say that risks have at least two dimensions.

Corporate-wide risk management practices that could enable the achievement of objectives within a company or organization will create negative and even counterproductive results if risks are attempted to be isolated. This implies that the risk management system itself poses a risk (threat) to the company. Based on this point, effective and agile supply chain risk management (SCRM) across the company should be designed to include the interdependence and interaction of potential risks within the scope of the entire supply chain process and management functions in a dynamic optimization process. This is possible by taking into account the company's needs and desires, in line with corporate strategies and a corporate risk management design specific to the company. Therefore, although the basic framework of corporate-wide (enterprise) risk management is similar to guidelines, it is essentially a unique design. The desired level of corporate risk management application performance also depends on the success of this design.

CEOs and executives in today's business world must evaluate opportunities in changing conditions, manage uncertain investments, direct resources to the right areas, and simultaneously provide assurance to stakeholders regarding value creation and preservation. In this context, ERM transforms risk management from an operational function into a strategic tool. ERM strengthens an organization's capacity to create sustainable value by ensuring that risks are systematically identified, analyzed, and effectively managed (Protiviti Inc, 2006).

ERM is a unique management system that creates value, such that its integrated nature and systemic design, along with its philosophy, which influences organizational culture, provide reasonable assurance that senior management decisions will optimize the overall risk-return profile by simultaneously enhancing the company's social, financial, and environmental profitability. It also develops the capacity to balance risk appetite with risk tolerance in achieving company objectives in line with corporate strategies. This is a critical point because if the company's risk appetite (willingness to take risks) is high but its risk tolerance (the level of risk-bearing and risk-taking) is low, loss and/or damage will occur. Based on all these considerations, corporate risk management, which will also be integrated into supply chain management, enables optimal decision-making in today's digital transformation environment, where there are numerous complex and interdependent risks. The success of companies in surviving is proportional to their ability to manage risks throughout the company.

Global supply chains are more interconnected and vulnerable than ever in today's digital transformation and artificial intelligence environment. A single disruption can create a ripple effect across sectors, leading to financial losses, compliance issues, and reputational damage. In situations such as geopolitical tensions, cyber threats, regulatory changes, or natural disasters, organizations must proactively manage risks to maintain stability and resilience. Traditional supply chain strategies prioritize efficiency over resilience, leaving businesses exposed to unexpected disruptions. Integrating a robust SCRM framework enables organizations to protect their operations, enhance compliance, and respond quickly to disruptions. Companies with effective SCRM frameworks are much better equipped to weather crises without suffering lasting damage (Protecht Group, 2025).

By identifying potential risks and disruptions in the supply chain, businesses can proactively develop contingency plans and mitigation strategies to minimize the impact of unexpected events. This allows them to be better prepared and respond quickly and effectively to any disruptions, ultimately increasing their resilience (DataGuard, 2024).

There is no standard size or allocation of resources for integrated risk management activities. Departments and agencies are encouraged to determine their own specific needs based on their current situation and adjust accordingly. In order to assess resource requirements for establishing and maintaining a risk management approach and process, it is important to identify the nature, adequacy, and usefulness of existing organizational tools, techniques, human resources skills, and expertise for managing risk and to determine incremental requirements. Key resource considerations could include, but are not limited to (Treasury Board of Canada Secretariat, 2001):

- the people, skills, experience, and competence necessary to design and implement the risk management approach and process throughout the organization, including determining the most appropriate approach and process, working with staff to embed risk management into their structures and processes, educating staff, and putting tools in place;
- the people, skills, experience, and competence necessary to conduct risk management activities on an ongoing basis;

- the people, skills, experience, and competence necessary to maintain the approach and process along with supporting procedures;
- the organization's existing processes, methods, and tools (including systems and technologies) that can be used for managing risk;
- incremental requirements with respect to processes, methods, and tools (including systems and technologies) needed for managing risk;
- the necessary training programs for the organization's staff to ensure a common understanding of and approach to risk management (e.g. common language and terminology);
- any resource constraints that could require trade-offs during the development and execution of risk management processes.

The enterprise (corporate) risk management framework prepares the appropriate ground for decision-making by taking into account all the interchangeable interaction between managerial functions and operational activities, and supports this with information, monitoring, reporting, and communication systems, enabling optimization to be approached. Corporate risk management, which is based on a strategy-based, lean, and agile philosophy, provides the opportunity to analyze risks by considering their interdependencies and effects. This is also the optimal way to achieve optimization. In future risk management models, attempting to manage siloed and isolated risks by focusing on them separately led to the reuse of resources separately for each risk. ERM eliminates this waste by managing to gather risks into main categories (Ai *et al.*, 2017).

ERM represents the most up-to-date state of risk management and is a strategic approach that identifies, evaluates, and manages organizational risks. This holistic approach supports the company's strategy and efficiency by addressing all types of risks rather than a narrow focus. Instead of addressing risks in silos, ERM transforms them into a strategic process at the management level. This requires the highest level of leadership to integrate risk assessments and management into key strategic planning and decision-making processes. The key components of ERM that increase transparency and stakeholder trust through senior leadership participation are as follows (Atlassian, 2025):

i. risk identification,
ii. risk assessment and evaluation,
iii. risk response strategies,
iv. risk monitoring, reporting, and control.

v. continuous communication and feedback throughout all stages. (Treasury Board of Canada Secreteriat, 2001).

6.2 Drive Corporate Value

Developing an understanding of risk and managing it effectively has become a critical requirement for leaders to succeed in the 21st century. Globalization, the geopolitical environment, technology, the internet, customer expectations, regulatory changes, mergers and reorganizations, accounting and reporting deficiencies, and complex financial instruments constitute the main risk areas organizations face. Traditionally, risk management has been approached in silos, addressed separately by finance, insurance, operations, information technology, and internal audit units. However, increasing complexity and global operations have revealed the interconnected nature of risks, thereby increasing the importance of the ERM approach. ERM addresses risks from a holistic perspective, enabling leadership to take conscious, calculated risks and ensuring that these risks are managed in a manner that benefits stakeholders (Shenkir and Walker, 2014).

ERM is a set of cultural practices, competencies, and practices that enable organizations to manage risks in alignment with strategy and performance. ERM does not only cover the listing of risks or internal control; it includes identifying and managing risks across the organization, setting strategy, strengthening governance, communicating with stakeholders, and measuring performance. ERM supports taking advantage of positive opportunities by reducing surprises and losses, minimizing performance variability, and effectively utilizing resources. It also enhances organizations' ability to adapt to change and enhance their long-term resilience. This approach ensures that risk is not just viewed as a constraint but as an element that can lead to strategic opportunities and competitive advantages. ERM can be applied to all organizations, regardless of size, and provides a holistic assessment of risk in decision processes (COSO, 2017).

Several ERM frameworks have been proposed by various professional associations and consulting firms, but most share similar core components. The differences between frameworks primarily arise from the terminology used and the number of steps involved in the process. When implementing ERM, companies can adapt a general framework to their own culture, management philosophy, competencies, needs, sector, and size. The organizational context necessary for effective ERM implementation includes the following elements:

- top-level commitment and ownership: top management's attitude (tone at the top);
- risk management culture, common language, set philosophy with values, and risk appetite balance with risk tolerance level;
- integration into managerial functions and operational process;
- design framework, which involves shaping ERM according to company;
- readiness level of company and initial infrastructure.

ERM's contributions are grouped into three key points: building sustainable competitive advantage, optimizing risk management costs, and improving business performance. Thus, management becomes more effective in both value preservation and value creation. Additionally, decision-making processes become more robust through the ownership of risks, timely development of risk responses, and risk-oriented preparation of business plans. However, this value proposition, defined at a general level, needs to be compared with organization-specific risk priorities and existing capacity. The true value of ERM, therefore, is embodied by clarifying the difference between the current state and the targeted risk management maturity. This process allows managers to find ERM investments more persuasive. From this point of view, an effective ERM infrastructure can be one of the factors that determine the difference between ordinary companies and those that shape the sector. The ERM approach not only simply manages risks; it also strengthens the organization's strategies, goals, and relationships with stakeholders, supporting corporate reputation and sustainable success (Protiviti Inc, 2006).

ERM is a business decision-making process to identify and manage uncertainty. The process used in ERM programs is the same as that used in traditional risk management programs, except that now the risk management professional seeks to create value and optimize risk opportunities, not just preserve assets. The steps in the risk management process (or a variety thereof) include risk and opportunity identification, risk evaluation and assessment, strategic risk response and implementation, and review, evaluation, and monitoring (American Society for Healthcare Risk Management, 2014).

ERM starts with what drives value for the entity. Because ERM seeks to provide information about risks affecting the organization's achievement of its core objectives, it is important to apply a strategic lens to the identification, assessment, and management of risks on the horizon. An effective starting point for an ERM process begins with gaining an understanding of what currently drives value for the business and what's in the strategic plan that represents new value drivers for the business. To ensure that the ERM process helps management keep an eye on internal or external events that might trigger risk opportunities or threats to the business, a strategically integrated ERM process begins with a rich understanding of what's most important for the business' short-term and long-term success (NC State University, 2025).

The purpose of businesses is to create value for their stakeholders. Value is created, protected, or eroded (reduced) by the management decisions taken by the organization through the achievement of its goals and the development of strategies for its activities. The risk and opportunity inherent in decisions must be recognized. Information about the internal and external environment needs to be taken into account by management. Changing conditions require reorganization of corporate activities and effective use of resources, for which up-to-date and timely information is required. Risks are considered when making decisions, and the decisions taken affect the business value through practices in line with these decisions and the results of these practices. The analysis of the probability and impact of risks has the potential to influence decisions and, therefore, business value. Value creation is achieved with resources that encompass people, capital, and technology. Businesses maintain their value through a focus on people, processes, systems, and activities. They create sustainable value through activities within the scope of product/service quality, production capacity, and customer satisfaction. Value is eroded through poor strategies and practices, inadequate knowledge of risks and opportunities, and incomplete activities (Kucuk Yilmaz, 2017).

A major difference between traditional risk management programs and the organization-wide ERM programs is the effort to create and recognize value. Previously, most of the effort was spent on value protection and other reactive strategies to mitigate risks. Little knowledge of the effect of uncertainty on value was understood and, therefore, not captured or enhanced. The value, if created, was serendipitous, unplanned, and solely by chance. ERM programs change that dynamic and consider value creation, recognition, and enhancement on the same level as value protection. The appropriate deployment of strategic risk response solutions becomes a critical function, given limited resources and other competing priorities, many of which are unfunded and unstaffed. The minimization of variability in care practices, reduction in duplicate efforts by differing units and departments, and a decrease in the volume of work to be redone can all help improve efficiency (American Society for Healthcare Risk Management, 2014).

Creating and maintaining value is the main goal of businesses because profitability can only be achieved when value is created and sustained. The decisions made by leaders as business managers in all activities, from strategy determination to the execution of daily work, create value for the business, preserve existing value, or cause these values to be lost or eroded. Values can be created through the use and strategic evaluation of production and management resources (people, capital, technology, and brand) to maximize their potential. These values are maintained through superior product quality, high production capacity, an uninterrupted supply chain, and therefore customer (internal and external) satisfaction. If these goals are not achieved as a result of poor strategy or inadequate execution, the value could be lost. In order to assess risks and opportunities when making decisions, management should review internal and external factors, utilize important resources and practices, and renew them in accordance with changing conditions. If management strives to find the optimal (best) balance between growth, earnings targets, and related goals when setting strategies and goals, and if it effectively implements them, it can maximize the value of the organization. If the goals are not reached, the value is lost. (Kucuk Yilmaz, 2007; COSO, 2005). Implementing ERM improves decision-making processes, aligns risk appetite with strategic initiatives, and strengthens business continuity by proactively mitigating risks. This approach also supports regulatory compliance, helps allocate resources optimally, and contributes to the company's resilience and sustainable growth by increasing stakeholder trust (Atlassian, 2025).

6.3 Enterprise Risk Management Design Challenge (to Size and Resources Allocation): One Size Does Not Fit All

Organizations have developed different frameworks and guidelines for the ERM framework and process. So why are they different? The ERM framework should be thought of like architectural drawings and plans when building a house: it provides high-level guidance on what the organization's purpose is for ERM, what objectives the risks will be managed toward, and where ERM will be positioned within the organizational structure. The framework defines roles, responsibilities, and the level of risk that senior management is willing to take (risk appetite). This ensures consistency in ERM implementation and clarifies why the ERM program was established. The ERM process is the implementation of the framework: it includes steps such as identifying, analyzing, prioritizing, assigning ownership, and reporting risks. The process determines the tools and methods used, but it should not be complex or documentation-heavy; the focus should be on creating results and value. Furthermore, the process should be flexible as the organization changes, allowing for additions or removals. The ERM framework with its processes must be adapted to the organization's culture, needs, and changing circumstances. A system set up once and left unchanged will not work in the long term; the framework and processes must be reviewed as leadership, products, or strategy change (Williams, 2019).

One size does not fit all. In this context, the same size does not fit everyone in the same way: every business is different. The fundamental difference begins with the fact that human resources are distinct in every company. Each person's background, attitudes, and behaviors, values that influence their decisions, ethical structures, and thought processes differ. Overall, no two individuals can be exactly alike. Since the people managing businesses are different, companies are also naturally different from one another. Even if they perform the same job in the same industry sector, they primarily differ in their approach. This fundamental reason alone is a strong indication of why risk management systems must be different and uniquely designed for each company. Therefore, the best ERM guidelines cannot be applied identically to any business like a prescription; even if applied, they will not be successful.

Appropriate resources (people, tools, etc.) need to be allocated for the design, implementation, and maintenance of the risk management approach and process, as well as for the ongoing conduct of risk management activities. With respect to resourcing, upfront investments may be necessary for the initial phases of design and implementation. Departments that have made substantial progress in implementing risk management have recognized the need for an initial investment of dedicated resources. Start-up costs (time, attention, training, systems, and communications) may be incurred until the practice becomes an integral part of organizational structures and processes. It may take time and effort to gain momentum, train managers and specialists, and establish effective tools and processes. Once fully implemented, initial start-up investments may be reallocated as appropriate (Treasury Board of Canada Secretariat, 2001).

In the ongoing management of risks, specific attention should be given to the allocation of resources for risk response activities. While identifying and analyzing risks are much easier to embed into day-to-day decision-making activities, specific resources may need to be assigned to risk response action items. These resources should be at the appropriate level given the severity of the risk and should take into account any necessary trade-offs due to resource constraints. It is important to note that resource allocations should be aligned with the level of risk to be managed, with resources being focused on the main risks—not necessarily every risk (Treasury Board of Canada Secretariat, 2001).

6.4 ERM Framework: Supply Chain Risks and Process

Organizational risks include inventory, operational, quality, and management risks. Inventory risk arises from excess or insufficient stock, leading to additional handling costs or lost opportunities, while operational risk emerges from process disruptions that hinder the flow of materials or information. Quality risks are often linked to supplier failures or outsourcing, and management risks result from weak capabilities to anticipate and respond to market demands. Network risks stem from interactions among supply chain partners, with supply risk, supplier default, and demand risk being the most studied issues. Supply risk refers to disruptions in inbound flows that prevent firms from meeting customer demand, while demand risk is associated with demand uncertainty or problems in outbound logistics. Environmental risks, on the other hand, are driven by external forces such as natural disasters, political and regulatory changes, or economic conditions (Ghadge *et al.*, 2012).

According to the framework published by COSO, ERM emphasizes the importance of risk in strategic planning and explains how it shapes strategy and performance across an organization. The framework consists of five core components (COSO, 2017):

- **Governance and culture:** This component sets the organization's approach to risk management and its ethical values, defining oversight responsibilities at the highest level.

- **Strategy and objective-setting:** During strategic planning, strategies and business objectives are developed in alignment with the organization's risk appetite. These objectives form the basis for identifying, assessing, and responding to risks.
- **Performance:** Risks that could affect strategy and objectives are identified, prioritized, and addressed within the risk-appetite framework. The results are then reported to stakeholders.
- **Review and revision:** The organization evaluates its performance over time and updates the ERM components in response to changes in the business environment.
- **Information, communication, and reporting:** This component requires the continuous sharing of critical information from internal and external sources throughout the organization.

The SCRM process consists of identifying, assessing, mitigating, and controlling risks. Most studies emphasize risk identification, but there is less focus on holistic processes. Risk mitigation strategies are categorized as proactive and reactive. Proactive strategies include supplier development, multi-sourcing, flexible contracting, product variety, and postponement, whereas reactive strategies involve disaster recovery, rebuilding supply chains, resource reallocation, demand shifting, and scenario planning. Although proactive approaches are more widely recommended in the literature, practitioners often find it difficult to justify their costs. Therefore, agility, flexibility, and preparedness are highlighted as essential overarching strategies for effective risk management (Ghadge *et al.*, 2012).

SCRM involves identifying potential vulnerabilities in supply chains by assessing factors such as supplier locations, transportation routes, political stability, and weather conditions. Once identified, risks are evaluated in terms of likelihood and impact using both quantitative and qualitative methods, including risk scoring, scenario analysis, and expert judgment. Based on these insights, companies can mitigate risks by diversifying suppliers, optimizing inventory, strengthening communication, investing in technology, and implementing contingency plans. As a continuous process, SCRM also requires regular monitoring of operations, policies, and key performance indicators while fostering strong supplier relationships and stakeholder engagement to ensure effective decision-making (McGrath and Jonker, 2023).

The first COSO framework was published in 2004, followed by an update in 2017. While the 2004 version focused more on identifying and controlling risks and preventing losses, the 2017 version integrates risk management with strategy and performance and treats risks as a source of opportunity and competitive advantage at the same time. The 2004 Enterprise Risk Management: Integrated Framework brought a more internal control-based and operational perspective to risk management. This approach, known for the "COSO Cube" model, explains the four categories of objectives: strategy, operations, reporting, and compliance, through eight components (internal environment, target setting, incident identification, risk assessment, risk response, control activities, information-communication, and monitoring). It also envisages the management of risks at the institution, unit, sub-unit, and process levels. Its primary purposes include aligning risk appetite with strategy, systematizing risk responses, reducing operational surprises, and improving capital allocation. Enterprise Risk Management: Integrating with Strategy and Performance, published in 2017, is more oriented toward strategy and performance. This framework integrates risk management into corporate culture, strategic decision-making, and value creation, rather than simply functioning as a control mechanism. It is based on five main components: governance and culture, strategy and goal setting, performance, review and revision, information-communication, and reporting. These components are divided into 20 principles, ensuring that risk management is integrated with ethical values, risk appetite, performance prioritization, adaptation to change, and transparent information flow across the organization (Kumar, 2022).

Supply chain risks can emerge from a variety of sources, both within the supply process and from external sources, including natural disasters, geopolitical events, supplier failures, quality issues, and cyberattacks. Disruption to the chain can be occasioned by seismic events, such as earthquakes, and hydrological events, such as floods. In addition, armed conflicts, trade disputes, and economic fluctuations can also have a significant impact. It is imperative to devise contingency plans to mitigate the potential repercussions of these risks. The establishment of robust supplier relationships is of paramount importance, as financial instability or capacity issues can compromise the chain, in which case firms may seek to diversify their supply. The increasing prevalence of digital systems has resulted in heightened vulnerability to cyberattacks, with ransomware and data breaches posing a significant threat to production and reputation. The significance of continuous and integrated risk management systems that analyze digital vulnerabilities and develop response plans has increased. Furthermore, in order to adapt to changing consumer demands, it is necessary to implement flexible production, accurate inventory management, and distribution strategies. Ensuring transparency against human rights, environmental damage, and labor violations in the supply chain is also part of risk management and should be supported by a rigorous audit process (McGrath and Jonker, 2023).

The traditional approach to SCRM, which focuses only on specific shocks or geographic footprints, is no longer sufficient. A more comprehensive strategy requires understanding two key components: vulnerabilities and exposures. Vulnerabilities are inherent weaknesses that make a supply chain fragile and can arise in planning and supplier networks, transportation and logistics, financial resilience, product complexity, and organizational maturity. For example, reliance on single-source components or a concentration of suppliers in a single region can be significant vulnerabilities. Exposure refers to unforeseen events that can exploit these weaknesses and disrupt the supply chain, including natural disasters, economic shocks, cyberattacks, and supplier issues. To manage these risks, companies need to map their entire supply chain, even beyond direct suppliers, to identify hidden relationships and weak points. Transparency can be enhanced through publicly available data and network-analytics algorithms, allowing firms to assess their fragility relative to peers and industry benchmarks. Companies should challenge established decisions by using financial modeling and scenario-building to quantify risks and adopt an insurance-like mindset to mitigate high-impact, low-probability events. A robust risk culture is essential for resilience, enabling organizations to respond quickly to severe crises. This culture requires clearly defined risk tolerance, open communication where employees feel empowered to share risks and lessons learned, and a sense of ownership where individuals take responsibility for outcomes and collaborate on rapid solutions. Ultimately, combining a risk-aware culture with investments in resilience and a mindset that prioritizes continuity over efficiency is critical for businesses to thrive in an increasingly unpredictable global environment (Alicke *et al.*, 2020).

6.5 Risk Categories in Supply Chains

Supply chain risk arises from both internal and external sources such as suppliers, vendors, transporters, retailers, and other external entities that may disrupt operations, performance, sales, or job functions.

If unmanaged, these risks can create quality problems, legal liabilities, and reputational damage (Safety Culture, 2025).

A supply disruption is any unforeseen event that disturbs the normal flow of goods and materials within a supply chain. These disruptions can lead to production issues, reduced productivity, and significant negative consequences for business operations, including an inability to meet customer demand and a negative impact on a company's financial performance, liquidity, and share price. Supply chain risks are broadly categorized as either internal or external (Golobrodska, 2024).

A. Internal risks

Internal risks are those that stem from within the organization or its immediate operations. While they are often manageable, they can cause serious disruptions if not properly controlled (Golobrodska, 2024). Internal risks stem from within the organization or its immediate operations. These can often be managed with a high degree of control but, if left unchecked, can cause severe disruptions (McAdoo and Ivalua, 2025).

Business risks/operational risks: These risks are potential disruptions that arise from internal processes, systems, or personnel. These include vendor risk and inventory management issues, both of which can impact the ability to deliver products and services on time and affect overall supply chain efficiency. Examples include a key supplier's sudden failure, which can halt production, or inventory management problems that lead to stockouts or overstocking. To mitigate these risks, organizations should implement robust vendor risk management strategies, including due diligence and contingency planning to identify alternative suppliers. The use of technology for real-time inventory tracking can also provide better visibility and enable proactive decision-making (Data Guard, 2024). Inefficiencies or poor management practices can lead to bottlenecks, quality control issues, and missed deadlines (McAdoo and Ivalua, 2025). Examples of operational risks are the following:

- **Material shortages:** Missing components, parts, or raw materials that halt or slow production—sometimes temporary but potentially long-term if alternative sources are unavailable (Safety Culture, 2025).
- **Delivery failures:** Late or missed shipments from suppliers or third-party vendors that result in production delays, missed deadlines, and customer dissatisfaction (Safety Culture, 2025).

- **Quality failures:** Defective or substandard inputs that lead to product recalls, rework costs, and reputational harm (Safety Culture, 2025).

Another good case is the semiconductor supply chain crisis: The automotive industry's reliance on single-source semiconductor suppliers led to severe production delays during and after the COVID-19 pandemic. According to S&P Global Mobility (see Protecht Group, 2025), over 9.5 million units of global light-vehicle production were lost in 2021 due to semiconductor shortages, with Q3 alone seeing an estimated shortfall of 3.5 million units. An additional 3 million units were lost in 2022. Although the situation improved in 2023, production remained disrupted. The growing demand for advanced driver assistance systems, infotainment, and autonomous vehicle technologies means semiconductor reliance will only increase. Diversification of suppliers, investment in long-term supply agreements, and the integration of predictive analytics for demand forecasting will be essential to avoiding similar disruptions in the future (Protecht Group, 2025).

Financial risks: Cost volatility, fluctuating demand, and cash flow issues create financial uncertainty, which can lead to compromised supplier relationships or cutbacks in inventory (McAdoo and Ivalua, 2025). Financial risks are potential financial losses stemming from factors such as market fluctuations, vendor performance, and compliance failures. These risks can be exacerbated by unforeseen events such as natural disasters or geopolitical tensions. They are interconnected with operational inefficiencies and demand fluctuations, not existing in isolation. To manage these risks, organizations are increasingly using sophisticated risk assessment tools to identify vulnerabilities and develop mitigation strategies, which helps ensure resilience and safeguards profitability (DataGuard, 2024). For example, price fluctuations are driven by changes in supply and demand, exchange rate volatility, or customs tariffs, which can undermine financial projections and profitability (Safety Culture, 2025).

Manufacturing risks: Delays in production, equipment malfunctions, and labor shortages have a domino effect on product availability (McAdoo and Ivalua, 2025).

Legal, contract, standards, regulatory, and compliance risks: Managing service-level agreements (SLAs) and upholding contract terms are vital to minimizing legal exposure. Non-compliance with terms such as right-to-audit clauses or regulatory requirements can lead to penalties, strained relationships, and costly legal challenges (McAdoo and Ivalua, 2025). This category of risks is the potential legal and financial consequences of failing to adhere to industry standards and regulations, such as ISO 28000. In a globalized market, it is essential to understand regulations such as the Foreign Corrupt Practices Act (FCPA) and the Sarbanes –Oxley Act. Non-compliance can lead to fines and a damaged reputation. Proactively assessing supply chains for adherence to standards and embracing a robust compliance management framework can help mitigate risks, enhance transparency, and foster trust with stakeholders (DataGuard, 2024). For example, supplier disputes, conflicts, litigation, or contractual disagreements with suppliers can disrupt delivery schedules and cause financial losses (Safety Culture, 2025).

B. External risks

External risks arise from factors outside the organization's direct control, such as third-party suppliers, geopolitical factors, or environmental changes. These risks require vigilant monitoring and adaptive strategies to mitigate anything potentially disrupting operations (McAdoo and Ivalua, 2025). External risks originate from factors outside the organization's direct control and require continuous monitoring and adaptive strategies (Golobrodska, 2024).

Reputational risks emerge when supply chain disruptions negatively impact an organization's public image and stakeholder trust. These risks often result from compliance failures or unethical practices within the supply chain. They can lead to diminished customer loyalty, reduced market share, and a reassessment of affiliations by stakeholders such as investors and partners. If not addressed proactively, reputational issues can hinder business performance and make future partnerships challenging. Therefore, organizations must prioritize transparency and ethical considerations to protect their reputation and build lasting relationships (DataGuard, 2024). A supplier's misconduct or failure to meet standards can significantly damage a brand's reputation (McAdoo and Ivalua, 2025). Reputational risks occur when supply chain disruptions negatively impact a company's public image and stakeholder trust (Golobrodska, 2024).

Cybersecurity risks: With an increase in ransomware and IT disruptions, cybersecurity risks are an escalating concern. The Colonial Pipeline incident, which led to significant fuel shortages in 2021, serves as a stark reminder of how vulnerable supply chains are to cyber threats (McAdoo and Ivalua, 2025). Cybersecurity risks that threats such as ransomware and other IT disruptions can severely affect operations. (Golobrodska, 2024)

Geopolitical risks: Tariffs, government instability, and trade wars can disrupt sourcing and increase costs. For example, the U.S.–China trade war resulted in added tariffs on $380 billion worth of Chinese goods, creating supply chain challenges and financial strain for companies reliant on those imports (McAdoo and Ivalua, 2025). External factors such as tariffs, trade wars, and political instability can disrupt sourcing and increase costs (Golobrodska, 2024).

Environmental risks: These include disruptions caused by natural disasters, climate change, and environmental regulations (Golobrodska, 2024). Climate change, natural disasters, and environmental regulations pose significant risks to supply chain continuity. In 2022 alone, the National Oceanic and Atmospheric Administration (NOAA) reported 18 separate billion-dollar climate and weather disasters in the United States, which led to widespread supply chain interruptions. Additionally, with the rise of ESG compliance requirements, companies are increasingly responsible for meeting environmental standards (McAdoo and Ivalua, 2025). Also, supply shocks are another one of the external risks. Large-scale disruptions from pandemics, natural disasters, labor disputes, geopolitical conflicts, or trade embargoes can abruptly reduce or eliminate supply availability (Safety Culture, 2025).

Supply chain risk categorization can also be shaped by industry type, company size, organizational structure, needs and objectives, organizational resources, risk management attitudes and understanding, or risk management needs. Risk categorization can also be approached from the perspective of different stakeholders. It is possible to examine the risk sources of all supply chain events, including both managerial functions and operational processes, by dividing them into three main categories. This categorization is particularly important and valuable for obtaining a holistic view of the overall risk environment, as seen in the following sample (Mukherjee and Padhi, 2022):

a. **Supply-side risks** (such as input prices).
b. **Demand-side risks** (such as product prices).
c. **Background risks** (such as setup costs).

The supply chain risk frameworks emphasize that risk categorization is essential, as it provides a holistic view of the overall risk landscape and uncovers risks often overlooked in traditional approaches. This ensures that mitigation strategies are not only company-focused but also account for system-wide interdependencies. Risks can be classified into three levels: (i) the supply chain level, covering risks within a focal company's supply chain, such as sourcing, demand, and internal processes; (ii) the industry or cross-supply chain level, addressing risks that spread across multiple supply chains within an industry, including competitive and cluster substitution risks; and (iii) the macro level, encompassing risks with broader impacts across industries and geographies, such as natural disasters or economic crises (Rong *et al.*, 2019).

6.6 Lean and Agile Framework Design for Enterprise Risk Management

"Lean Process to Save Production Sources"

The integration of lean principles with risk management is designed to support decision-making processes through the quantitative assessment of risks and their relationships. In this context, lean-specific risk factors such as miscommunication, lack of knowledge of lean principles, low employee participation, insufficient human resources, and weak leadership commitment have been identified as key risk factors. These factors directly impact critical risk events, such as failure to meet performance targets, delays in implementing lean initiatives, and ineffective knowledge transfer. By implementing a structured risk assessment process, organizations can prioritize mitigation strategies and align them with lean objectives. This approach ensures a more resilient implementation process by proactively addressing the underlying causes of failure in the lean transformation and reinforcing continuous improvement through data-driven risk control.

It is important to be aware of and understand exactly what ERM is. Therefore, it is necessary to proceed from the best definitions. Corporate risk management is:

> "… established to identify potential events that may affect the company, to manage risks in accordance with the company's corporate risk-taking profile, and to provide a reasonable degree of assurance regarding the company's achievement of its objectives, the reliability of financial reporting, the effectiveness and efficiency of operations, and compliance with applicable laws and regulations; it is defined as a systematic process influenced by the board of directors, managers, and all other employees of the company and applied throughout the entire business within a certain strategy, including internal control". (COSO, 2004)

Instead of managing financial and operational risks separately with a siloed approach, ERM is founded on the idea that the firm should address all risk exposures in a single framework and does not limit risk management to specific departments. It considers ERM as a holistic structure that spans all functional areas of the organization. In this context, ERM should not only be limited to reducing or preventing risks but also should be strongly integrated with company strategies, business goals, and value creation processes (Hunziker *et al.*, 2002). According to the COSO Treadway Commission, the benefits of effective enterprise risk management are as follows (COSO, 2005, 2017):

(a) expand the range of opportunities;
(b) identify and manage risks across the organization;
(c) increase positive outcomes and advantages while reducing negative surprises;
(d) reduce performance variability;
(e) optimize resource distribution;
(f) enhance organizational resilience.

However, while ERM enables businesses to anticipate and manage risks, it has some fundamental limitations. The inherently uncertain nature of the future means that even the most comprehensive ERM systems cannot eliminate all risks. The effectiveness of the process depends on factors such as the competence of decision-makers, human errors, and the system's vulnerability to manipulation. Additionally, excessive control increases costs, while insufficient control can magnify risks. Therefore, ERM does not provide certainty; it only serves to manage risks reasonably and increase the resilience of the business (Kucuk Yilmaz, 2007, 2017).

Integrating lean management tools into risk management processes increases the effectiveness of methods that comply with risk standards, such as ISO 31000:2018. The Ishikawa diagrams enable identifying and preventing the root causes of risks, while Hoshin Kanri enables strategic risk-taking to capitalize on opportunities. PDCA, a continuous improvement cycle, supports the systematic elimination of risk sources, while Poka Yoke reduces the likelihood of error-induced risks through error prevention. Teamwork fosters collaboration and mitigates the impact of risk outcomes, while outsourcing facilitates risk sharing by delegating responsibilities to external parties. Lastly, Nemawashi contributes to the informed assumption of risks through its inclusive and consensus-based decision-making processes. This integration supports a culture of proactive and continuous improvement, aligning risk mitigation with operational excellence and organizational agility.

Lean thinking offers a practical framework for transforming risk management from a compliance-driven formality into an integrated, value-adding activity within product development. Applying lean principles such as value identification, value stream mapping, and flow optimization allows risk management to support project objectives by aligning with actual engineering needs rather than bureaucratic expectations. A lean approach emphasizes delivering timely and relevant risk insights to internal stakeholders, promoting early identification and mitigation of uncertainties, reducing wasteful iterations, and fostering continuous learning. It also enhances collaboration by encouraging a participatory culture where engineers are empowered to manage risks as part of their daily responsibilities. Ultimately, lean-aligned risk management enhances project adaptability, decision-making quality, and outcome predictability (Willumsen *et al.*, 2017). The integration of the lean approach with risk management is designed to support decision-making by quantitatively assessing risks and their interrelationships. Lean-specific risk factors, such as a lack of communication, poor understanding of lean principles, low employee engagement, inadequate human resources, and weak leadership commitment, are identified as primary risk agents. These factors directly contribute to critical risk events, including the failure to meet performance targets, delays in executing lean initiatives, and ineffective knowledge transfer. By implementing a structured risk evaluation process, organizations can prioritize mitigation strategies and ensure they are aligned with lean objectives. This approach fosters a more resilient implementation process by proactively addressing the underlying causes of lean failure and reinforcing continuous improvement through data-driven risk control (Widiasih *et al.*, 2015).

In conclusion, ERM can create great value for businesses when it is well-designed, but when poorly designed, it becomes a bureaucratic burden and may lose its main purpose. The major challenge faced by companies is to make ERM a tool that supports flexible and strategic decision-making rather than a restrictive internal control mechanism. Continuous improvement (Kaizen) and a data-based decision-making culture, underlying lean management, make it possible to make risk management not simply a prescription style or a standard process. With the support of the Kaizen philosophy, risk management can transform into a more dynamic and proactive mechanism, "updating itself in accordance with developments and changes, willing and flexible to development." Thus, by focusing on risk culture, organizational behavior, and human factors, which are often ignored in traditional risk management, lean management aims to identify the root causes of these risks and manage them with an appropriate strategy. This integration not only mitigates or reduces the negative effects of risks but also strengthens operational capacity building and, most importantly, corporate agility.

6.7 The Interrelationship Between Corporate Performance and Enterprise Risk Management

Proactive and effective risk management is not merely a defensive function aimed at preventing negative outcomes; it is also a strategic driver that significantly contributes to improved corporate performance and enhanced financial stability. Organizations that embrace strategic risk management are demonstrably more likely to deliver greater stakeholder confidence and achieve better overall business outcomes (Harvard Business School, 2025).

6.8 Case Studies from Best Practices

D-CEET Project by Eidgenössische Technische Hochschule Zürich (ETH Zürich)

Current airline crew training is conducted through physical cabin mockups and simulators, known as cabin emergency evacuation trainers (CEETs). The D-CEET project aims to transform these trainings by creating a "digital twin" of an Airbus A320 CEET. Funded by the German Federal Ministry of Digital Affairs and Transport with a budget of approximately €1.5 million, this three-year project aims to deliver all educational content in a fully immersive manner through virtual reality (VR) and tablet-based applications. In addition to improving training efficiency, this digitalization will also reduce environmental impact by reducing the operating costs of CEET devices, which reach €200,000 per year, and decrease crew travel requirements due to their fixed location. The project explores the potential of digital twins to simulate and test real processes in advance, addressing the question of how efficient emergency training can be, particularly for cabin and cockpit crews, in a VR environment. The research team utilizes advanced technologies, such as eye tracking and physiological sensors, to assess the cognitive load of participants and the effectiveness of training. This three-year D-CEET project, funded by the German Federal Ministry for Digital Affairs and Transport with approximately €1.5 million, was launched at Frankfurt Airport on June 11–12 (ETH Zürich, 2024, 2025).

We emphasize the key points of this best practice as follows:

- **The D-CEET project**, developed by ETH Zürich, serves as a pioneering best practice in transitioning from physical to digital risk management environments in aviation. By creating a "digital twin" of traditional simulators, the project addresses the logistical and financial burdens of conventional crew training. The core elements and strategic impacts of this digitalization are summarized here:
- **The Problem:** Traditional airline crew training relies on expensive, fixed physical simulators (CEETs), which involve high maintenance costs, significant environmental impact, and complex logistical challenges for global crews.
- **The Digital Twin Solution:** The D-CEET project replaces physical infrastructure with VR and tablet-based environments. This digital twin approach allows for portable, scalable, and highly accessible training modules.

- **Economic and Operational Benefits:** Digitalization is estimated to reduce operational costs by approximately €200,000 per year per unit. Additionally, it eliminates the need for crews to undertake long-distance travel, significantly lowering the environmental footprint.
- **Risk Management & Cognitive Analytics:** A critical aspect of D-CEET is the integration of eye-tracking and physiological sensors. These technologies allow the research team to measure cognitive load and training effectiveness in real time, ensuring that virtual security and emergency scenarios meet or exceed the safety standards of physical training.

When analyzed in terms of risk management, it is seen that this application aims to optimize the scope of managing training performance risks, training cost risks, environmental impact risks, and logistics risks. As a cost-effective project, it provides savings by reducing the costs of all processes related to education. As is known, simulations also provide the opportunity to recognize systemic gaps. This is important in terms of preventing irreparable losses. It also creates the opportunity to increase the performance of human resources by reducing their cognitive load. Experiencing every negative scenario is not feasible for corporate resources and human resources. For this reason, it is one of the strategies of risk management to strengthen both the business and human resources by experiencing security and security vulnerabilities in the digital environment. In these respects, value can be created by producing nature-friendly and human-friendly results, incorporating risk management.

Johnson & Johnson Enterprise Risk Management Framework

Johnson & Johnson takes a consistent, collaborative, and forward-looking approach to its ERM practice, aimed at increasing risk awareness across the entire organization. This approach is **shaped by core principles such as compliance**, reporting, and business conduct, helping the company identify potential incidents and manage associated risks and opportunities. The ERM framework is designed to support strategic objectives, protect and grow the business, optimize resource allocation, and enable data-driven decision-making. The five main components of the framework are as follows (Johnson and Johnson, 2024):

A. **Strategy and objectives:** ERM objectives are set and risk information is provided to support strategic decisions.

B. **Governance and audit:** There is a comprehensive governance structure, and risk management is the responsibility of the entire company. This is supported by a "Lines of Responsibility" model that extends from the board level to all employees.
C. **Risk identification and prioritization:** Risk is defined as a potential uncertain event or situation that could impact business objectives. Risks are classified as strategic, operational, financial, or compliance-oriented and are prioritized using quantitative and qualitative data.
D. **Risk management and monitoring:** Risk management is a critical process for understanding risks, identifying mitigation options, and executing actions. Risks are regularly monitored and discussed at top-level management meetings.
E. **Information, communication, and reporting:** Channels are in place to keep business leaders and employees aware of the risks they are responsible for. Risk management functions meet regularly with senior leaders to ensure visibility and ownership. This structure, which enhances stakeholder trust by protecting company assets and reputation, supports sustainable growth.

Johnson & Johnson uses an ERM framework to manage various risks, ensuring continuity and safeguarding assets. For supply chain risks, they may diversify suppliers or create contingency plans (Atlassian, 2025).

Netflix: Inspire to Innovation

Netflix is a striking example of how risk management can inspire innovation. While the company was mainly known for its DVD rental service in the early 2000s, it faced increasing competition from video rental stores. Seeing this strategic risk situation as an opportunity, Netflix reversed the course of the industry by launching its **video streaming service**, an uncommon idea at the time. This bold move created an industry that exploded nearly a decade later, radically altering the dynamics of the market.

Netflix's innovation journey did not stop there. With the video streaming market becoming highly competitive, the company has once again pivoted to gain a competitive edge. This time, it took the risk of producing original content. This strategic move has helped set its platform apart, increase subscriptions, and solidify its position as a market leader. Both significant transitions by Netflix (from DVD to streaming and streaming to original content) involved significant risks, but these risks were turned into successes by creating innovative solutions and constantly adapting to market dynamics (Gibson, 2023).

References

Ai, J., Brockett, P., and Wang, T. (2017, December). Optimal enterprise risk management and decision making with shared and dependent risks. *Journal of Risk & Insurance* (The American Risk and Insurance Association), 84(4), 1127–1169. https://doi.org/10.1111/jori.12140.

Alicke, K., Barriball, E., Lund, S., and Swan, D. (2020, May). Operations practice, is your supply chain risk blind—or risk resilient? McKinsey & Company. https://www.mckinsey.com/~/media/McKinsey/Business%20Functions/Operations/Our%20Insights/Is%20your%20supply%20chain%20risk%20blind%20or%20risk%20resilient/Is-your-supply-chain-risk-blind-or-risk-resilient.pdf.

American Society for Healthcare Risk Management. (2014). Enterprise risk management: A framework for success. American Society for Healthcare Risk Management ASHRM. chrome-extension://efaidnhttps://www.ashrm.org/sites/default/files/ashrm/ERM-White-Paper-8-29-14-FINAL.pdf.

Atlassian. (2025). What is enterprise risk management (ERM)? https://www.atlassian.com/work-management/project-management/enterprise-risk-management. Accessed at 07/09/2025.

Committee of Sponsoring Organizations of the Treadway Commission (COSO). (2017). Enterprise risk management integrating with strategy and performance executive summary. coso.org. https://www.coso.org/_files/ugd/3059fc_61ea5985b03c4293960642fdce408eaa.pdf. Retrieved September 09, 2025.

COSO. (2005, August). Enterprise risk management framework, executive summary, p. 2. Committee of Sponsoring Organizations of the Treadway Commission (COSO). www.erm.coso.org.

DataGuard. (2024, August 20). Supply chain risk assessment: A critical tool for business resilience. DataGuard Insights. https://www.dataguard.com/blog/supply-chain-risk-assessment/.

ETH Zurich. (2025, September 09). Digital twin for safety training. http://www.ethz.ch/. https://baug.ethz.ch/en/news-and-events/news/2024/06/digital-twin-for-safety-training.html. Accessed at August 29, 2025.

Ghadge, A., Dani, S., and Kalawsky, R. (2012). Supply chain risk management: Present and future scope available to purchase. *The International Journal of Logistics Management* (Emeral Group Publishing), 23(3), 313–339. https://doi.org/10.1108/09574091211289200.

Gibson, K. (2023, October 24). What is risk management & why is it important? *Harvard Business Review*. https://online.hbs.edu/blog/post/risk-management.

Golobrodska, M. (2024). 7 basic types of supply chain risks. PRECORO. https://precoro.com/blog/7-basic-types-of-supply-chain-risks/.

Harvard Business School. (2025, May 12). What is risk management & why is it important? HBS Online - Harvard Business School. https://online.hbs.edu/blog/post/risk-management.

Johnson & Johnson. (2024). Enterprise risk management framework. https://www.jnj.com/about-jnj/enterprise-risk-management-framework. Accessed August 28, 2025.

Kucuk Yilmaz, A. (2017). *Enterprise Risk Management in International Businesses: Strategy and Organizational Culture Focused Paradigm. Konya: Literatürk Publications.* Literatürk Publishing House, Konya. https://www.amazon.com.tr/Uluslararasi-%C4%B0%C5%9Fletmelerde-Kurumsal-Risk-Y%C3%B6netimi/dp/6053371238.

Kumar, S. (2022). COSO, ISO 31000, risk appetite, three lines of defence and risk management policies, risk management framework (Chapter-4). Research Gate. https://www.researchgate.net/publication/355978926_Risk_Management_Framework.

McAdoo, J. and Ivalua. (2025, February). Mastering supply chain risk management strategies & solutions. Ivalua. https://www.ivalua.com/blog/supply-chain-risk-management/.

McGrath, A. and Jonker, A. (2023, December 2). What is supply chain risk management (SCRM)? IBM. https://www.ibm.com/think/topics/supply-chain-risk-management.

Mukherjee, S. and Padhi, S. (2022). Sourcing decision under interconnected risks: An application of mean–variance preferences approach. *Annals of Operations Research*, 313, 1243–1268.

NC State University, Enterprise Risk Management Initiative. (2025, August 19). What is enterprise risk management (ERM)? NC State Poole College of Management. Erm.ncsu.edu. https://erm.ncsu.edu/resource-center/what-is-enterprise-risk-management/.

Protecht Group. (2025, February 26). Vendor risk management a comprehensive guide to supply chain risk management. Protecht Group. https://www.protechtgroup.com/en-us/blog/supply-chain-risk-management-guide.

Protiviti. (2006, January 1). Guide to enterprise risk management. Frequently asked questions; Risk consulting, business risk, technology risk, internal audit. FAQ.

Sarbanes-Oxley Act of 2002, H.R. 3763, 2006. https://erm.ncsu.edu/resource-center/erm-frequent-questions/; https://www.researchgate.net/profile/Jorge-Gomes-4/post/The-effect-on-firm-value-of-enterprise-risk-management-May-I-link-the-between-firm-value-and-enterprise-risk-management-Which-methods-can-I-apply/attachment/59d61f7e79197b807797df00/AS%3A283726362759170%401444657044341/download/Guide+ERM.pdf.

Ratter, E., Kalbarczyk, M., and Pietrzyk-Wiszowaty, K. (2024). The utilization of lean management tools in the application of risk management methods according to ISO 31000:2018. *European Research Studies Journal, 27*(1), 65–81.

Rong, Z., Souza, R. D., and Goh, M. (2019). Risk management of complex supply chains part 1: Supply chain risk and complex systems. TLI Asia Pasific White Paper Series Volume 12 Nov-SCI09. https://tliap.nus.edu.sg/wp-content/uploads/2019/04/12-Nov-SCI09_Supply-Chain-Risk-and-Complex-Systems.pdf.

Safety Culture. (2025, September 09). A guide to supply chain risk management, supply chain disruptions. Safety Culture. https://safetyculture.com/topics/supply-chain-disruption/supply-chain-risk-management/.

Shenkir, W. G. and Walker, P. L. (2014). *Enterprise Risk Management, Frameworks, Elements and Integration, United States of America by Institue of Management Accountants.* United States of America by Institue of Management Accountants, USA.

The Institute of Internal Auditors (IAA). (2025). Enhanced enterprise risk management and strategic decision-making. https://www.theiia.org/en/content/research/foundation/2025/enhanced-enterprise-risk-management-and-strategic-decision-making/.

Treasury Board of Canada Secreteriat. (2001). *Integrated Risk Management Framework.* President of the Treasury Board, Canada, Cat. No. BT22-78/2001. https://publications.gc.ca/collections/collection_2019/sct-tbs/BT22-78-2001-eng.pdf. Accessed September 9, 2025.

Widiasih, W., Karningsih, P. D., and Ciptomulyono, U. (2015). Development of integrated model for managing risk in lean manufacturing implementation: A case study in an Indonesian manufacturing company. *Procedia Manufacturing, 4*, 282–290. https://doi.org/10.1016/j.promfg.2015.11.042.

Williams, C. (2019, October 21). ERM fundamentals, ERM maturity & frameworks. Strategic Decision Solutions. https://strategicdecisionsolutions.com/erm-framework-vs-process/.

Willumsen, P., Oehmen, J., Rossi, M., and Welo, T. (2017). Applying lean thinking to risk management in product development. In *Proceedings of the 21st International Conference on Engineering Design (ICED17)*, Vol. 2: Design Processes. Design Organisation and Management, Vancouver, Canada, 21–25 August 2017, pp. 269–278.

Chapter 7

NOTECHs to RAgile Supply Chain Risk Management

7.1 Growing Need for NOTECHS Skills in the Supply Chain Ecosystem

Integration is pivotal to managing today's supply chain ecosystem in accordance with objectives. This is because human resources, in particular, possess both technical and non-technical skills, and each—either individually or in interaction with other elements—creates risks for the supply chain. In order to effectively manage risk, it is essential to integrate both technical and non-technical skills. The human factor is a dual-meaning concept within systems, representing both positive and negative aspects. As human beings, we both create risks and are simultaneously sources and managers of risk. Non-technical skills (NONTECHs) are more challenging to manage than technical skills and are also notoriously difficult to measure. At this stage, risk management involves quantifying the probability and severity of impacts, along with other relevant factors, through a process of risk analysis. The most common methods for assigning values are risk matrices.

The success of the supply chain and, indeed, supply chain risk management is determined by a combination of human factors, technical systems, and digitalization. Human resources are the determining factor in the success of supply chain and risk management. Humans, with their unique skill sets, are a strategic asset. It is essential to develop the NONTECHs of leaders, employees, and stakeholders. It is vital to develop awareness and relevant skills, as well as technical knowledge and expertise, in order to improve motivation and performance. This will help ensure the supply chain is closer to achieving its goals. Furthermore, with employees and stakeholders equipped with both technical and non-technical skills and a high level of awareness and perception, the supply chain will become more flexible, efficient, and resilient. This will enhance supply chain risk management performance and improve agility. Resilience and agility are among the main goals of supply chain risk management. By equipping human resources with NONTECHs, both the performance of supply chain processes and operations and the company's resilience and agility against potential risks are enhanced.

Recruitment processes powered by artificial intelligence (AI) are currently on the agenda, but it is important to note that NOTECH capacity development strategies and practices are just as important as recruitment itself.

A strategic approach to human resources management is adopted, with a focus on developing leadership, communication, problem-solving, decision-making, and motivational skills.

These competencies are highly sought after by hiring managers and are a key objective of recruitment strategies. Furthermore, providing employees with diverse training in areas covered by NOTECHs is a good strategy to empower them. However, training alone is not sufficient; it is essential that employees internalize what they learn and develop, incorporating it into their work style and workplace behaviors so that it becomes part of their work style.

7.2 NOTECHs

NONTECHs are very important for managing safety risks in different sectors, such as healthcare, rail, maritime, aviation, and engineering. These skills are important for making sure that operations are safe and efficient. For example, it seems that many problems in healthcare are caused by people not being able to communicate, work as a team, lead others, or make decisions (Lewis *et al.*, 2012). NONTECHs are cognitive, social, and personal resource skills that complement technical skills and contribute to the safe and efficient performance of tasks. They are cognitive (e.g. decision-making) and social (e.g. teamwork). Analyses of incidents have revealed that the underlying causes are commonly due to behavioral or non-technical aspects of performance (e.g. communication errors) rather than a mere lack of technical expertise. Therefore, while technical skills seem essential, they are not sufficient to ensure safety and quality (Royal College of Surgeons of Edinburgh, 2019).

Attention to NOTECH "soft" skills such as teamwork, leadership, situational awareness, decision-making, and communication will increase the likelihood of maintaining high performance levels over time. The four main skill categories of the NONTECH system are:

i. situational awareness,
ii. decision-making
iii. communication and collaboration or team skills,
iv. leadership.

These four core skills, categorized under the heading "NOTECH Soft Skills: Bridging Gaps in Supply Chain Risk Management", demonstrate the critical role of the human factor beyond technological systems in managing supply chain risks. Furthermore, the complexity and virtualization of supply chains, and the uncertainties inherent in the supply ecosystem, extend supply chain risk management beyond technological solutions and their implementation. Risk management requires NONTECHs. Making accurate and timely decisions and developing risk leadership are essential components of risk management. Risks cannot be managed without spreading and internalizing a risk culture throughout the company, that is, without communication. Furthermore, while senior management is ultimately responsible, every employee and stakeholder has a responsibility in risk management because "everyone is a risk manager!" Therefore, situational awareness and collaboration accelerate risk management performance by bringing it closer to its target level. People have a very limited tolerance for uncertainty. In fact, some cultures cannot tolerate uncertainty at all. It is leaders who guide them through uncertainty. In this way, the company can improve its supply chain resilience capabilities. To effectively manage risks and increase both the agility and resilience of the supply chain in a lean manner, people-focused skills are needed as much as technical proficiency. For these reasons, the four NOTECHs highlighted in the figure are included within the scope of supply chain risk management (see Fig. 7.1).

The four main categories are divided into two subcategories: two soft skills (collaboration/team & communication, leadership, and management)

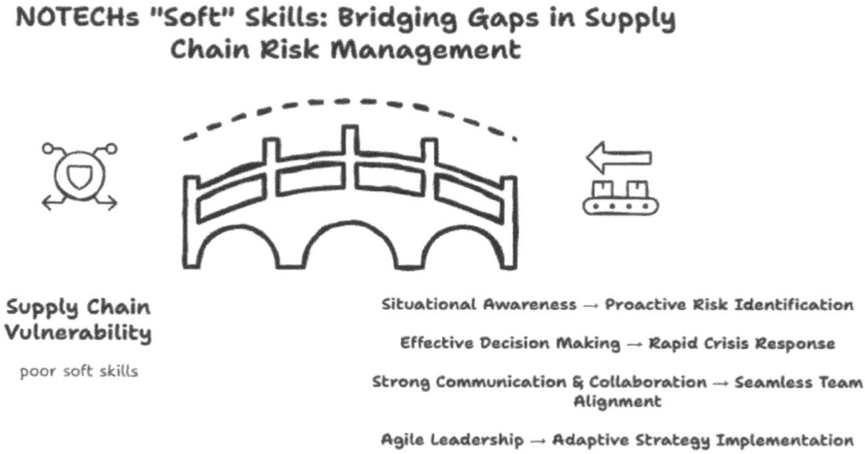

Fig. 7.1. NOTECH "soft" skills: Bridging gaps in supply chain risk management.

Source: The original design is by the authors; Napkin AI was used for visualization purposes only. https://app.napkin.ai/page/CgoiCHByb2Qtb251 EiwKBFBhZ2UaJDYwNThkNGZiLTY5 MzQtNDcz MC05Nzk2LWYzODE3MWM4ZDc1NQ.

and two cognitive skills (situational awareness and decision-making). For social skills, behaviors are generally seen to be in the form of communication that can be observed directly. Cognitive skills, on the other hand, are not directly observable since they do not occur directly in explicit behavior (Flin *et al.*, 2017).

In increasingly digitalized industries and supply chains shaped by AI, technological skills are considered a critical skill in safety risk management. Technological advancements play a significant role in the implementation and maintenance of safe and secure supply chain operations. Therefore, technological skills represent the human ability to use, manage, and maintain technological systems and equipment. Therefore, all supply chain stakeholders must develop their technological mastery and expertise in using technology in direct proportion to technological advancements. Otherwise, the gap between the digitalized and AI-influenced operating environment and the human factor will widen. This increase will reveal areas of vulnerability in the supply chain and risk management. Therefore, technological skills capacity must be developed in line with technological advancements. Therefore, risk management also encompasses the topic of technological skills capacity development.

7.2.1 *Situational Awareness*

Situational awareness (SA) can be described as "knowing what's happening in the environment". This is the first of the cognitive skills considered, with the other being decision-making. The system performs three functions: it gathers information, interprets it, and predicts future situations (Flin *et al.*, 2008). SA is widely regarded as a pivotal component of safety risk management, given its capacity to enhance awareness, thereby enabling individuals and organizations to discern and mitigate potential hazards and risks. Within the domain of aviation management, situational awareness is characterized by the capacity to discern and interpret prevailing circumstances and their ramifications, discern critical components of the environment pertaining to business and safety risks, and extrapolate the prevailing situation based on this information, in addition to anticipating future outcomes. SA in safety risk management is defined as a holistic understanding of the operating environment, the identification of hazards and opportunities, and the prediction of their potential consequences. Consequently, as SA is enhanced, the implementation of safety risk management will be optimized, thereby contributing to improved performance.

SA is a necessary ingredient of effective decision-making, influencing the understanding of current circumstances and situation, and the identification and selection of the most appropriate alternatives to manage or resolve the situation. From a safety risk management perspective, situational awareness refers to understanding circumstances, awareness of current and future business environment events, and an understanding of their implications for both the present and future. The process demands concentration, observation, interpretation (i.e. judgment), and awareness. For flight crews, for instance, the process of mastering a flight plan necessitates a comprehensive understanding of potential scenarios, the capacity to anticipate possible encounters, and maintaining situational awareness within prevailing circumstances. Consequently, SA is regarded as a pivotal component within the overarching framework of safety risk management and strategies. The ability to make sound decisions is associated with this.

SA is also a key factor in the decision-making process. Without awareness, accurate understanding, sound decision-making, and effective management are impossible. To maintain the highest level of AS, it is essential to clearly define and manage the factors influencing it (both positive and negative) in a supportive manner. SA is based on the principle that, in the face of technical skill requirements and complex structures in aviation, pilots can accurately assess situations and make appropriate decisions, thus enabling technical maintenance crews to make the right decisions to manage the situation and operations. SA should not be understood solely at a technical level; it should be integrated with managerial, social, environmental, and psychological disciplines. The implementation of awareness risk management is envisioned (Flouris *et al.*, 2019).

Increasing SA also supports good and effective decision-making because it increases people's readiness to focus their attention, identify areas of the work environment to pay particular attention to, and recognize changes and developments within those areas. In this regard, SA is recognized as a key skill area for safety risk management. It is important to note that each person's perceptions and the sources that influence them vary depending on a number of factors. These include their experience, demographic characteristics, education, and risk culture. Therefore, comprehensive strategies are developed, and integrated techniques are implemented to increase situational awareness across all employees. Furthermore, as is well known, SA is not merely a technical matter; it is both influenced by and influences people's psychological and sociological characteristics. The way in which people perceive and interpret events and processes, both on an individual basis and as part of a group, is influenced by their level of SA.

For example, in civil aviation, maintaining a high level of SA is one of the most critical and challenging aspects of a flight crew's job. SA can be regarded as an internalized mental model of the current state of the flight environment. This integrated picture forms the central organizing feature where all decision-making and action occur (Endsley, 1999). SA is a cognitive phenomenon that resides in the minds of human operators and is a fundamental truth that can be known. In order to achieve good SA, it is helpful to use expert or normative performance standards as a reference point (Nguyen *et al.*, 2019). The improvement of SA appears to be centered on two primary strategies: the design of the system interface to encourage improved sampling and reduce cognitive workload, and the implementation of SA training at the individual and team levels (Stanton *et al.*, 2001). SA involves perceiving critical factors in the environment (Level 1), understanding what these factors mean, particularly when combined with the flight crew's objectives (Level 2), and, at the highest level, understanding what will happen in the system in the near future (Level 3).

These higher SA levels enable pilots to function in a timely and effective manner (Endsley, 1999).

7.2.2 *Decision-Making*

"Decision-making" can be defined as the process of making a judgment or selecting an option. The process involves the following steps: first, the situation is assessed and the problem defined; second, one or more response options are generated and considered; third, a response option is selected and its consequences reviewed (Flin *et al.*, 2008).

Decision-making is an everyday occurrence within the supply chain. Decisions regarding the management of its stakeholders are made at every stage of the supply chain and in every managerial function. Making a decision invariably involves taking a risk. Taking a risk involves selecting from a range of options. In order to make the best choice, it is crucial to identify all the good and correct alternatives. When selecting from among options, the choice is made based on the objective, in accordance with the risk management philosophy. If a risk is deemed necessary to achieve the goal, a decision is made to take it; otherwise, a decision is made not to take the risk. Making a choice means rejecting all other possible options for that task or situation. Indeed, a high level of SA is paramount to making an informed decision.

Decision-making is also fundamental to information processing. Decision-making is the process of selecting a course of action from a set of alternative options. It typically involves (a) multiple competing options, (b) a certain amount of information, (c) a certain timeframe, and (d) a certain level of uncertainty (Carroll, 2023).

7.2.3 *Communication and Collaboration/Team Skills*

"Communication" is a word we use frequently in everyday conversation, but our ability to communicate effectively is open to discussion. Achieving effective communication is one of the most challenging aspects of any business. It is imperative to investigate whether people who speak the same language or work in the same place communicate effectively with each other.

In today's complex, noisy, and fast-paced digital environment, people may not be willing to listen to each other, or if they do, their understanding may differ due to differing cultures and values. It has been noted that messages conveyed in the field of communication cannot be delivered verbatim to the recipient; they will inevitably change as they travel from sender to receiver and will be influenced by both the recipient and the environment.

Effective communication involves multifaceted skills such as active listening, sensitive expression, and the ability to adapt communication to different audiences. In project management, a project manager who can communicate clearly and concisely prevents misunderstandings and ensures that all team members remain fully aligned on the project's objectives. This operational clarity is the first line of defense in preventing costly mistakes. Communication skills encompass both speaking and listening; this means being able to express thoughts clearly and concisely while also understanding the opinions and feelings of others. For example, a project manager who is a good communicator can clearly define the client's expectations and ensure the team receives all necessary information (Munich Business School, 2024).

Communication skills include the ability to present and defend opinions and the results of one's work, both orally and in writing, and in formal and informal settings. They also include the ability to locate, obtain, organize, and use information from print, human, or electronic sources (Montano *et al.*, 2001). Effective communication plays a critical role in achieving goals, and it is especially crucial in high-stakes situations. Working in today's airspace is a profession of high responsibility, with human life and significant asset costs at stake on every flight. As with other complex human–machine systems, effective communication is essential for achieving goals, coordinating team members, and executing tasks harmoniously (Kanki *et al.*, 1995). The key components of communication are sending information clearly and concisely; incorporating context and intent when exchanging information; receiving information, especially by listening; and identifying and addressing barriers to communication (Montano *et al.*, 2001). There are many diverse stakeholders involved in the supply chain. In interactions among different stakeholders, communication is a multifaceted tool that serves various purposes (Fjeld *et al.*, 2018).

Being multifaceted is also an indicator of communication difficulties. "Speaking the same language" is a common expression in our lives. Communication styles vary from person to person, and the facial expressions, idioms, and emphasis used in communication across cultures are also different. A communication gesture or word that indicates sincerity in one culture may be considered rude or disrespectful in another.

Many people are now working from home, and numerous companies are using digital tools. With the rise of remote work and the proliferation of digital tools such as Slack, Teams, and WhatsApp, effective communication is a critical foundation for high-performing organizations. However, many managers fail to establish clear lines of communication, leading to burnout, poor onboarding, wasted time, and undermined productivity. For example, a manager might discover their detailed memo goes unread; an employee might miss a meeting because of a Slack reminder they rarely check; a CEO might delay approval of a six-page memo due to a lack of summary; or a leader might spend hours consolidating incompatible reports. These problems arise when communication lines are blurred. As the volume of written communication increases with the proliferation of AI-powered writing tools, establishing clear guidelines that prioritize readability and ensure readers can easily digest information becomes even more crucial (Rogers and Dorison, 2025).

Communication in aviation is vital to flight safety and security. Because communication serves many functions, it provides an effective indicator of crew performance. By listening to communications during a flight, many indicators can be obtained as to whether tasks are being performed according to normal procedures or whether any problems are occurring (Montano *et al.*, 2001).

Where there are people, every problem is solved through communication, and every communication problem or malfunction causes problems. In order for leaders and decision-makers to manage, they need to communicate with stakeholders in a healthy, continuous manner and using the right strategy. Communication skills play a critical role in achieving goals, and effective communication is of great importance, especially in high-risk situations. For example, working in air transportation, whether in an air traffic control tower, cabin, airport, or aircraft maintenance center, Maintenance, Repair, and Overhaul (MRO) is a field of work that requires high responsibility and has very low fault tolerance, as human life and costly assets are involved in accidents.

It is noteworthy that communication skills are inherent in all four categories in the NOTECHS system, and all of the behaviors listed include communication (Flin *et al.*, 2008). On the other hand, collaboration (or team skills) is when all team members combine their strengths and work together harmoniously to achieve a common goal, much like a marketing team developing a joint campaign. In a successful team project, everyone contributes their strengths and works together to achieve the goal. These skills include sharing information, a willingness to work together, and the ability to resolve conflict (Munich Business School, 2024).

Collaboration is the ability to work together with rhythm to achieve objectives, which needs establishing teams. Teamwork is defined as a "distinguishable set of two or more people who interact dynamically and adaptively towards a common and valued goal, objective or mission" and are based on the other NONTECHs (Hagström, 2023).

Teams need to be willing to adapt to each other and maintain a positive attitude to function well. Teamwork achieves success through shared effort, clear goals, and coordinated action, with each member having a specific role. Team breakdowns can lead to serious incidents due to role misunderstandings, poor coordination, disagreements, conflicting goals, and communication problems. Teams support one another, resolve conflicts and exchange information, and coordinate activities to perform well. This requires four key inputs (NSW Government Trade & Investment, 2011):

i. individual inputs (individual contributions, how well strategies fit the task, and the knowledge and skills applied),
ii. leadership inputs (leadership style, knowledge and skills, and personality),
iii. organizational work task and environmental inputs (task design, availability of information, resources, rewards, management style, and culture),
iv. team structure inputs (team size, actual roles and responsibilities, status of each team member, balance of personality types, and team unity).

In most productions in industries, employees work in teams. Maintenance in aviation is done by teams. In the health sector, work is carried out by surgical teams, that is, health teams. In the education, tourism, and automotive sectors, many jobs that come to mind that require teamwork. The key to achieving teamwork is communication. The leader impresses employees with his oratory and communication skills, and he guides and inspires them in line with goals. Life is based on communication. In the supply chain, the quality of communication between stakeholders is proportional to the performance of the chain. Motivation in human resources management and communication success in performance management are decisive.

Supply chains require collaboration and teamwork from stakeholders. The basis of establishing and maintaining this cooperation is communication.

7.2.4 *Leadership*

Other NONTECHs will be effective in approaching goals through leadership. However, the leadership skills of individuals themselves are also important in this regard.

Leadership is one of the most important and influential concepts in human history. Definitions of leaders, including the different types of leadership, are diverse. While definitions share a common foundation, the qualities emphasized differ.

One notable definition is that offered by Bennis (1989), for example, who defines leadership as a guide in the process of formulating a vision, implementing ideas, and achieving set goals. In this context, a leader must possess the ability to influence and inspire those around them toward the desired goal (Bennis, 1989).

Jaques *et al.* (1994) define leadership as a process that guides a group of individuals and employees with high efficiency and commitment to the set goal. This definition emphasizes the role of the leader in bringing the team to the goal. While leadership is primarily important for team leaders, other team members must also possess both leadership and follower skills. Team leaders perform essential tasks such as setting a vision, providing direction, establishing working conditions, building and maintaining a team, and supporting it to achieve success. An effective leader must be able to utilize a variety of leadership styles, such as delegating, consultative, democratic, or directive, to suit different situations, as no single style is effective in all situations. In emergencies, the team leader may assume the role of "commander", which requires management under stressful circumstances. Leadership competence can be developed through training, guided feedback, and assessment of personal experiences (Flin *et al.*, 2008).

Leadership is a multifaceted concept that encompasses various attributes, behaviors, and skills. At its core, leadership is about influencing others, guiding teams, and driving organizational success. Risk leaders also lead human behavior and their motivation. The psychology of leadership offers valuable insights into what makes a good leader. By understanding and cultivating key characteristics such as self-awareness, emotional intelligence, effective communication, vision, adaptability, integrity, and empowerment, individuals can enhance their leadership effectiveness (London of School of Business, 2025). Leadership concepts include meaning that having leaders possess other NONTECHs, and it should be. It requires a variety of qualities in leaders, such as strong communication skills, emotional intelligence, adaptability, and decisiveness (Anyanugo *et al.*, 2024) so that they can lead.

Good, clear communication is a leadership hallmark. Some fundamental tools for effective communication include defining and articulating long-term goals; listening to and understanding stakeholders; creating openings for dialogue; and communicating proactively. Furthermore, in times of uncertainty, these elements are important for risk leaders who are crisis communicators: giving people what they need, when they need it; communicating clearly, simply, and frequently; choosing candor over charisma; revitalizing a spirit of resilience; distilling meaning from chaos; and supporting people, teams, and organizations to build the capability for self-sufficiency (McKinsey, 2024).

Effective leaders can create empowering organizational cultures that produce successful long-term outcomes (Sasikala and Kumari, 2023). Leadership styles should align with organizational culture and values to create a positive workplace environment and improve overall performance (Gomathy, 2023). A high-risk industry, such as aviation, is exposed to risk every day, and as such, its employees are also exposed to aviation risks from the moment they begin their jobs. Moreover, safety is costly and difficult to achieve without the input of all employees and leadership. Aviation safety is closely related to leadership styles. The transformational leadership style has a higher safety climate score compared to transactional and unleashing leadership styles. However, some leadership factors, especially passive management and laissez-faire approaches, reduce the level of safety (Bastola, 2020).

Today, capacity building of leaders has been a situational issue, and all leaders need to build their capacity of their digital skills to act as "digital leaders". Digital leadership must be able to utilize digital environments, communicate through these platforms and tools, manage risk, leverage these tools for motivation, and share leadership using digital platforms and tools. Leaders should always be flexible and open to innovation. They should be able to use "digital transformation" as an enabling and supportive tool and environment to be faster, more agile, more impressive, and more inspiring.

AI and digital transformation also affect and improve leadership. We say "developing" because leaders develop their capacities by meeting existing leadership qualities with digital skills. Since digital transformation eliminates the boundaries of time and space, leaders are also more agile, faster, more accurate, and more diverse—that is, they need to diversify and increase their talents and skills so that they can seize the day and be ready for tomorrow.

Leaders need to be able to perform their oratory skills in face-to-face conversations with the same effectiveness on digital platforms and environments, develop their competencies in using digital instruments, and manage digital and AI-related risks while developing strategies. Supply chains are also digitalizing, and even virtual supply chain applications are becoming widespread. A leader must have high maneuverability, flexibility, and the ability to adapt to new variables according to the dynamics of the environment and to know how to benefit from digital technologies and even artificial intelligence in decision-making.

AI is significantly transforming leadership practices and organizational dynamics in several ways. AI technologies are reshaping traditional leadership paradigms, fostering more adaptive, data-driven, and personalized approaches to leading teams and organizations (Madanchian *et al.*, 2024). In this new era, it's important for leaders to focus on their unique strengths, such as strategic thinking and emotional intelligence. AI should be used as a tool to support these strengths and empower leaders to achieve more efficient outcomes (Brown, 2024). In this way, leaders can manage more effectively by using both technology and human talent together. AI supports leaders by providing data-driven decision-making, operational efficiency, and insights. It saves time by automating routine tasks, allowing for a focus on human creativity. AI also reduces biases, promoting inclusivity and diversity within teams. Leaders need to develop their AI skills to prepare their teams for the future. When used responsibly, AI offers innovative solutions to leaders and their teams, giving them the opportunity to achieve higher levels of success in the business world (Khatri, 2023). AI systems can significantly improve decision-making processes by providing data-driven insights and analytical capabilities (Bao *et al.*, 2023; Li *et al.*, 2025). AI can assist with tasks such as resume screening, marketing decisions, and product design (Cai *et al.*, 2024; Pathirannehelage *et al.*, 2024).

However, the application of AI in leadership roles raises important considerations. While AI can process vast amounts of data and generate recommendations, human leaders still play a crucial role in interpreting these insights, considering ethical implications, and making final decisions (Smith and Green, 2018).

Advances in AI are expanding the scope of leadership into exciting new areas. But these advances also create some very real risks. The main one is "cognitive laziness". This means that it's easy to find information and ideas, but it can make it difficult to think in a critical way, to learn, to make judgments, and to be creative. As AI becomes smarter and capable of thinking like a human, people will find it less necessary to develop their own thinking skills. Another risk is the bias multiplier. AI systems often have built-in biases that are hidden from users. If leaders are unaware of these biases and accept AI-generated decisions without question, it becomes impossible to protect their employees and customers from them. Finally, there is the danger that AI could trap leaders in an echo chamber; systems could restrict access to different points of view by presenting content tailored to what leaders want to see and hear. This could have a negative effect on leaders' ability to develop themselves and make decisions that are more inclusive (Potential Project, 2024).

The relationship between AI and leadership is complex and involves decision-making processes, ethical issues, and the development of leadership competencies. AI technologies are increasingly integrated into organizational structures due to their impact on leadership decision-making, particularly in the business world. For example, one study highlights the use of AI in decision-making across various leadership styles and its importance in improving leadership effectiveness within organizations in Pakistan. This integration allows leaders to leverage AI's analytical capabilities, improving the quality and speed of their decisions. Furthermore, AI applications such as artificial neural networks (ANNs) serve as valuable tools for managerial decision support systems, streamlining information flow and improving management performance. These technologies not only aid in decision-making but also serve as information sources that leaders can use to enhance their strategic capabilities. AI's ability to process big data allows leaders to make informed decisions aligned with organizational goals, contributing to a more effective leadership environment (Walczak, 2016). AI can enhance self-awareness among leaders, improving their ability to adapt and respond to dynamic organizational environments (Mansour *et al.*, 2019).

Digitalization in aviation has integrated technologies such as artificial intelligence, machine learning (ML), digital twins, and advanced communication systems. These innovations have not only improved operational efficiency but also played a significant role in developing safety procedures and reducing human error. In aircraft design and manufacturing, digital twins are used for virtual assembly and assembly estimation, allowing engineers to optimize complex aerospace structures. The technology is also driving technological innovation in aerospace manufacturing by supporting the development of reusable spacecraft and smart rockets (Wang *et al.*, 2022). Digital twins are used in the power distribution systems of civil aircraft, facilitating real-time monitoring, fault detection, and health management (Liu *et al.*, 2023). The use of AI in modern applications related to aircraft operations, aircraft maintenance, and engine maintenance improves fuel efficiency, reduces emissions, improves dispatch and airline crew effectiveness, and prevents maintenance issues on aircraft and engines (Pilon, 2024). For example, Air France will use "Sky Breathe" technology, which employs "Big Data Algorithms, Artificial Intelligence and Machine Learning" to analyze "billions of data records" from flights (Caswell, 2020). However, although AI-powered systems in crisis management strengthen leaders' decision-making processes, human intuition, experience, and ethical responsibility remain critical in situations full of uncertainties due to the nature of aviation. Therefore, while technology optimizes leaders' decisions, the human factor still remains an indispensable component.

Automated systems, AI-powered analysis, and the use of big data make it possible to create safer and more efficient processes by minimizing human errors. In the aviation industry, thanks to digitalization, error rates have decreased in many areas, from flight planning to maintenance processes (Schneider *et al.*, 2013; Humza, 2023), while decision support systems provide more accurate and timely information to pilots and air traffic controllers (Airbus, 2020; NASA, 2021; EASA, 2020).

Advanced simulations and virtual training technologies reduce operational risks and ensure better preparation of personnel (CAELUM, 2020), while the Internet of Things (IoT) and sensor technologies prevent potential accidents by detecting equipment failures in advance (NexusIntegra, 2022; Sarma, 2018). Despite all these technological advancements, the importance of the human factor persists. In crisis situations, unexpected variables, emotional intelligence, intuition, and ethical decision-making play a critical role. Therefore, while AI systems may strengthen leaders' decisions, human leadership remains indispensable for the accountability and viability of final decisions.

The incorporation of AI into decision-making processes has led to mixed perceptions of fairness. In some cases, applicants view AI-based resume screening as less fair than human screening (Cai *et al.*, 2024). Additionally, the use of AI in courtrooms has raised concerns about the right to a fair trial, with AI assistants being preferred over fully autonomous "robot judges" (Ulenaers, 2020). These findings underscore the importance of maintaining human involvement in critical decision-making processes. Despite the advantages AI offers, human leadership remains critical, especially in unexpected crises. The Air France Flight 447 crash in 2009 demonstrated the dangers of overreliance on automation systems and the weakening of pilots' manual response capabilities. Furthermore, the trend known as automation bias can cause people to overtrust the recommendations of automated systems and neglect their own evaluations (Harford, 2024).

Today's technology and AI cannot completely replace human leaders. While this is debatable for the future, the human role will always remain unique. AI excels at analyzing big data, quickly evaluating scenarios, and ranking options. However, in situations such as crisis management, where uncertainty is high, immediate decisions are required, and human-centric elements like ethics and emotional intelligence come into play, the role of the leader remains indispensable. For example, in the 2009 Hudson River ditching incident, "Sully" Sullenberger's flight computer recommended returning the flight to the airport. However, the captain quickly assessed the situation, made a "manual decision" and successfully landed the plane in the water. Today's AIs cannot yet make such decisions with ethical and intuitive layers.

Critical decisions such as managing a crisis during a disaster, controlling and guiding individuals who have gone astray, calming crowds during a stampede, or saving lives are based not only on technical knowledge, digital tools, or AI but also on conscientious responsibility and ethical reasoning, caring about humanity, and a belief in the primacy of human life. While AI provides clear results by working with past or provided data and performing powerful analyses through rapid, complete coding, the ability to manage uncertainties and generate creative solutions in previously difficult scenarios remains uniquely human.

Trust is one of the most crucial issues for people and stakeholders. In panicked, difficult, and disruptive situations, what people most need is a person or people they can trust. For example, instilling confidence in passengers and crew during a crisis, controlling panic, and managing morale still require entirely human skills. Therefore, no matter how advanced technology becomes, we believe that elements such as ethics, intuition, and leadership will remain the most critical and indispensable elements of the human factor in any system. In conclusion, while AI-powered decision-makers could significantly enhance human leadership capabilities, it is unlikely that human leaders will be completely replaced in the near future. The most effective approach appears to be a synergy between human leaders and AI systems, where AI provides valuable insights and support, while human judgment, ethical considerations, and interpersonal skills remain essential. As AI technologies continue to evolve, organizations will need to carefully consider how to integrate these tools while preserving the critical human elements of leadership. AI can support efficiency in supply chains and operational processes, increase speed, and strengthen decision-making processes for managerial functions. Therefore, from our perspective, the most appropriate and effective approach is a secure and flexible collaboration model where humans and AI complement and support each other. AI accelerates decisions and reduces the risk of error, but ultimately, it is humans who make and implement those decisions.

The introduction of AI and ML in existing factories can provide significant benefits, including increased efficiency, reduced costs, and improved product quality. AI can be used for predictive maintenance, quality control, and supply chain optimization, while machine learning can also be used for security purposes such as anomaly detection, user authentication, and intrusion detection (Meena *et al.*, 2023). Businesses must leverage AI to process and analyze large datasets; this enables them to identify subtle trends and emerging risks that traditional methods might miss. This proactive approach to risk management is crucial for staying ahead of potential disruptions and ensuring business agility (Kalogiannidis *et al.*, 2024). While natural language processing (NLP) has little impact on business continuity, it significantly speeds up the risk assessment process, allowing for faster and more accurate detection of potential threats. By incorporating NLP into their risk assessment frameworks, businesses can use it to rapidly process vast amounts of unstructured data. As a result of this automation, risk assessments become more streamlined and reliable, increasing productivity and reducing the likelihood of human error (Kalogiannidis *et al.*, 2024).

Alongside AI, other digital technologies, such as blockchain technology, are significantly improving supply chain transparency, traceability, and security. By providing immutable record-keeping, smart contracts, and real-time visibility into product movements, blockchain is making a significant difference in reducing the risk of fraud and counterfeit goods by increasing trust and accountability among supply chain partners (Naveena *et al.*, 2024).

AI is becoming increasingly integrated into supply chain management, creating a paradigm shift in how businesses optimize their operations. With the ever-increasing complexity of global supply chains, traditional methods often struggle to adapt to the dynamic demands of the market. However, AI-driven solutions offer a transformative approach to addressing these challenges (Naveena *et al.*, 2024). The COVID-19 pandemic has highlighted significant vulnerabilities in global supply chains, increasing the importance of adaptive risk management strategies. In this process, the integration of AI stands out as a critical solution for making supply chains more resilient to future shocks. AI-powered demand forecasting algorithms produce more accurate forecasts by analyzing historical data and external factors, while inventory management optimization algorithms prevent excess inventory and stockouts by dynamically adjusting stock levels. Furthermore, AI-based route optimization improves delivery processes by reducing transportation costs. Thus, AI increases supply chain efficiency, contributing to the creation of faster and more resilient systems against disruptions (Bidin *et al.*, 2024). All these examples indicate that when NONTECHs are combined with digital technology, optimization can be approached, that is, risks can be managed through timely and appropriate strategies in line with supply chain goals.

AI facilitates better decision-making in supply chain planning by considering various constraints, risks, and opportunities in real time. By simulating different scenarios and assessing potential risks, AI-powered planning tools help companies optimize resource allocation, reduce lead times, and increase overall supply chain agility. In addition to AI, robotics and automation technologies transform warehouse operations, enabling companies to increase efficiency, accuracy, and productivity. Automated storage and retrieval systems (AS/RS), robotic arms, and automated guided vehicles (AGVs) reduce labor costs and cycle times by optimizing inventory management, order picking, and packaging processes (Naveena *et al.*, 2024).

AI technologies enable organizations to assess supplier performance, identify potential risks, and optimize supplier selection and contract management processes. AI-powered risk management systems analyze various data sources, including historical performance data, market trends, and geopolitical events, to identify and assess potential risks across the supply chain. Predictive analytics algorithms can forecast the likelihood and impact of various risk scenarios, enabling organizations to prioritize risk mitigation efforts and allocate resources effectively (Bidin *et al.*, 2024).

Senior managers have traditionally prioritized technical skills (hard skills), often treating non-technical competency development programs as a "cost", leading to program budget constraints. However, these expenditures on NONTECHs should be perceived as an "investment" because when managers view an activity as an investment, they are more willing to maintain, increase, and expand the budget. This strategic investment perspective, ironically, maximizes the corporate value of NONTECHs, which, as managers themselves recognize, makes organizations more sustainable, more innovative, and more appreciated by their corporate cultures (Phillips *et al.*, 2020).

The supply chain ecosystem requires NONTECHs at least as much as technical skills. NONTECHs are key to risk management, and they are difficult to imitate; they are core competencies, but they can be developed and learned. However, the application of each skill is unique to each individual. Each writer on our team is excellent, but their style is inimitable. Companies also have their own unique applications of NONTECHs, giving them competitiveness and agility. As technical skills and technology become commonplace, the key differentiators are increasingly NONTECHs. Such capabilities, which also emphasize human characteristics, should be viewed as opportunities to break free from routine. The more capacity is developed in NONTECHs, the more people and, therefore, supply chains become solution-oriented, creative, resilient, and agile. These are the characteristics that support the creation of a sustainable supply chain. As NONTECHs become more advanced, the cost of errors will decrease, opportunities will emerge, and a healthy work environment can be created in this complex and multifaceted environment.

References

Airbus. (2020). Autonomous flight technologies: The future of aviation. Airbus.

Anyanugo, M. O., Ololube, N. P., and Okuru, C. L. (2024). Establishing the basis for organizational success through effective leadership. *South Asian Research Journal of Humanities and Social Sciences*, 6(04), 156–169. https://doi.org/10.36346/sarjhss.2024.v06i04.003.

Bao, Y., Gong, W., and Yang, K. (2023). A literature review of human–AI synergy in decision making: From the perspective of affordance actualization theory. *Systems*, 11(9), 442. https://doi.org/10.3390/systems11090442.

Bastola, D. P. (2020). The relationship between leadership styles and aviation safety: A study of aviation industry. *Journal of Air Transport Studies*, 11(1), 71–102. https://doi.org/10.38008/jats.v11i1.155.

Bennis, W. (1989). *On Becoming A Leader.* New York, NY: Basic Books.

Bidin, M. F., Espinosa-Jaramillo, M. T., Martínez, D. C., Hashim, N. A., Chauhan, D. S., and Karmode, S. (2024). Adaptive supply chain risk management using AI mitigating disruptions and enhancing resilience in the post-pandemic era. *Tuijin Jishu/Journal of Propulsion Technology*, 45(2), 2655–2664. https://doi.org/10.52783/tjjpt.v45.i02.6294.

Brown, A. (2024, April 18). The impact of AI on the past, present, and future of leadership - Part 1. Oxford Group. https://www.oxford-group.com/insights/the-impact-of-ai-on-leadership/.

CAELUM. (2020). AI in pilot training and simulation. CAELUM Aviation Systems.

Cai, F., Zhang, J., and Zhang, L. (2024). The impact of artificial intelligence replacing humans in making human resource management decisions on fairness: A case of resume screening. *Sustainability*, 16(9), 3840. https://doi.org/10.3390/su16093840.

Carroll, M. (2023). Decision making in aviation. In *Human Factors in Aviation and Aerospace*. (pp. 563–588). San Diego, CA: Academic Press.

Caswell, M. (2020). Business traveller. Business Traveller. https://www.businesstraveller.com/business-travel/2020/07/15/air-france-to-use-artificial-intelligence-to-reduce-co2-emissions/#:~:text=Air%20France%20has%20announced%20a,50%20per%20cent%20by%202030.

EASA. (2020). Artificial intelligence roadmap: A human-centric approach to AI in aviation. EASA.

Endsley, M. R. (1999). Situation awareness in aviation systems. In Wise, J. A., Hopkin, V. D., and Garland, D. J. (eds.), *Handbook of Aviation Human Factors* (pp. 257–276). Boca Raton, FL: CRC Press.

Fjeld, G. P., Tvedt, S. D., and Oltedal, H. (2018). Bridge officers' non-technical skills: A literature review. *WMU Journal of Maritime Affairs*, 17, 475–495.

Flin, R., O'Connor, P., and Crichton, M. (2008). *Safety at the Sharp End a Guide to Non-Technical Skills.* Boca Raton, FL: CRC Press.

Gomathy, C. (2023). The effect of leadership on organisational behaviour. *International Journal of Scientific Research in Engineering and Management (IJSREM)*, 7(5), 1–8.

Hagström, C. (2023). Non-technical skills and how it may influence the prehospital care, a qualitative study in Swedish ambulance care. Degree project in nursing care, 15 högskolepoäng. Malmö University: Faculty of Health and Society, Department of nursing, 2023. https://www.diva-portal.org/smash/get/diva2:1727757/FULLTEXT02.

Harford, T. (2024). Financial Times. https://www.ft.com/content/2a3e05a3-c50c-4193-8a3d-4fac79183b22?utm_source=chatgpt.com.

Humza, M. (2023). Optimizing passenger experience: A technological preference analysis in turkish airports. *International Journal of Business Ecosystem and Strategy*, 5(4), 1–20. https://doi.org/10.36096/ijbes.v5i4.460.

Jaques, E., Clement, S. D., and Lessem, R. (1994). *Executive Leadership: A Practical Guide to Managing Complexity.* Oxford, UK: Blackwell.

Kalogiannidis, S., Kalfas, D., Papaevangelou, O., Giannarakis, G., and Chatzitheodoridis, F. (2024). The role of artificial intelligence technology in predictive risk assessment for business continuity: A case study of Greece. *Risks*, 12(2), 19. https://doi.org/10.3390/risks12020019.

Kanki, B. G., Helmreich, R. L., and Anca, J. (1995). *Crew Resource Management.* San Diego, CA: Academic Press.

Khatri, R. (2023, July 22). The impact of artificial intelligence on leadership. Open Growth. https://www.blogs.opengrowth.com/the-impact-of-artificial-intelligence-on-leadership.

Lewis, R., Strachan, A., and Smith, M. M. (2012). Is high fidelity simulation the most effective method for the development of non-technical skills in nursing? A review of the current evidence. *The Open Nursing Journal*, 6, 82–89. https://doi.org/10.2174/1874434601206010082.

Li, Z., Zhu, H., Lu, Z., Xiao, Z., and Yin, M. (2025). From text to trust: Empowering AI-assisted decision making with adaptive LLM-powered analysis. In *Human Factors in Computing System,* Yokohama, Japan. https://doi.org/10.48550/arxiv.2502.11919.

Liu, W., Li, X., Shen, Z., and Ma, C. (2023). A digital twin method for civil aircraft power distribution system based on Unity3D and Simulink. *Journal of Physics: Conference Series*, 2615, 012017. https://doi.org/10.1088/1742-6596/2615/1/012017.

London of School of Business. (2025, September 28). The phsycology of leadership: Understanding what makes a good leader. https://londonsba.org.uk/blog/the-psychology-of-leadership-understanding-what-makes-a-good-leader/#:~:text=Leadership%20is%20a%20multifaceted%20concept,teams%2C%20and%20driving%20organisational%20success.

Madanchian, M., Taherdoost, H., Vincenti, M., and Mohamed, N. (2024). Transforming leadership practices through artificial intelligence. *Procedia Computer Science*, 235, 2101–2111. https://doi.org/10.1016/j.procs.2024.04.199.

Mansour, N., Rafeh, W., Afram, G., and Zaatari, G. (2019). The role of self-awareness, augmented artificial intelligence and enhanced leadership competencies in developing future academic physicians. *Middle East Journal of Family Medicine*, 24(5), 605–628.

McKinsey. (2024). https://www.mckinsey.com/featured-insights/mckinsey-explainers/what-is-leadership#/.

Meena, R., Ravi, and Madan, P. A. (2023). Using AI for predictive maintenance in CAM. *International Journal of Research Publication and Reviews*, 4(4), 5712–5722.

Montano, J. L., Donoso, J. A., Hassall, T., and Joyce, J. (2001). Vocational skills in the accounting professional profile: The Chartered Institute of Management Accountants (CIMA) employers' opinion. *Accounting Education: An International Journal*, 10(3), 299–313. http://dx.doi.org/10.1080/09639280210122339.

Munich Business School. (2024). Soft skills. Business Studies Dictionary. https://www.munich-business-school.de/en/l/business-studies-dictionary/soft-skills.

Naveena, M., Ellaturu, N., Kumari, T. L., and Rajalakshmi, M. (2024). AI-driven solutions for supply chain management. *Journal of Informatics Education and Research*, 4(2), 861–868. https://doi.org/10.52783/jier.v4i2.849.

NASA. (2021). AI in air traffic management: Enhancing flight safety and efficiency. NASA.

NexusIntegra. (2022, April 11). *Akıllı Havalimanları, havalimanlarının dijital dönüşümü*. NexusIntegra. https://nexusintegra-io.translate.goog/smart-airports-the-digital-transformation-of-airports/?_x_tr_sl=en&_x_tr_tl=tr&_x_tr_hl=tr&_x_tr_pto=wa.

Nguyen, T., Lim, C. P., Nguyen, N. D., Gordon-Brown, L., and Nahavandi, S. (2019). A review of situation awareness assessment approaches in aviation environments. *IEEE Systems Journal*, 13(3), 3590–3603.

NSW Government Trade & Investment. (2011). March 2011 – Factsheet 9 Black Diamond Training. ANTS Factsheet No. 9: Teamwork. ANTS. https://courses.blackdiamondtraining.com.au/sites/all/resources/ANTS/ANTS-factsheet-No-9-Teamwork.pdf; www.nswminesafety.com.au.

Pathirannehelage, S. H., Shrestha, Y. R., and Krogh, G. V. (2024). Design principles for artificial intelligence-augmented decision making: An action designresearch study. *European Journal of Information Systems*, 34(3), 207–229. https://doi.org/10.1080/0960085X.2024.2330402.

Phillips, P. P., Phillips, J. J., and Ray, R. (2020). *Proving the Value of Soft Skills: Measuring Impact and Calculating ROI*. Association for Talent Development (ATD), The United States of America.

Pilon, R. V. (2024). *Artificial Intelligence in Commercial Aviation*. New York, NY: Routledge.

Potential Project. (2024, November 18). AI is becoming more human. So, why aren't we? Potential Project. https://cdn.prod.website-files.com/5ff86e09616 5bce79acc825c/66e197c7b27e514c8ae81370_Potential%20Project-Human%20Leader%20Report-Vol8.pdf.

Rogers, T. and Dorison, C. (2025, September 25). It's time to strengthen our communication at work, communication. Harvard Business Review Turkey. https://hbrturkiye.com/blog/isteki-iletisimimizi-guclendirmenin-vakti-geldi?utm_source=dengage&utm_medium=email&utm_campaign=BLOG_290925&dn_channel=email&dn_send_id=733.

Royal College of Surgeons of Edinburgh. (2019). The non-technical skills for surgeons (NOTSS) system handbook v2.0. Structuring observation, feedback and rating of surgeons' behaviours in the operating theatre. Royal College of Surgeons of Edinburgh: rcsed.ac.uk. https://www.rcsed.ac.uk/media/ypmnkyhn/notss-handbook.pdf.

Sarma, G. (2018, July 13). *Akıllı Havalimanı*. Lojistik Kulübü. https://www.lojistikkulubu.ist/akilli-havalimani/.

Sasikala, B. and Kumari, S. V. (2023). A study on workers effectiveness and business performance with reference to leadership style and their influence. *Tuijin Jishu/Journal of Propulsion Technology*, 44(4), 5738–5742. https://doi.org/10.52783/tjjpt.v44.i4.1977.

Schneider, S., Spieth, P., and Clauss, T. (2013). Business model innovation in the aviation industry. *International Journal of Product Development*, 18(3), 286–310. https://doi.org/10.1504/ijpd.2013.055010.

Smith, A. M. and Green, M. (2018). Artificial intelligence and the role of leadership. *Journal of Leadership Studies*, 12(4), 85–87. https://doi.org/10.1002/jls.21605.

Stanton, N., Chambers, P., and Piggott, J. (2001). Situational awareness and safety. *Safety Science*, 39, 189–204.

Ulenaers, J. (2020). The impact of artificial intelligence on the right to a fair trial: Towards a robot judge? *Asian Journal of Law and Economics*, 11(2). http://doi.org/10.1515/ajle-2020-0008.

Walczak, S. (2016). Artificial neural networks and other AI applications for business management decision support. *International Journal of Sociotechnology and Knowledge Development (IJSKD)*, 8(4), 1–20. http://doi.org/10.4018/IJSKD.2016100101.

Wang, X., Bao, C., Sun, Z., and Wang, X. (2022). Research on the application of digital twin in aerospace manufacturing based on 3D point cloud. In *2022 International Conference on Electronics and Devices, Computational Science (ICEDCS)*. http://doi.org/10.1109/ICEDCS57360.2022.00076.

Chapter 8

Supply Chain Risks in Electric Vehicles and Sustainable Aviation Fuels: The Chains of the Green Future

From Raw Materials to Batteries & Sustainable Fuels…

8.1 Electrical Transformation

The electric vehicle (EV) market is growing at an accelerating pace, and this has begun to fundamentally transform not only consumer behavior but also global industrial infrastructure. Carbon neutrality targets, sustainability regulations, and energy efficiency policies are the primary drivers of this transformation. The automotive sector, moving away from internal combustion engines (ICEs), is redefining its energy sources, supply chains, investment priorities, and competitive landscape (Baban, 2025).

The EV transformation is progressing in tandem with "Automotive 2.0" processes such as autonomous driving and digitalization. While these processes contribute to reducing emissions and accidents, they require significant investments in advanced technology, data processing capacity, and software development. Billions of dollars in investments by automotive manufacturers (e.g. VW and GM) demonstrate the speed and scale of the transformation. Holistic, long-term, and responsible investor engagement is critical for managing environmental, social, and governance (ESG) risks and capitalizing on opportunities in the EV ecosystem (O'Connell, 2022). The automotive industry is undergoing a historic transformation from ICE vehicles to EVs. This transition is fundamentally changing not only vehicle technologies but also the supply chain ecosystem (Jagani *et al.*, 2024). This situation is a shock for traditionally automotive-based economies and suppliers, posing a significant risk of disruption for companies that manufacture key components such as exhausts, fuel systems, and transmissions. As new value creation shifts to battery production and the critical minerals required for batteries, the supply chain risk management (SCRM) framework is also being reshaped to address the needs for sustainable fuels (PwC, 2025).

The transition from traditional production resources to electric power and sustainable biofuels is fundamentally reshaping supply chain risk profiles. This shift mandates that risk management capabilities evolve to effectively handle the emerging "green" supply chain landscape. Changes in core resources immediately transform all associated functions, from storage and transport to safeguarding and final delivery. Ensuring the supply chain is agile, flexible, and resilient is crucial, especially considering the valuable energy sources and critical minerals involved (see Fig. 8.1).

Fig. 8.1. Supply chain risks in green transport.

Source: The original design is by the authors; Napkin AI was used for visualization purposes only. https://app.napkin.ai/page/CgoiCHByb2Qtb25lEiwKBFBhZ2UaJGZmNzBkN2RmLWQ3NjAtNDc4NS1hZDZkLTQ4NTk0NzJmOTJiMA.

EV production requires a complex and strategically important new ecosystem of components, far beyond simply an "electric" vehicle. This is forcing countries to restructure their industrial strategies, supply security approaches, and technology investments. Ten key components with high external dependencies play a particularly critical role. These components carry strategic value in terms of cost, technology, know-how, and R&D. Therefore, supply dependencies directly impact not only industrial policies but also geopolitical risks and critical raw material strategies (Baban, 2025):

- *battery cells and modules,*
- *battery management systems (BMS),*
- *inverter/converter systems,*
- *electric motors,*
- *power electronics modules,*
- *thermal management systems,*
- *electronic control units (ECUs),*
- *telematics and connectivity modules (TCUs),*
- *chargers and infrastructure systems,*
- *EV-specific tires.*

This retailoring and the components offered also indicate a structural transformation. EVs have completely changed our perception of the "car". Such a radical transformation poses a powerful risk, capable of creating a crisis. It affects manufacturers, suppliers, and customers—every stakeholder in the supply chain. This means that supply chains are being reshaped. Flexibility in the design of new supply chains and supply chain risk strategies is crucial for survival and adaptation in such a volatile environment. Furthermore, such a volatile environment means resilience and durability are essential. The potential vulnerabilities of next-generation supply chains must be thoroughly identified and managed. However, because technological transformation and human adaptation to digitalization are not keeping pace, a chasm, or gap, is emerging between humans, next-generation resources, and next-generation vehicles/fuels. Risks created by uncontrolled or poorly understood events cannot be fully identified and managed. Therefore, leaders and stakeholders need to develop their knowledge and analytical skills, albeit at different levels, in the areas of next-generation energy resources and supply chains.

The transition to EVs is driving radical supply chain changes in the automotive industry and raising significant ESG challenges. While EV engines require fewer parts, they use much heavier and more complex batteries. These batteries consume approximately six times more minerals and a wider variety of minerals than conventional vehicles. The increasing demand for copper, aluminum, cobalt, lithium, nickel, and rare earth elements, in particular, poses risks of environmental pollution, waste, and high emissions. Mineral extraction and processing are the most critical areas for responsible investors. However, risks are not limited to mining; responsible management and financing are required at all stages of the supply chain, including battery production, assembly, energy infrastructure, and vehicle manufacturing. Therefore, it is important for investors to foster sustainable practices by engaging in constructive dialogue with both companies and governments (O'Connell, 2022). The EV supply chain is characterized by different and more intense risks than the traditional automotive industry. This vulnerability stems largely from dependence on specific geographies and companies, financial volatility, and increasing regulatory burdens. EVs and batteries are heavily dependent on critical minerals (including lithium, cobalt, and nickel), which form the foundation of the modern economy and are used everywhere, from mobile phones to satellite technologies. This dependence on critical minerals underpins supply chain fragility (Blakemore and Engelke, 2025). Clean, green, or sustainable energy technology supply chains (including EVs) are typically more geographically concentrated than traditional energy sources such as oil and natural gas. Vulnerability arises from dependence on a single actor at critical stages of the supply chain, rather than from the physical absence of the resource (International Energy Agency, 2022).

The primary objectives of SCRM are to provide reasonable assurance of strategy achievement, establish and maintain an agile and resilient supply chain, identify, analyze, and prioritize risks, develop and implement risk management strategies, and monitor and report on these strategies. Furthermore, it should maintain multifaceted communication with stakeholders throughout the entire process. Achieving these risk management objectives requires identifying events that impact supply chain resilience and the resulting risk factors. For the lithium supply chain example, risk factors were identified as geopolitical dependencies (especially on China), excessive reliance on a single supplier, inadequate diversification, and supply chain bottlenecks. The strategies were developed as follows (He *et al.*, 2025):

i. *diversification strategy,*
ii. *sourcing from trusted countries,*
iii. *domestic market capacity,*
iv. *recycling.*

Minerals and metals are the fundamental elements that make today's modern economy possible. From cell phones and solar panels to satellites and semiconductors, mineral-based components are essential components of nearly all of today's technologies. Critical minerals range from high-volume commodities such as nickel and copper to niche elements such as tungsten, indium, lithium, and cobalt, as well as rare earths needed for permanent magnets and alloys. These minerals are transformed into usable precursors like chemicals or alloys through complex supply chains from the mines where they are mined to the final product. Numerous stakeholders, including private sector companies and government agencies, shape these supply chains based on market demand, profit margins, and national security concerns (Blakemore and Engelke, 2025). It is important to develop optimal strategies for risk management, taking into account these "shapers" so that the objectives can be achieved.

These strategies have been developed to make the lithium supply chain more resilient, which is crucial for electric vehicle batteries. Each strategy directly targets specific risk factors. Diversification reduces the vulnerability of over-reliance on a single source, while sourcing from reliable countries limits dependence on actors with high geopolitical risks, such as China. Domestic market capacity reduces the risk of production disruptions, while recycling provides additional protection against the risks of resource scarcity and price fluctuations. For example, GM experienced low supply chain resilience in 2022 because it met almost all of its lithium needs from a Chinese supplier. However, in 2023, it increased its resilience by shifting to purchasing refined lithium from South Korea and expanding battery assembly capacity in the US. In contrast, Tesla's supply chain is more complex and less transparent, with the majority of its lithium imports still coming from battery packs. Tesla is also striving to increase its strategic resilience through joint gigafactory investments with Panasonic and recycling projects with Redwood Materials (He *et al.*, 2025). The supply of critical minerals such as copper, lithium, nickel, cobalt, and rare earth elements will be particularly important. These critical minerals are essential for many clean energy technologies. The world's resources for these minerals are undoubtedly large enough to accommodate this increase, but production and processing for many of them are currently concentrated in a small number of countries, making supply vulnerable to political instability, geopolitical risks, and potential export restrictions (International Energy Agency, 2022).

It is important to understand that these risk factors can have a strategic impact on the company and the supply chain. This means that they should be considered when making important decisions. Strategic risks are increasing in the supply chains of developed countries for mineral resources essential to their economic prosperity and national security. This situation is further exacerbated by geopolitical pressures stemming from the dominance of some countries in global supply chains. Managing these risks necessitates investment incentives, the development of reliable partnerships, and the implementation of sensitive policies in a fragmented global trade environment. However, multifaceted factors such as mineral criticality, trade fragmentation, geopolitical uncertainties, and natural disasters make simple and uniform methods inadequate in risk mitigation strategies. Failure to consider these nuances risks further increasing developed countries' dependence on rival countries in their supply chains (Blakemore and Engelke, 2025). The automotive supply chain is vast and complex. The transition to electric vehicles, particularly due to the specific requirements for battery production and charging infrastructure, presents new investment risks and opportunities from an ESG perspective. As governments and companies strive to implement sustainable practices throughout the supply chain, investor engagement is yielding positive results. With increasing global investor interest in this area, sustainability performance across the automotive sector and its suppliers is expected to accelerate (O'Connell, 2022).

8.2 Industry Sample: Xiaomi

Supply Chain Strength in a New Market Entry: Xiaomi EV (Xiaomi, 2025; Tobin and Fu, 2025)

Modern supply chains are facing increasing risks to ESG. It is very important for companies to have a plan for how they will deal with these risks. Xiaomi manages the risks to its supply chain by using company management structures and strategies that address risk at every stage. It creates and puts into action general plans to reduce risks and make sure the company is following the rules. Xiaomi, a global technology leader, sees sustainability as important for business and the environment. Xiaomi is a leader in technology and electric vehicles. It is one of the best at managing its supply chain in a sustainable way. Xiaomi has a step-by-step plan, from choosing suppliers to checking and rewarding them, and it balances doing things the right way with looking after the environment and acting ethically.

The following case sample presents Xiaomi's multi-layered approach, spanning from Responsible Business Alliance (RBA) membership to red-line violations and responsible minerals traceability. This risk management system and practices are also considered a best practice sample of how Xiaomi builds supply chain resilience. This case is remarkable for demonstrating how Xiaomi secures its complex supply chain using corporate governance structures and full-cycle risk mitigation strategies.

8.2.1 *Corporate Structure and Commitment to Sustainability*

Xiaomi is committed to integrating sustainability principles such as labor rights, environmental protection, and ethics into its management to enhance supply chain resilience. To this end, it has established separate management structures (purchasing committees, operation centers, etc.) for its smartphone and EV businesses, and it has categorized its suppliers based on performance criteria. To ensure compliance with international standards, it joined the RBA in March 2025 and published a mandatory Supplier Social Responsibility Code of Conduct (Xiaomi, 2025).

8.2.2 *Full-Cycle Risk Mitigation Strategies*

This management structure is supported by comprehensive risk mitigation strategies that span the entire supplier lifecycle. During the selection and recruitment process, not only technical capacity but also potential risks such as geopolitical, financial, operational, and raw material shortages are holistically assessed, along with CSR performance. Suppliers with "red flag" violations such as child labor, forced labor, minimum wage violations, and occupational safety deficiencies are required to complete remediation prior to hiring. Management conducts comprehensive written and on-site audits covering Tier 1, key Tier 2, and selected Tier 3 suppliers, while unannounced spot checks are implemented in key processes to ensure production stability. A robust remediation mechanism is in place, providing remote and on-site support to quickly resolve any issues identified after the audit. Successful and environmentally responsible suppliers are rewarded and incentivized with annual performance evaluations (Xiaomi, 2025).

8.2.3 *Supply Chain Risk Strategies*

Consumer electronics giant Xiaomi's rapid and successful entry into the EV market was driven by the critical role of supply chain access when entering a new industry. This contrasts starkly with the challenges faced by tech giant Apple, which canceled its EV project despite spending $10 billion. While Apple failed to make progress in EV production despite nearly a decade of effort, Xiaomi launched its first EV model, the SU7, after just three years of development, and it set ambitious delivery targets in its first year. A key difference behind Xiaomi's success is its strategic leveraging of China's robust EV supply chain ecosystem. Rather than building its own supply chain from scratch, Xiaomi leveraged China's established manufacturing infrastructure and critical suppliers, which dominate the global EV market (Tobin and Fu, 2025):

- **Speed and cost-effectiveness:** Chinese companies specialize in EV component production. Thanks to this ready-made infrastructure, Xiaomi has accessed the necessary components quickly and cost-effectively.
- **Partnership with critical suppliers:** Xiaomi has established direct partnerships with key suppliers such as BYD and Contemporary Amperex Technology Company (CATL), the world's largest manufacturers of vehicle batteries.
- **Government support:** By integrating into an ecosystem that benefits from the Chinese government's multi-billion-dollar support for the EV sector, Xiaomi has leveraged supply chain control down to the minerals within the batteries.
- **Rapid manufacturing agility:** These advantages have enabled the company to rapidly begin manufacturing the SU7 in its own factory and bring new models to market much faster than traditional automakers.

"*Responsible Minerals*"

Xiaomi has a strict policy on responsible minerals. This means that it will not support companies that have been involved in human rights violations. 3TG strictly follows the OECD Due Diligence Guidance and RMI standards when sourcing minerals such as cobalt and mica. In this context, it checks that supply chains can be traced every year; it received a full response from Tier-1 and Tier-2 suppliers in 2024 (Xiaomi, 2025). This case underlines Xiaomi's brand strength in consumer electronics, as well as its strategic supply chain access, and it is preparing to rapidly enter the global automobile market (Tobin and Fu, 2025).

8.3 Industry Example 1: Agility and Vertical Integration in Tesla's EV Supply Chain Risk Management

Creating its own brand and ecosystem is one of the best risk management strategies, but it is a very difficult and expensive strategy that needs to be well thought out. Tesla, which has the only system that can eliminate supplier dependency, succeeds in supplier selection and eliminating the source of supplier-related risks. Let's discuss this in detail.

Tesla's rapid rise in the EV market owes its importance not only to its technological innovations but also to its unique resilience strategy in the face of global supply chain crises. While traditional automotive giants grappled with shocks such as the global semiconductor shortage or raw material price fluctuations in 2021, Tesla maintained production continuity and rapidly gained market share. This created significant risks to the supply of raw materials, particularly battery cells, semiconductors, and lithium/nickel, which are critical for EVs. The global COVID-19 pandemic and the 2021 chip crisis were key challenges that tested Tesla's supply chain (Scott, 2024). Tesla's approach is to position supply chain management (SCM) not as a mere support function but as a strategic cornerstone that enables the company's rapid growth and unparalleled flexibility (Adebola Oluwafunmilayo and Talabi, 2024). The basis of this strategic approach is to balance environmental sustainability, social responsibility, and economic benefits, along with cost and efficiency targets in SCM processes (Zheng, 2024).

A cornerstone of Tesla's supply chain strategy is vertical integration and complete control over critical EV components. The decision to manufacture battery cells in-house (via Gigafactories), the most critical and long-lasting component in the automotive industry, has largely protected the company from the risk of battery supply shortages. Similarly, developing its vehicle software in-house has given the company unparalleled agility. For example, during the chip crisis, unlike its competitors, Tesla was able to quickly rewrite its software to integrate alternative, more readily available chips into its vehicles, thus eliminating the risk of production shutdowns (Scott, 2024). This vertical model carries its own risks, as internal control over resources increases, and the impact of any internal bottleneck in battery assembly or on the assembly line escalates more rapidly and severely than in a traditional supply chain, as seen during the Model 3 "production hell" period (Lövenich, 2025). To support these operational advantages, Tesla effectively minimizes costs and optimizes resource allocation by using lean production methods and automation technology in its production processes (Zheng, 2024).

Despite its strong investment in vertical integration, Tesla maintains strategic partnerships with key suppliers to enhance the flexibility of its supply chain. This collaborative approach is particularly evident in its long-term partnership with Panasonic for battery production. This partnership has not only provided Tesla with a stable and reliable battery supply but has also succeeded in improving battery performance and significantly reducing costs through joint innovation efforts. This collaboration demonstrates that, even in its relationships with external suppliers, Tesla is not only cost-conscious but also focused on technological development and risk reduction (Adebola Oluwafunmilayo and Talabi, 2024). However, the prolonged supply delays experienced in the early years of its relationship with Panasonic (during the production ramp-up of the Model 3 in 2018), the company faced significant challenges, a period Elon Musk famously described as "production hell." This period, famously exemplified by the challenges in Tesla's history during the Model 3 mass production acceleration process, revealed that Tesla failed to adequately analyze the risk of persuading the supplier to establish a new production site (Gigafactory). This demonstrated the importance of a proven track record and reliable production infrastructure, rather than cost, in supplier selection (RiskWatch, 2019).

Another key strategy in risk management has been diversification and localization. By locating its production facilities (Gigafactories) close to key markets such as the US, China, and Germany, Tesla has minimized logistics costs, transit times, and the risk of geopolitical tensions. It has also committed to sourcing raw materials (such as lithium and nickel) from multiple sources, rather than relying on a single region (Scott, 2024). However, despite Tesla's global footprint and diversification efforts, its intensifying reliance on sourcing raw materials, particularly in the extraction of critical minerals like lithium and cobalt, and production volume in China, still makes the company vulnerable to geopolitical vulnerabilities such as trade tensions and regulatory changes. Tesla has extended its innovative approach in the supply chain to the distribution channel. By bypassing traditional dealership networks with its direct-to-consumer (DTC) sales model, it has both reduced costs and strengthened the alignment between demand and production. In this way, agility and efficiency were gained at the last stage of the supply chain by ensuring that the vehicle leaving production was delivered to the customer quickly. In this process, the so-called "production hell" experienced during the Model 3's mass production acceleration period clarified the risks associated with relying on excessive automation. This course led Tesla to rebalance automation and precise human oversight/labor in its processes, challenging it to combine technology with a more pragmatic and flexible approach to manufacturing (Lövenich, 2025).

Tesla has made technology and sustainability an integral part of risk management. The use of artificial intelligence (AI) and the Internet of Things (IoT) has enhanced the ability to make instantaneous decisions by improving demand forecasting and providing real-time visibility into the supply chain (Scott, 2024). AI, in particular, predicts market needs more accurately, allowing for dynamic production adjustments, while blockchain technology enhances transparency and traceability of ingredients in the supply chain, reducing the risk of fraud (Adebola Oluwafunmilayo and Talabi, 2024). In the field of sustainability, its investment in battery recycling facilities has created financial and operational resilience by reducing external dependence on critical minerals and increasing resource security in the long term (Scott, 2024). To embody these efforts, Tesla employs methods such as lifecycle assessment (LCA) to thoroughly measure environmental impact, use low-carbon materials, and actively promote a circular economy model by recycling used batteries (Zheng, 2024). This commitment is reflected in its logistics and labor supply chain operations. For example, with the "Giga Train" application launched at the Berlin Gigafactory, the electric train service provided free and environmentally friendly transportation to employees. This innovation not only supports environmental goals by reducing approximately 50 tons of CO_2 emissions per week but also indirectly improves the efficiency and delivery times of Tesla's logistics operations by alleviating regional traffic congestion (Hargreaves, 2024).

The most critical point we need to learn from Tesla is that a supply chain is not simply a cost. Supply chains serve as the strategic cornerstone of industrial success and resilience. Supply chains and the creation of the company's own production ecosystem are the most determining factors for the strategic superiority and sustainability of industries.

As can be seen from the above examples and other best practices, one of the best strategies for a supply chain is to create its own ecosystem. Of course, this requires significant resources and powerful support, such as government support. Developed countries have neglected the importance of creating a supply chain ecosystem and instead focused on cost reduction or profit. However, logistics is the most critical element of the supply chain. Sustainability-based strategies should be developed to manage risk factors related to both external and internal issues. However, a company's primary goal should be redefined not as financial profit but as sustainable profitability. It is valuable to develop risk management strategies and design applications to ensure sustainability under the most adverse conditions.

8.4 SAF as Sustainability Driver and Supply Chain Relations for Industries

SCM design involving sustainable aviation fuel (SAF) is a multi-dimensional, multi-risk, and multi-criteria decision-making problem. Supply chains face numerous and diverse risks. Changes to resources in areas such as fuel that directly impact operations create new risks. Furthermore, and more importantly, all risks have the potential to interact and/or conflict with each other. As risks increase and become more complex, management will require more advanced tools than traditional instruments or methods. In this respect, SCRM is a next-generation application. New-generation risk management and solutions are also needed for new-generation fuel risks.

Sustainable fuels are energy sources used to power vehicles and equipment that are produced and consumed in ways that minimize environmental impacts. These fuels, derived from renewable or low-carbon sources, are critical to meeting global decarbonization goals (DHL Group, 2025). Supply chains feature a managerial system whose strategy consists of a combination of operational, functional, and information management, which involves a large number and variety of stakeholders, starting from the supplier of the production resources necessary for the production of the product and service to the final consumer. Supply chain risk is the probability and consequences of events occurring at any stage of the entire chain (Supply Chain Risk Leadership Council, 2011).

Sustainable fuels offer an alternative to fossil fuels, enabling faster decarbonization of existing fleets, particularly in the transportation sector. While aviation and maritime transport are expected to play a significant role, passenger cars and commercial vehicles will increasingly shift to electrification. Sustainable fuels create a closed carbon cycle by releasing CO_2 previously absorbed during production into the air during combustion, resulting in no net increase in atmospheric CO_2 (DHL Group, 2025). The efficient configuration of supply chains is a current challenge for deploying SAF, a key element of the decarbonization of the aviation industry (Martinez-Valencia *et al.*, 2021).

The transportation sector has been one of the most resilient sectors to emission reductions to date due to its high dependence on fossil fuels and increasing demand. Due to its dependence on fossil fuels, the transportation sector is one of the most challenging areas for emission reductions and accounts for approximately 20% of the EU's greenhouse gas (GHG) emissions. The EU, aiming for an 80–95% reduction by 2050, sees the rapid deployment of alternative fuels as essential in the face of shrinking oil supplies. In this context, the European Commission is developing clean transportation systems and long-term fuel strategies. Because no single fuel can meet all transportation needs, the combined use of options such as electricity, hydrogen, biofuels, synthetic fuels, methane, and LPG is envisioned. The scaling of these fuels should be supported by improved supply chain efficiencies, infrastructure investments, harmonized standards, and incentive mechanisms (European Commission, 2011). SAF stands out as one of the most critical tools for reducing the aviation sector's carbon emissions. However, the SAF supply chain faces significant challenges due to high production costs, limited and variable raw material supplies, scalability issues, the complexity of multi-stage production processes, and regulatory uncertainty. In this context, recent studies have focused on advanced modeling and optimization methods to increase cost-effectiveness, reduce emissions, and strengthen supply chain resilience. Linear and mixed-integer programming, metaheuristic algorithms, and machine learning-based optimization techniques enable integrated management of supply sources, production, logistics, and distribution stages. Furthermore, Aspen Plus, GAMS, and Python-based software are widely used in lifecycle analysis, logistics optimization, and policy scenario assessment. Ensuring the SAF supply chain becomes efficient and scalable will be possible not only through technological and logistics solutions but also through the integration of AI big data, resilient planning under uncertainty, and strong policy support (Liang *et al.*, 2025).

The production, resources, storage, transportation, composition, use, and emergency response of different fuel types can vary. Therefore, when faced with problems, the fuel's characteristics may need to be taken into account. Therefore, a thorough understanding of fuel properties is crucial for identifying and managing potential threats. In the sustainability of this system, which is extremely complex in these respects, it is necessary to identify and consider a very large number and variety of risks. However, it is critical that the supply chain, which is also sensitive in terms of "time", should decide which risks should be allocated resources and add them to its agenda. Therefore, prioritizing risks by creating a risk map is the decisive step in the process of managing risks.

Sustainable fuels are categorized into two main types (DHL Group, 2025):

i. ***Biofuels:*** *These include traditional and "drop-in" fuels such as ethanol, biodiesel, and hydrolyzed vegetable oil (HVO). Because the raw materials used in their production (such as agricultural waste) absorb* CO_2*, the amount of* CO_2 *released upon combustion is equal to the amount absorbed, making the combustion process carbon neutral.*
ii. ***Synthetic fuels (e-fuels):*** *These are more advanced fuels, such as electrofuels and e-kerosene. They are produced using captured* CO_2 *emissions and hydrogen. If the hydrogen is produced with green electricity, these fuels are considered carbon neutral.*

Many of these fuels are "drop-in" fuels that can be used directly without requiring any modifications to existing vehicles and infrastructure (unlike "non-drop-in" fuels, such as liquefied natural gas, which require modifications). In response to demand and proposed regulations, sustainable fuel production capacity is expected to grow significantly in the coming years. Over $150 billion in production capacity investment has been announced to date. Synthetic fuels, currently in the experimental phase and with very limited availability, will take time to become widespread until sufficient green electricity becomes available. However, biofuels are already available and are rapidly scaling up in air, sea, and road transport sectors. The belief that it is time for companies to transition from fossil fuels to sustainable fuels to achieve environmental goals is growing (DHL Group, 2025). Investments are also trending in this direction, and this trend is increasing. Investments are directed to industries, impacting their operational activities, management functions, and therefore their supply chains. The resources used vary and change depending on the investment. Investments are directed to industries which impact their operational activities, management functions, and therefore their supply chains. The resources used vary and change depending on the investment.

Current research and experiments on SAF provide evidence of their compatibility with existing jet engines and the absence of any need for modifications to aircraft, representing a significant advantage for airlines. But importantly, using SAF is currently experimental and limited to a few flights. For this reason, we cannot be sure of the long-term impact on aircraft systems. Nonetheless, alternative fuels and their sources definitely present different advantages. Their ability to be produced from a variety of different products, reducing dependence on petroleum, providing fuel efficiency gains of 1.5–3%, and reducing carbon emissions are among their strengths, both environmentally and in terms of their business image. However, their high cost (both production and supply chains and other costs) increases ticket prices, leading to the risk of lost revenue. Furthermore, the lack of sufficient production capacity raises supply issues. Meanwhile, the increased demand generated by ICAO targets and environmentally friendly approaches offers new business and employment opportunities, while high prices also threaten to reduce demand and lower occupancy rates in the sector. Therefore, while SAF offers significant environmental and strategic opportunities, it requires careful investment evaluation due to cost and supply constraints.

8.5 New Alternatives to Sources of Business: Sustainable Aviation Fuel

Sustainability and carbon neutrality are crucial in the logistics and supply chain sector due to its multitude of transportation modes. While excessive carbon emissions from traditional fossil fuels pose environmental threats, sustainable alternatives such as biodiesel, methanol, hydrogen, natural gas (CNG/LNG), P-series fuels, and solar-based fuels aim to achieve an emissions-free future in this sector. The large-scale use of these fuels plays a key role in decarbonizing the economy by reducing global emissions (Beiträge, 2022). The aviation industry consumes energy to sustain its economic and cultural catalyzing effect, but it also generally creates negative environmental impacts: noise pollution, emissions, etc. The risk management philosophy tries to maximize the positive impacts, i.e. opportunities, while it tries to reduce (minimize) or, if possible, eliminate adverse impacts and their sources. One of these minimization solutions proposed is the use of renewable energy sources in aviation. However, again from the risk management framework, no risk is one-dimensional. In other words, each risk has yin-yang sides, encompassing both opportunity and threat dimensions.

At present, there are three widely researched and highly feasible energy alternatives globally: electrification, hydrogen energy, and SAF. From a technical perspective, it is difficult to achieve significant progress in the short to medium term and provide effective assistance for carbon reduction through methods such as electrification and hydrogen energy. SAF are further divided into sustainable aviation biofuels and sustainable aviation synthetic fuels. SAF is an alternative fuel made from renewable raw materials. It comes from a variety of sources, including biofuels such as second-hand edible oil, household waste, and energy crops, as well as synthetic fuels made from carbon dioxide captured from the air or industrial emissions. Compared to general aviation fuel, SAF not only provides power for flight but also reduces carbon emissions by 80%, and airlines can use it directly without the need for aircraft modifications. Therefore, most countries view sustainable aviation fuels as the key to breakthroughs in emissions reductions in the aviation industry. Directive (EU) 2018/2001 of the European Parliament and of the Council and its predecessor set out overarching targets across all transport modes to be supplied with renewable fuels. As aviation is a relatively small fuels market for which renewable fuels are more costly to produce in comparison to other transport modes and operates in a highly competitive and integrated EU air transport market, the regulatory framework should be complemented with aviation-specific measures to effectively boost the deployment of SAF (The European Parliament and The Council of The European Union, 2023). There are risks of creating significant fragmentation in the EU air transport market, where national rules on SAF would set out widely differing targets. This would be expected to further exacerbate the issues of a level playing field in air transport (Delli, 2022).

With the introduction and ramping up of SAF at EU airports, practices of fuel tankering could be exacerbated as a consequence of rising aviation fuel costs. Tankering practices are unsustainable and should be avoided, as they undermine the EU's efforts to reduce the environmental impact from transport. Those would contradict the aviation decarbonization objectives, as increased aircraft weight would increase fuel consumption and related emissions on a given flight. Tankering practices also put at risk the level playing field in the EU between aircraft operators and between airports. This regulation should therefore require aircraft operators to refuel prior to the departure from a given EU airport. The amount of fuel uplifted prior to departure from a given EU airport should be commensurate with the amount of fuel necessary to operate the flights departing from that airport. The requirement ensures that equal conditions apply to EU and foreign aircraft operators across the EU, while ensuring a high level of environmental protection. As the regulation does not define maximum shares of SAF in all aviation fuels, aircraft operators and aviation fuel suppliers may pursue more ambitious environmental policies with higher SAF uptake and supply in their overall network of operations, while avoiding fuel tankering. Nevertheless, this regulation should also take into account the fact that fuel tankering at times occurs in order to comply with fuel safety rules in line with Commission Regulation 965/20128 and, in such cases, is justified by safety reasons (The European Parliament and the Council of the European Union, 2023).

Carbon dioxide emissions are considered one of the main causes of global warming. Industries are also responsible for the emergence and increase of these emissions. Especially the transport sector, where transport vehicles are used, plays a role as a source of emissions at different rates in air, sea, and land environments. However, since economic and cultural sustainability cannot be achieved without transport, a risk management strategy is adopted by changing emission sources used in transport rather than the transport itself. Within the scope of this strategy, it is envisaged that the production, supply, and subsequent widespread use of renewable energies will support the goal of managing the risk of global warming.

Traditional fuels remain a matter of debate due to their environmental damage and cost. However, the sustainability of energy is directly proportional to its ability to support people and their lives in all economic, social, operational, and environmental aspects in the short, medium, and long term. At this point, the risk of a sustainable, uninterrupted, and effective supply of sustainable energy is at a decisive position.

Enterprises are constantly experiencing higher levels of supply chain disruptions in their operations due to the expansion of industries' business networks. It becomes highly necessary for enterprises to continually assess risks in their business operations (Abdul Ganiyu *et al.*, 2020). It is foreseen that SAF, which is presented as a solution for environmental sustainability and energy independence, has both remarkable opportunities and threat potential. Therefore, the economic, strategic, and operational risks should be analyzed, and a prioritized risk list should be taken into account in investment decisions and resource allocation. In this chapter, the risks of renewable energy sources in the aviation sector are identified and prioritized. This prioritized risk list is designed to serve as an instrument for managers to consider in critical decision-making.

8.6 Sustainable Energy for a Sustainable Supply Chain and Managing Risks

SCRM is the coordination of activities to manage and control a company's end-to-end supply chain, from raw material sources to customer end-use, within the context of supply chain risks. Supply chain risk is defined as the probability and consequences of events that can occur at any point in the chain. While globalization and long supply chains have increased efficiency, they have also made supply chains more fragile and increased the risk of disruptions; therefore, effective SCRM is vital to business success. The SCRM process begins with risk identification and assessment, where managers map the supply chain and identify critical components, including risks at second-tier suppliers. Risks include both intentional and unintentional disruptions, such as natural disasters, political uncertainty, supplier production issues, distribution restrictions, and internal uncertainties. The goal of SCRM is to mitigate these disruptions and support business continuity (Supply Chain Risk Leadership Council, 2011).

SCRM is a process by which companies identify, assess, and mitigate risks associated with their supply chains. These risks can arise from a variety of sources, including natural disasters, geopolitical tensions, supplier issues, or fluctuating market demand. Effective SCRM helps businesses minimize disruptions, ensure operational continuity, and enhance long-term resilience. A thorough and accurate understanding of SCRM, along with its core components, enables companies to effectively respond to risks and maintain robust supply chain performance (IFS, 2025):

(a) **Risk identification:** Identifying potential vulnerabilities in the supply chain.
(b) **Risk assessment:** Prioritizing risks by evaluating their likelihood and impact.
(c) **Risk mitigation:** Developing strategies such as supplier diversification, creating inventory buffers, or using advanced technology.
(d) **Continuous monitoring:** Regularly reviewing and improving the process, remaining flexible to new threats.

SCRM analyzes alternative energy sources, encompassing all critical steps, from fuel certification and logistics to ultimately integrating the fuel into the existing airport system and establishing the mechanism (mass balance) that will allow the airline to claim environmental benefits, as every step ultimately relates to the supply chain.

Supply chain risk is defined as the probability and consequences of events that can occur at any stage of an end-to-end supply chain network, extending from raw material sources to end-customer use. With increasing globalization, supply chains have become more widespread and complex, exposing key linkages to risk and causing businesses to consistently experience high levels of supply chain disruptions throughout their operations. Analyses have empirically proven that supply chain risks are negatively correlated with business performance. This suggests that businesses with high levels of supply chain disruptions will experience lower performance compared to their competitors. Implementing SCRM strategies is essential to mitigate these negative consequences. SCRM is a well-structured and organized approach that aims to mitigate supply chain disruptions by identifying and analyzing risks. SCRM strategies are designed to mitigate the negative consequences of supply chain fragility and have a positive impact on business performance. In particular, businesses with specialized organizational structures designed to mitigate SCRM have been found to outperform their competitors. These strategies include elements such as collaboration with suppliers, emergency/business continuity plans, product differentiation to mitigate demand risks, and acquiring insurance against risks (Abdul Ganiyu *et al.*, 2020).

The increasing difficulty in predicting the business world and economic drivers means that systematic management of supply chain resilience and risks is required in this context. It is stated that the way to cope with fragility is to increase supply chain resilience. As governments and companies strive to implement sustainable practices, investor engagement is yielding positive results, with global interest expected to further accelerate sustainability performance across the automotive sector and its suppliers (O'Connell, 2022). Then, SCRM is defined as the effective coordination and management of all business activities to regulate an enterprise's end-to-end supply chain network placing higher priorities on supply chain risks (Abdul Ganiyu *et al.*, 2020; Supply Chain Risk Leadership Council, 2011).

Supply chain risks are events that may cause the flow not to go as planned due to interruption and/or damages (Oliveira *et al.*, 2019). Therefore, there is a potential to deviate from business objectives. The sources of risk include the occurrence of a certain event and the consequences of the events and effects, the severity of the effects, and the environmental conditions that trigger the event and its occurrence.

Supply chains are the dynamic and strategic links that connect companies and their vendors. The supply chain includes research, selection, planning, control, purchasing, logistics, and transportation, as well as product development, marketing, distribution, and customer service. As SCRM is such a strategic management process that is multi-stage and integrates many activities, it is particularly important to identify and manage risks that can disrupt or stop this process and its flow. These risks can disrupt the supply chain flow and cause serious disruptions for both supplying and receiving companies (Oliveira *et al.*, 2019). Supply chain risks, which consist of natural and man-made disasters, have been broadly identified as organizational, network, and other risks (Oliveira *et al.*, 2019; Ghadge, 2012).

At the same time, since supply process risk sources are also present in different business areas such as product sales process, material supply, inventory management, distribution process, and customer services, it is important to include these areas in the scope of risk management and to make the relevant planning in the most appropriate way. In SCRM, it is important to plan activities such as stakeholder relations, supply and demand balance, cost–benefit analysis, production planning, logistics, transport, finance, and resource management in a correct and harmonious manner. As it is also valid for supply chain-related strategies, it is especially important that SCRM strategies are shaped specific to the organization and designed according to the wishes and needs of the organization.

Organizations are open systems that outsource their product and service sourcing needs through outsourcing and hence supply chains. Therefore, almost all organizations are exposed to supply chain risks and operate in a more complex and uncertain environment that increases their risk profile. Global sourcing trends are making supply chains longer and more fragmented, and this is exposing firms to greater costs and risks (Christopher *et al.*, 2011). When planning a potential facility for an SAF supply chain, relevant parameters should be considered to accurately assess bio-oil feedstock costs in the biorefinery. Risk analysis is a fundamental requirement of this assessment. The dependent and independent parameters of supply chain activities, such as the supply of SAF from the refinery to the airport, encompass critical stages such as raw material production, transportation, conversion, and product shipment. This comprehensive analysis will reveal the profit potential for economic actors in the potential supply chain. For the financial viability of a sustainable SAF supply chain, a risk analysis related to the cost of profit is essential (Dyk and Deshpande, 2025).

8.7 Risk Taxonomy and Raising Risk from Alternative Energy Sources

Taxonomies are useful for risk analysis and prioritization and, more importantly, for seeing the holistic picture and creating risk maps. In the taxonomy we developed, potential risks in the SAF supply chain are grouped into five main areas. The first group focuses on SAF cost risks. This specifically includes fuel costs, operational comparison with other alternative fuels, and availability and accessibility issues across all systems, such as aviation, maritime, and rail systems. Technological, operational, and usage costs are also considered within this risk group.

The second group of risks relates to the logistics of sustainable fuels such as SAF. This encompasses risks arising from managing the systems and processes of logistics activities within the supply chain.

The third group relates to technology and production risks (operational category) required to produce fuels such as SAF. All these risks are directly linked to the resilience and agility of the supply chain. Risks in the operational group in supply chains include both internal and external process events, problems, interruptions, disruptions in the scope of effectiveness and efficiency, and the performance adequacy of activities and the risks in this area (Yılmaz, 2017).

The fourth group of risks encompasses social and environmental aspects (or green risks), specifically examining the impacts of SAF use on global resources. These risks should be considered because they have the potential to indirectly impact economic and political factors.

Finally, the fifth group of risks includes demand risks and comparison with alternatives. These risks address the demand side, such as customer willingness to bear higher costs, economic usage costs, and customer preferences and attitudes.

The SAF supply chain risk taxonomy categorizes five main risks: cost, supply, technology/production (flexibility and agility), environment/ social (green), and demand. By classifying them into categories, it reveals the multifaceted challenges in the adoption and dissemination of SAF. The risk management strategies required for each category differ and require resources. Therefore, categorization must be made carefully and include all administrative, environmental, economic, and operational risk groups within the scope of sustainable fuels such as SAF. The impact of risks within these categories must then be assessed. Furthermore, risks can combine to create different and new risks. Regardless of the topic, the integrated impact should be one of the outputs considered and calculated in risk management. Since risk management strategies will be developed based on this impact, they must be calculated with accurate and complete analyses.

It is imperative to prepare for the future and make the necessary adjustments, ensuring a well-functioning air transport sector that fully contributes to achieving the Union's climate goals, with high levels of connectivity, affordability, safety, and security. The Union has established legal obligations under Regulation (EU) 2021/1119 of the European Parliament and the Council to achieve climate neutrality by 2050 at the latest and to achieve a reduction in net GHG emissions by at least 55% compared to 1990 by 2030. In order to achieve this, all economic sectors, including the transport sector, have to take rapid steps to decarbonize. For the air transport sector, this necessitates a strong ramp-up of the production, supply, and uptake of SAF (The European Parliament and the Council of the European Union, 2023). In addition, SAF-based risks can be taxonomized in terms of the frequency with which they are encountered or occur, the severity of their impact, the size of their impact area when they occur, and their predictability. Regulations may encourage alternatives for flight operators in other non-regulated areas. This situation may lead to distortion of competition and risk of carbon leakage at the expense of Union airports and operators using these airports (Delli, 2022). Therefore, increasing the scope of regulations within the scope of SAF in terms of countries and regions is important for the manageability of this risk.

8.8 Investment and Decision-Making on Alternative Energy Sources

Renewable energy sources exhibit fluctuating energy production depending on weather conditions and seasonal changes. This fluctuation increases the need for excess energy storage to meet energy consumption. This requires energy storage systems to have greater capacity, which increases costs and reduces efficiency. The fact that renewable energy sources are not a stable energy source complicates the planning of energy supply and operations in the aviation industry (Ali *et al.*, 2023). Increasing production of low-emission fuel by leveraging technology and infrastructure will be possible through developing supply chain design technology and creating alternatives to expand its use. For example, ExxonMobil is engineering proprietary methanol-to-jet technology that will produce SAF when renewable methanol is used as a feedstock. In this way, ExxonMobil's portfolio of technology solutions designed to produce SAF from other biological feedstocks is expanded (Exxon Mobil, 2022).

The EV transformation is progressing in tandem with "Automotive 2.0" processes such as autonomous driving and digitalization. While this process contributes to reducing emissions and accidents, it requires significant investments in advanced technology, data processing capacity, and software development. The multibillion-dollar investments of automotive manufacturers (e.g. Volkswagen and General Motors) demonstrate the speed and scale of the transformation. Holistic, long-term, and responsible investor engagement is critical for managing ESG risks and capitalizing on opportunities in the EV ecosystem (O'Connell, 2022).

The use of renewable energy sources in industries has significant potential in terms of environmental sustainability and energy independence. However, energy storage challenges pose significant drawbacks that limit the full realization of this potential. Factors such as storage capacity, energy density, infrastructure requirements, and energy stability make it difficult to adopt renewable energy sources in the aviation industry. These challenges require a focus on forward-looking solutions and technological advances.

There are two types of emissions that need to be considered:

- **Production emissions:** GHG emissions generated during the chemical or biological conversion processes.
- **Resource-specific emissions:** The carbon footprint and GHG emissions associated with the extraction, collection, and transport of raw resources and feedstock.

This is particularly important, as insufficient raw materials for sustainable fuel production can create many risks. Because limiting production to a certain area may lead to soil diversity and loss of productivity, it may also lead to pollution of soil and water due to production waste. Since the composition of wastes changes, waste management systems may also need to be revised, which draws attention as a separate cost and management problem.

Changing energy production sources also means that production centers, access to what is produced, and the balance of access will be affected. In this respect, it can lead to serious and widespread negative economic effects, such as a rapid increase in prices and different effects on the economies of different countries.

All these potential threat areas and risks are also important for SAF supply chain management as areas of disruption and resilience. It reflects the difficulty of sourcing suitable raw materials and waste for sustainable fuel production. Therefore, it is important to carefully manage the supply of raw materials for sustainable fuel production, taking environmental and social impacts into account and ensuring that resources are used sustainably. In addition, policies and practices regarding sustainable fuel production should focus on minimizing these risks.

These identified risks should be considered in investment decisions regarding the production of sustainable fuels and the use of agricultural lands, as well as in risk management decisions regarding resource allocation and the sustainability of these investments. A SAF supply chain is a multi-criteria decision-making problem. It is envisaged that taking these risks into account when making this decision will contribute to seeing the holistic picture and applying optimization. This list of risks identified in our research requires considering important environmental and social factors such as food security, protection of water resources, sustainability of forests, and conservation of biodiversity when managing the SAF supply chain and promoting the production of sustainable fuels for the sustainability of production. Therefore, it is important to design policies and practices regarding sustainable fuel production in a balanced way.

The air transport market is subject to strong competition between economic actors globally and across the Union, for which a level playing field is indispensable. The stability and prosperity of the air transport market and its economic actors rely on a clear and harmonized policy framework where aircraft operators, airports, and other aviation actors can operate based on equal rules and opportunities, leading to a vibrant sector and job opportunities. Where market distortions occur, aircraft operators or airports are at risk of being disadvantaged by internal or external competitors. In turn, this can result in a loss of competitiveness for the air transport industry, putting air transport businesses and jobs at risk, and a loss of air connectivity and transport choices for citizens and businesses (Delli, 2022). Despite advances in biorefinery site selection, transport network design, and modeling of by-product utilization, current supply chains and business models for renewable fuel production do not result in costs competitive with fossil fuels. The current approach to supply chain design for SAF is unique in that it can be enriched with business models and methods used by other industries to design and analyze supply chains to increase process efficiency, reduce risk, lower total cost, and maximize profit. The SAF business model can be enhanced by incorporating ecosystem and social services for revenue enhancement, which can be achieved through new strategies that take into account the dynamic interactions between the components of the SAF supply chain (Martinez-Valencia *et al.*, 2021). Although airlines want to use fuel derived from waste to reduce emissions by up to 70%, the high cost and limited supply of materials needed to make SAF make large-scale production difficult. SAF accounts for less than 0.1% of the total global jet fuel used today and costs three to five times as much as regular jet fuel. These production difficulties, quantity constraints, and production costs emerge as risks in the (threat) group considered in investment decisions related to SAF (Young and Plucinska, 2023).

It is therefore important that the Union sustain efforts made at international, multilateral, and bilateral levels to promote a high level of ambition and convergence in the uptake of SAF, while providing for an international level playing field (Delli, 2022).

The development of SAF is not only a critical step for the aviation industry to achieve carbon neutrality but also offers far-reaching environmental, economic, and social benefits. From an environmental perspective, thanks to the use of renewable raw materials and improved processes, SAF has the potential to reduce GHG emissions by up to 80% over its lifecycle; it also improves air quality by reducing particulate matter and sulfur emissions. From an economic and strategic perspective, a mature SAF market strengthens energy security and geopolitical stability by reducing dependence on fossil fuels while also protecting the sector from oil price volatility. Furthermore, investments in SAF infrastructure create jobs and fuel innovation toward sustainable bionomies, while from a social perspective, they enhance the social standing of the aviation industry by supporting global Sustainable Development Goals, such as climate change and clean energy. Ultimately, SAF is a catalyst that will play a crucial role in shaping the sustainable future of global transportation (Wang *et al.*, 2024).

Global warming causes severe and sudden extreme meteorological events, destabilization of seasons, reduction of biodiversity, water pollution, and water scarcity, thus negatively affecting both the comfort of today's life and the resources of future generations. There are increasing studies suggesting that the use of new energy sources will be effective in combating global warming. However, new energy sources face the threat of not being widespread in terms of sustainable access and use unless supply issues are addressed. Therefore, the sustainability of SAF production and resources, storage, stockpiling, and accessibility are considered basic needs. Therefore, even if SAF is produced, if it cannot be supplied or the supply chain cannot be managed, it will not be widespread at the desired level and will not provide the expected benefit in terms of the climate crisis.

The identification, prioritization, and analysis of the risks of sustainable fuels in terms of the supply chain is of vital importance due to the decisive risk in their use and dissemination in the aviation industry. The aviation industry is expected to be more difficult to decarbonize than the road transport industry. The aviation industry generates approximately 2–3% of global carbon emissions. Engines in commercial use are not yet certified to fly with more than 50% SAF, and the vast majority of flights mix much lower amounts of SAF with conventional jet fuel (Young and Plucinska, 2023).

All transport modes, including air transport, need supply chains and SCRM to provide services to their users. It should be kept in mind that these fuels, which are still relatively new, may lead to the premature obsolescence of engine and fuel system components over the medium and long term. Aircraft and engine manufacturers should prepare more detailed and clear research and reports on the subject and present them to the public. An accident caused by alternative fuels has the potential to affect investment sustainability and durability. The ability of sanctions alone to prevent supply chain risks is open to discussion.

Since the production of sustainable fuels from biological or agricultural products will require changes in procurement, logistics, storage, and stocking processes, there is a risk of increasing the costs of logistics activities, as it creates significant pressure on the supply chain. In order to prevent fuel deterioration in warehouses, it may be necessary to develop special warehouses incorporating appropriate technologies through R&D studies. This situation will increase the costs and authorization responsibilities on the airline company due to the time pressure.

The development and deployment of SAF, which has a high potential for sustainability, commercial maturity, and innovation and growth to meet future needs, should be promoted. This should support the creation of an innovative and competitive market for SAF and ensure the sufficient supply of SAF for aviation in the short and long terms to contribute to Union transport decarbonization ambitions, while strengthening the Union's efforts toward a high level of environmental protection. Incentives for the use of renewable fuels of non-biological origin in transport granted under other Union laws will have a positive impact on the uptake of such fuels in aviation. A single, clear, and robust sustainability framework is necessary to provide legal certainty and continuity for aviation and fuel industry actors regarding the eligibility of SAF under this regulation (Delli, 2022).

In the SAF risk analysis, the risk that ranks first at the end of the research is the cost risk. The price of SAF depends on technology and the trajectory of oil prices. The market price of current SAF from biogenic residues is currently three to five times the price of fossil kerosene. The next generation of SAF is currently ten times more expensive than fossil kerosene. The Lufthansa Group is involved in numerous projects to make SAF available in larger quantities as soon as possible. As production is industrialized, prices are likely to fall (Lufthansa, 2024).

The widespread adoption of SAF is crucial for the green transformation of the aviation sector, and its success depends on the establishment of robust supply chains. SAF's direct compatibility with existing fuels offers a significant advantage in supply chain integration, allowing existing infrastructure and equipment to be used without additional costs. However, the biggest challenge facing commercialization is the supply problem caused by insufficient production capacity. To address this issue and overcome economic and logistical challenges, investment in production facilities and supply chains is essential. On the feedstock side, which is the starting point of the supply chain, the production of SAF from various sources, such as renewable biomass and organic solid waste, increases supply security. However, as seen particularly in China, improved infrastructure is needed to support the rural supply chain, meet growing production demands, and ensure efficient raw material collection and distribution. Finally, to verify the environmental benefits of SAF, lifecycle emissions must be carefully monitored throughout the supply chain, including raw material cultivation, processing, and transportation (Wang *et al.*, 2024).

Effective stakeholder relationship management and stakeholder involvement in risk management efforts are required to fully identify, prioritize, and manage manufacturing and distribution-wide risks. To reduce bottlenecks in SAF supply and supply chain, incentive regulations regarding SAF investment and measures that support risk sharing and risk reduction should be taken.

The majority of research on sustainable or alternative fuels appears to focus on the technical feasibility and composition of these fuels. Efforts to reduce environmental damage resulting from all operations and activities in industries, aviation, and the supply chain ecosystem are commendable. It appears possible to mitigate environmental damage and resource use, but whether it can be eliminated as a "net-zero future" is debatable. Let's assume that this is desired by all stakeholders and that efforts are made to achieve it. Even then, zero emissions may not be possible. This is because environmental systems, the factories and facilities where they are produced, the vehicles used for supply and transport, and all facilities used in the supply chain can create negative environmental impacts during production. However, while net zero is an impossible goal, efforts should at least be made to minimize harmful effects. Reducing the costs of alternative fuels in the short or medium term does not appear feasible. However, if alternatives to the source of production can be developed in the long term, costs can be relatively reduced.

Potential risks associated with sustainable new energy alternatives, along with issues related to global warming, are prompting new investment opportunities. To expand the use of alternative energy sources such as electricity, hydrogen, and biomass within industries, a detailed risk analysis should be conducted, and stakeholders should be included in risk management. New fuel alternatives have the potential to create risks in operational, economic, and social areas. This issue should be considered in conjunction with organizations' corporate social responsibility. In this context, investments in alternative energy sources by senior managers should be undertaken with the goal of contributing to capacity building in an environmentally and socially responsible approach, considering the associated risks.

8.9 Sustainability of Supply Chains: Future Projections

Well-formulated energy risk management systems, including processes such as data collection and route optimization, are essential for successfully operating sustainable supply chains and logistics. Green supply chain and logistics practices, such as the use of EVs, can create a sustainable revolution in the economic sector, depending on the effective collaboration of businesses, consumers, and governments. While this transition may require additional initial costs, it will be beneficial in the long run for both environmental sustainability and controlling business costs (Beiträge, 2022).

Considering the uncertainty in the design of supply chains, it is necessary to fully and accurately identify and prioritize the risks arising from cooperation within the mostly global managerial and operational network and the interactions between stakeholders to understand the impact areas and intensities, as well as to minimize the negative effects of the risks and, where possible, the threat effects. It has been emphasized that developing proactive mitigation capabilities should become the golden rule for eliminating them (adopted by Colicchia and Strozzi, 2012).

DHL and World Energy Partnership: In October 2023, DHL Express and World Energy agreed to accelerate aviation decarbonization through SAF certifications (SAFc) in a seven-year global partnership. This agreement aims to provide 668 million liters (0.6 Mt) of SAF and will enable DHL to reduce approximately 1.7 million tons of CO_{2e} on a lifecycle basis (equivalent to one year of carbon-neutral operation of the entire DHL Americas aviation network) (DHL Group, 2025).

The development of SAF, as the primary decarbonization tool for the aviation sector, requires integrating technological and economic feasibility with supply chain management strategies. Analyses guide investment decisions by evaluating the techno-economic performance of various raw material and technology combinations. In this context, a transformative supply chain configuration is proposed to ensure the cost competitiveness of second-generation SAF. This model involves integrating small-scale production facilities (which convert feedstock into intermediate products) located close to biomass sources with a larger, centralized refinery to reduce raw material logistics costs. This innovative approach serves as an example of effective supply chain management that optimizes the balance between economies of scale and logistics costs, mitigating the environmental and financial risks associated with long-distance biomass transportation. Furthermore, the need for strategic interventions to reduce investment risk and increase efficiency is emphasized; in particular, incorporating green hydrogen from renewable sources into synthesis processes offers the potential to increase SAF efficiency by up to 70% and reduce production costs by up to 18%. Such supply chain optimizations and technological integrations provide essential guidance for SAF project developers, policymakers, and investors to achieve critical cost reduction and sustainability goals (Wang *et al.*, 2024).

Supply chain management and resilience play a central role in the success of global lithium supply, which is critical for both next-generation fuels, including SAF, and US automotive EV battery production. Supply chain risks are particularly concentrated in the areas of raw material supply and logistics. The fragmented structure of used cooking oil (UCO) supply chains, low collection efficiency, and a lack of awareness point to a critical raw material supply risk. Furthermore, the use of bulky biomass feedstocks such as agricultural residues significantly increases logistics costs, making supply chain management challenging and a constraint on achieving commercial-scale efficiency. To mitigate these risks and increase supply chain efficiency, implementing policies that facilitate raw material access and incentives for transportation processes is considered essential. Furthermore, another report on lithium supply indicates the need to develop a supply chain resiliency index (SRI) to inform strategic decision-making. Ensuring supply chain resilience and efficiency at all stages, from raw material procurement to the delivery of final products, is a fundamental prerequisite for achieving national and global industrial targets (Dyk and Deshpande, 2025; He *et al.*, 2025).

Production sustainability is inextricably linked to supply chain resilience. Even if the end product is inherently sustainable, such as SAF, any disruption to the supply of critical production resources such as raw materials and/or semi-finished products presents a supply risk that disrupts the product's production potential. Furthermore, because supply chains frequently cross international borders and involve numerous stakeholders, each cross-border transition presents a distinct source of geopolitical and operational risk, with the type and degree of risk varying significantly across different segments of the chain.

Considering all these risks and the challenges they create, ensuring continuity, reliability, and transparency in the supply of critical materials needed to produce electric vehicles—particularly lithium and SAF, which are essential for their batteries—is a prerequisite for achieving global emissions targets. Managing this multilayered risk environment, in which the supply chain plays a key role, is only possible through strategic investments in both production and supply chains, collaborations built on trust and transparency among stakeholders, and the analysis, prioritization, and integration of supply risks into the risk management system. SCRM develops its strategies by also considering new and emerging current risks.

References

Abdul Ganiyu, S., Yu, D., Xu, C., and Mongo, P. (2020). The impact of supply chain risks and supply chain risk management strategies on enterprise performance in Ghana. *Journal of Business and Management*, 8, 1491–1507. https://doi.org/10.4236/ojbm.2020.84095.

Adebola Oluwafunmilayo, I. and Talabi, S. (2024). Tesla's supply chain management model: A lesson for smart manufacturing. *International Journal of Engineering Research & Technology*, 13(5), 1–3. https://doi.org/10.5281/zenodo.18138716. https://www.ijert.org/teslas-supply-chain-management-model-a-lesson-for-smart-manufacturing.

Baban, C. (2025, August 02). The electric vehicle supply chain: The geopolitics of critical components. Bogazici Ventures. https://bogaziciventures.com/tr/makale-detay/elektrikli-araclarda-tedarik-zinciri-kritik-bilesenlerin-jeopolitigi.

Beiträge, A. (2022, December 14). The green energy revolution: A guide to sustainable fuels in logistics. GRYM: gryn.com. https://www.gryn.com/post/the-green-energy-revolution-a-guide-to-sustainable-fuels-in-logistics.

Blakemore, R. and Engelke, P. (2025, July). A US framework for assessing risk in critical mineral supply chains. Atlantic Council Scowcroft Center for Strategy and Security. https://www.atlanticcouncil.org/in-depth-research-reports/issue-brief/a-us-framework-for-assessing-risk-in-critical-mineral-supply-chains/.

Christopher, M., Mena, C., Khan, O., and Yurt, O. (2011). Approaches to managing global sourcing risk. *Supply Chain Management: An International Journal*, 16(2), 67–81.

Colicchia, C. and Strozzi, F. (2012). Supply chain risk management: A new methodology for a systematic literature review. *Supply Chain Management: An International Journal*, 17(4), 403–418.

Delli, K. (2022). Amendments by the European Parliament Regulation (EU) 2023/… of the European Parliament and of the Council of … on ensuring a level playing field for sustainable air transport (ReFuelEU Aviation). THE EUROPEAN PARLIAMENT AND THE COUNCIL OF THE EUROPEAN UNION AM\P9_AMA(2022)0199(137-137)_EN.docx 1/90 PE733.796v01-00. https://www.europarl.europa.eu/doceo/document/A-9-2022-0199-AM-137-137_EN.pdf.

DHL Group. (2025, 09 29). Trend overview relevance to the future of logistics. DHL: dhl.com. https://www.dhl.com/tr-en/home/innovation-in-logistics/logistics-trend-radar/sustainable-fuels.html.

Dyk, S. V. and Deshpande, A. (2025). Feasibility study on the use of sustainable aviation fuels in India. ICAO: https://www.icao.int/sites/default/files/environmental-protection/Documents/ACT-SAF/Feasibility_Study_India.pdf.

European Commission. (2011, January 25). Alternative fuels for transport press release. European Commission. https://ec.europa.eu/commission/presscorner/detail/el/memo_11_41.

Exxon Mobil Corporation. (2022, June 20). ExxonMobil methanol to jet technology to provide new route for sustainable aviation fuel production. https://www.exxonmobilchemical.com/en/resources/library/library-detail/101116/exxonmobil_sustainable_aviation_fuel_production_en?utm_source=google&utm_medium=cpc&utm_campaign=cl_downstream_none&ds_k=&gclsrc=aw.ds&&ppc_keyword=saf%20fuel&gclid=Cj0KCQiA35ur: https://www.exxonmobilchemical.com/en/resources/library/library-detail/101116/exxonmobil_sustainable_aviation_fuel_production_en?utm_source=google&utm_medium=cpc&utm_campaign=cl_downstream_none&ds_k=&gclsrc=aw.ds&&ppc_keyword=saf%20fuel&gclid=Cj0KCQiA35ur.

Ghadge, A., Dani, S., and Kalawsky, R. (2012). Supply chain risk management: Present and future scope. *International Journal of Logistics Management*, 23(3), 313–339.

Hargreaves, L. (2024, August 23). Tesla: Transforming supply chain sustainability. *SupplyChain Digital Magazine*. https://supplychaindigital.com/articles/tesla-transforming-supply-chain-sustainability. Retrieved September 2025.

He, H., Brush, T., Cai, H., Thakkar, D., Dunlop, S., and Biller, S. (2025). Developing a strategic supply chain resiliency index: An assessment of the global lithium supply for U.S. automotive EV battery production. *International Journal of Production Research*, 1–23. https://doi.org/10.1080/00207543.2025.2534842.

IFS. (2025, September 30). What is supply chain risk management (SCRM)? IFS: https://www.ifs.com/tr: https://www.ifs.com/tr/what-is/supply-chain-risk-management.

International Energy Agency. (2022). Securing clean energy technology supply chains. International Energy Agency (IEA). https://iea.blob.core.windows.net/assets/0fe16228-521a-43d9-8da6-bbf08cc9f2b4/SecuringCleanEnergyTechnologySupplyChains.pdf. Retrieved September 2025.

Jagani, S., Marsillac, E., and Hong, P. (2024). The electric vehicle supply chain ecosystem: Changing roles of automotive suppliers. *Sustainability*, 16(4), 1570. https://doi.org/10.3390/su16041570.

Liang, Y., Shahabuddin, M., Ahmed, S. F., Tan, J., and Ali, S. M. (2025, December 15). Optimizing sustainable aviation fuel supply chains: Challenges, mitigation strategies and modeling advances. *Fuel*, 402, 135972. https://doi.org/10.1016/j.fuel.2025.135972, https://www.sciencedirect.com/science/article/pii/S0016236125016977.

Lövenich, A. (2025, February 12). Tesla's supply chain in detail: Innovation, challenges, and lessons. All Things Supply Chain. https://www.allthingssupplychain.com/teslas-supply-chain-in-detail-innovation-challenges-and-lessons/.

Lufthansa. (2024). Frequently asked questions concerning Sustainable Aviation Fuel (SAF). Lufthansa.com. https://www.lufthansa.com/ae/en/discover-lufthansa/carbon-offsetting/faq-saf.

Martinez-Valencia, L., Garcia-Perez, M., and Wolcott, M. P. (2021). Supply chain configuration of sustainable aviation fuel: Review, challenges, and pathways for including environmental and social benefits. *Renewable and Sustainable Energy Reviews*, 152, 111680. https://doi.org/10.1016/j.rser.2021.111680, https://www.sciencedirect.com/science/article/pii/S1364032121009540.

O'Connell, P. (2022, October 22). Sustainable investing through the supply chain: Electric vehicles. AllianceBernstein L.P. https://www.alliancebernstein.com/corporate/en/insights/investment-insights/sustainable-investing-through-the-supply-chain-electric-vehicles.html.

Oliveira, J., Jin, M., Lima, R., Kobza, J., and Montevechi, J. (2019). The role of simulation and optimization methods in supply chain risk management: Performance and review standpoints. *Simulation Modelling Practice and Theory*, 92, 17–44. https://doi.org/10.1016/j.simpat.2018.11.007.

PwC. (2025, September 25). Merge ahead: Electric vehicles and the impact on the automotive supply chain. PricewaterhouseCoopers: pwc.com. https://www.pwc.com/us/en/industries/industrial-products/library/electric-vehicles-supply-chain.html.

RiskWatch. (2019, June 5). Supply chain issues and what we learned from Tesla. Risk Watch. https://www.riskwatch.com/tesla-supply-chain-issues/.

Scott, A. (2024, June 19). Building resilience: Lessons from Tesla's supply chain strategies. Supply Chain 360. https://supplychain360.io/building-resilience-lessons-from-teslas-supply-chain-strategies/.

Supply Chain Risk Leadership Council. (2011, August). Supply chain risk management: A compilation of best practices. Supply Chain Risk Leadership Council. https://www.scrlc.com/articles/Supply_Chain_Risk_Management_A_Compilation_of_Best_Practices_final%5B1%5D.pdf.

The European Parliament and the Council of the European Union. (2023). 2023/2405 31.10.2023 Regulation (EU) 2023/2405 of the European Parliament and of the Council of 18 October 2023 on ensuring a level playing field for sustainable air transport (ReFuelEU Aviation). http://data.europa.eu/eli/reg/2023/2405/oj. *Official Journal of the European Union*. https://eur-lex.europa.eu/legal-content/EN/TXT/PDF/?uri=CELEX:32023R2405.

Tobin, M. and Fu, C. (2025, February 28). Why a Chinese gadget company can make an electric car and Apple can't. The New York Times: https://www.nytimes.com/. https://www.nytimes.com/2025/02/28/business/china-xiaomi-apple-electric-cars.html#.

Wang, B., Ting, Z. J., and Zhao, M. (2024). Sustainable aviation fuels: Key opportunities and challenges in lowering carbon emissions for aviation industry. *Carbon Capture Science & Technology,* 13, 100263. https://doi.org/10.1016/j.ccst.2024.100263, https://www.sciencedirect.com/science/article/pii/S2772656824000757.

Xiaomi. (2025). Sustainable supply chain supply chain management system. https://www.mi.com/csr#/supplychain: https://www.mi.com/csr#/supplychain.

Yılmaz, A. K. (2017). *Uluslararası İşletmelerde Kurumsal Risk Yönetimi: Strateji ve Örgütsel Kültür Odaklı Paradigma.* Nüve Kültür Merkezi, Konya.

Young, S. and Plucinska, J. (2023, November 29). Virgin Atlantic jet lands after maiden transatlantic flight on low-carbon fuel. Reuters. https://www.reuters.com/sustainability/virgin-atlantic-jet-lift-off-maiden-transatlantic-flight-low-carbon-fuel-2023-11-28/.

Zheng, S. (2024). Analysis of the Tesla's sustainable supply chain management. *Advances in Economics, Management and Political Sciences* (EWA Publishing), 84, 49–55. https://doi.org/10.54254/2754-1169/84/20240780.

Index

www.ingramcontent.com/pod-product-compliance
Lightning Source LLC
LaVergne TN
LVHW051051210926
848486LV00002B/76

* 9 7 8 1 8 0 0 6 1 9 1 9 7 *